Interactive Multiple Goal Programming

International Series in Management Science/Operations Research

Series Editor:

James P. Ignizio
The Pennsylvania State University, U.S.A.

Advisory Editors:

Thomas Saaty
University of Pittsburgh, U.S.A.
Katsundo Hitomi
Kyoto University, Japan
H.-J. Zimmermann
RWTH Aachen, West Germany
B.H.P. Rivett
University of Sussex, England

Jaap Spronk

Erasmus University
Rotterdam

Interactive
Multiple Goal
Programming

Applications to Financial Planning

Martinus Nijhoff Publishing
Boston/The Hague/London

658.152
S 771

DISTRIBUTORS FOR NORTH AMERICA:
Martinus Nijhoff Publishing
Kluwer Boston, Inc.
190 Old Derby Street
Hingham, Massachusetts 02043, U.S.A.

DISTRIBUTORS OUTSIDE NORTH AMERICA:
Kluwer Academic Publishers Group
Distribution Centre
P.O. Box 322
3300 AH Dordrecht, The Netherlands

Library of Congress Cataloging in Publication Data

Spronk, Jaap.
  Interactive multiple goal programming.

  (International series in management science/op-
perations research)
  Includes bibliographies and indexes.
  1. Capital investments—Decision making—Mathematical models. 2. Corporations—Finance—Decision
making—Mathematical models. 3. Decision-making—
Mathematical models. I. Title. II. Title: Multiple
goal programming. III. Series.
HG4028.C4S67   658.1'52   81-1202
                                AACR2

ISBN 0-89838-064-2

In memory of my father

CONTENTS

LIST OF FIGURES

LIST OF TABLES

1. INTRODUCTION

1.1. Motivation

This book is based on the view-point that both public and
private decision making, in practice, can often be improved upon
by means of formal (normative) decision models and methods. To some
extent, the validity of this statement can be measured by the
impressive number of successes of disciplines as operations research
and management science. However, as witnessed by the many discussions
in the professional journals in these fields, many models and methods
do not completely meet the requirements of decision making in practice. Of all possible origins of these clear shortcomings, we mainly focus on only one: the fact that most of these models and methods
are unsuitable for decision situations in which multiple and possibly conflicting objectives play a role, because they are concentrated on the (optimal) fulfilment of only one objective.

The need to account for multiple goals was observed relatively
early. Hoffman [1955], while describing 'what seem to be the principal areas (in linear programming) where new ideas and new methods
are needed' gives an example with conflicting goals. In this problem, the assignment of relative weights is a great problem for the
planning staff and is 'probably not the province of the mathemati-
cian engaged in solving this problem'. These remarks were true pre-
cursors of later developments. Nevertheless, the need for methods
dealing with multiple goals was not widely recognized until much
later.

Of course, there are always early risers: Koopmans [1951]
formulated the production allocation decision as a vector maximum
problem, which is nowadays generally considered to be a problem in
multiple criteria decision making (cf. also Chapter 3). Relatively

early too, Charnes and Cooper [1961] stressed the need to deal with
multiple goals in formal decision models (see Chapter 4). Moreover,
they made important contributions to meet this need by providing
a new technique which was called goal programming. In spite of these
early examples, however, the main part of the academic interest in
multiple criteria decision making was developed in the last decade,
and it is still rapidly growing.

An important impetus for this development came from the public
sector. By nature, many of the decisions made there are intended
to serve multiple goals. In many countries, the expenditures of this
sector have grown significantly, and consequently, the desire for
efficiency and equilibrium in serving the public became manifest.
Discussions on political issues such as the improvement of public
transport facilities, health care, aid to the Third World, and so
forth need not be described here. The existence of multiple goals
in the public sector is obvious.

Another impetus was given by the societal developments in the
late sixties, when the role of private enterprise in society became
criticized and discussed once more. Negative effects of economic
growth, limits to this growth, democracy within the firm and many
other topics, together with their effect on entrepreneurial behaviour,
drew the attention of people representing a wide and colourful
political spectrum. These discussions were obviously rather normative.
They concentrated on what private enterprise's goals should be, or
more often, what they should not be: in the latter case usually
narrow-minded profit maximization was mentioned.

In many micro-economic approaches of the firm, it is assumed
that the firm's goal is, in one form or another, to maximize profits.
Depending on the point of departure chosen, profit maximization is,
broadly speaking, translated as the maximization of short-term
profits, the maximization of the net present value of future profits
or, more generally the maximization of the wealth of current stockholders. In many economic theories these assumptions are sufficient

to lead to conclusions which can be tested empirically. These
theories are generally considered worthwhile as long as their implications (and not necessarily their underlying assumptions) are
not contradicted by the facts observed in reality. If the implications of these theories do not correspond to reality, one can
'identify the specific departures from the idealized conditions
which give rise to various real world institutions whose functions
require analysis and explanation' (cf. Copeland and Weston [1979,
p. 111]).

In earlier times of economic analysis (e.g. in the days of
Adam Smith) when many of the product markets were thought to be
reasonably described by the model of perfect competition, it was not
completely illogical to adopt the goal of profit maximization as
the only objective, among other things because the actual allocation
of goods and services induced by a general acceptance of this very
objective was generally understood to have some well-known advantages, at least from a strictly economic point of view.

Things have, however, changed. Most markets have lost their
seemingly 'perfect' character. Von Neumann and Morgenstern [1953,
p. 11] have shown that profit maximization is mathematically not
well-defined in oligopolistic markets (which in fact most markets
are nowadays). Thus, part of the individual firm's logic to maximize profits has disappeared.

In a discussion on *laissez-faire*, Keynes [1926] argued that
'One of the most interesting and unnoticed developments of recent
decades has been the tendency of big enterprise to socialize itself.
A point arrives in the growth of a big institution ...... at which
the owners of the capital, i.e. the shareholders, are almost entirely
dissociated from the management, with the result that the direct
personal interest of the latter in the making of great profit
becomes quite secondary'. Indeed, modern enterprise has become a
complex organization in which many factors other than profit alone
play a role. In empirical studies, the goal of profit maximization -

in a variety of manifestations - is seldom mentioned as the only one.
And if it is, there is generally a multiplicity of subgoals, though
seldom with an exact definition of the relationships between these
subgoals and the main goal.

The problem of the firm's goals has engaged many prominent
researchers. To mention just a few, the work of Simon [1958], Cyert
and March [1963] and Williamson [1974] is well-known. Until now, the
academic world has reached little consensus on the nature and role
of the firm's goals. Nevertheless, because the firm in general has
multiple parties to serve, and because the claims of each of them
change over time, it is clear that the firm has to deal with a
complex of multiple goals, also changing over time.

A firm which should be aiming at such a dynamic goal complex
and which uses decision techniques designed for profit maximization
only runs the risk of neglecting the interests of some of the parties
involved. Unfortunately, most of the formal decision methods and
models are based on precisely this assumption. In our opinion,
multiple criteria decision methods offer a closer correspondence
to decision making in practice. Therefore, we hope to contribute to
the use and understanding of multiple criteria decision methods, not
only in the public sector but also in the realm of the private enterprise.

1.2. Scope of the Study

The main purpose of this study is to investigate the usefulness
of multiple criteria decision methods for capital budgeting and
financial planning. Both the private and the public sector have to
undertake capital investment projects. Obviously, in order to choose
the 'right' projects, the effects of the proposed projects must be
evaluated. In the public sphere, the existence of multiple goals in
project selection has been recognized for a long time, as is

witnessed by the widespread use of cost-benefit and cost-effective-
ness analyses.[1] In this study we will mainly focus on the private
sector. As indicated in the preceding section, we are taking the
position that private decision making in general, and private
project selection in particular, should be aimed at the fulfilment
of multiple goals. The question now arises whether existing methods
for private project selection are well suited to deal with this
multiplicity of goals.

An important theoretical framework for private project selection
is being offered by the discipline of finance, which starts from the
a priori position that the firm's single goal should be to maximize
the wealth of its current stockholders. For quoted companies, stockholders' wealth is being determined on the stock exchange by means
of supply and demand for the firm's stock. As described by finance
theory, the stock value depends on the expected levels and the risk
characteristics of the future streams of income which will be distributed among the stockholders, and on the interest rate of a
risk-free asset. Since the decision rules for project selection have
been placed in an equilibrium framework, they have been subject to
revolutionary changes.

However, the theoretical background of these decision rules as
such is far from complete. The underlying capital market model has
not been extended to the multiperiod case (at least not in a generally accepted way). In addition, severe problems arise in applying
these rules.

If other goals are involved, they can, within this approach,
be only accounted for by formulating criteria (or restrictions) and
applying them to the set of alternative investment proposals before
the mentioned goal of wealth maximization can be served.

We will investigate whether such an approach can be used safely
to maximize the stockholders' wealth and whether other goals can be
incorporated in an adequate way. Our position will be that neither

1) See Nijkamp [1979] for a critical discussion.

the first nor the second question can be answered affirmatively
except in some very sophisticated, theoretical cases.

Next we will examine whether existing multiple criteria decision
methods can offer some help. In doing so, we will conclude that the
existing set of methods shows a gap. We will try to fill this gap
by proposing a new, interactive variant of one of the existing methods,
viz. goal programming. It will be shown how this new variant can be
used within capital budgeting and financial planning.

The same approach will prove to be applicable to other fields
of interest, bot inside and outside the realm of project selection.
In fact, we will show that, compared with existing methods, the
proposed technique is applicable for a broader class of problems.

1.3. Outline of the Contents

In this section we present a brief description of the contents
of each of the following chapters.

In Chapter 2 we give some reasons for considering capital
budgeting and financial planning as decision problems involving
multiple goals. We do not claim to offer any new insights into the
firm's behaviour. On the contrary, we try to synthesize some almost
generally accepted and sometimes old ideas into a frame of reference
which can serve for the evaluation of the normative decision models
being developed in subsequent chapters. Within this framework, we
try to integrate the goal of the firm as it is seen in financial
theory. We are then able to formulate some desiderata for decision
methods which could possibly serve to support the capital budgeting
decision, and financial planning in general.

In Chapter 3 we give a brief account of normative decision
making, including its way of thinking in terms of 'means and ends'
(or 'instruments and targets') and its possibility to incorporate
concepts as 'uncertainty' and 'fuzziness'. We then turn to a brief
overview of multiple criteria decision methods with some special
emphasis on programming techniques. In doing so, we also elucidate

a number of concepts and definitions used in the multiple criteria decision making literature.

Chapter 4 is devoted to one of the earliest methods in this field. This is goal programming, established and further developed mainly by Charnes and Cooper. In our opinion, it is to this day one of the stronger methods available. We will show that it has some properties which are in close agreement with decision making in practice. Furthermore, many goal programming problems can be solved by means of linear programming, a well-known technique for which many excellent software packages are available. However, depending on the problem formulation, other solution procedures (e.g. generalized inverses) may also be used. In this chapter we try to give an impression of the variety of problems which can be handled by goal programming.

An important drawback of goal programming is its need for fairly detailed *a priori* information on the decision maker's preferences. As will be shown in Chapter 5, we agree with those scholars advocating interactive approaches to the goal programming problem. These are based on a mutual and successive interplay between decision maker and expert. They neither require an explicit representation or specification of the decision maker's preference function nor an explicit quantitative representation of trade-offs among conflicting objectives. A sample of interactive goal programming methods will be presented and discussed.

It appears that the evaluation of an interactive decision model is itself a multiple criteria problem. In order to illustrate this statement we shall propose some criteria which may be important in evaluating interactive decision models. We will see that most of the usual interactive approaches lack some of the advantages of 'traditional' goal programming, such as for instance the possibility to include pre-emptive priorities. Furthermore, in contrast with most existing interactive methods, goal programming is particularly suitable in situations of satisficing behaviour. This situation, combined with the repeatedly shown power of the traditional approach to inclu-

de piecewise linear functions (cf. Charnes and Cooper [1977]) justi-
fies the effort to seek an interactive variant of this approach.

In Chapter 6, we present a detailed description of a new method
which we have termed Interactive Multiple Goal Programming (IMGP).
This method includes all advantages of goal programming. For instance,
pre-emptive priorities and piecewise linear functions can be handled
in a straightforward way. Furthermore, the interactive process
imitates practice in formulating aspiration levels, assessing
priorities, seeking a solution and readjustment of the aspiration
levels. The method needs no more *a priori* information on the decision
maker's preference structure than other interactive multiple objective programming models. However, all available *a priori* information
can be incorporated within the procedure.

In Chapter 7, to illustrate the properties of IMGP, we describe
a number of possible applications in various fields of decision
making. In order to give an impression of the 'game of questions and
answers' induced by this procedure, we introduce an 'imaginary
decision maker'. With the help of this fictitious creature we are
able to discuss the convergency properties of the method.

In Chapters 8 and 9, we describe how IMGP can be used in capital
budgeting and financial planning. In Chapter 8 we first review some
applications of multiple criteria decision methods in capital budgeting and financial planning, as reported in the literature. We then
list a number of general problems occurring in these applications
and demonstrate how IMGP might help.

In Chapter 9, we present a detailed example of a financial
planning model with multiple goals. We show how such a model can be
handled within the Interactive Multiple Goal Programming framework,
while the possible   (dis)advantages of such an approach are also
exposed.

The final chapter deals with an evaluation of the properties
of interactive multiple goal programming, especially when applied
to capital budgeting and financial planning.

References

Antosiewicz, H.A. (ed)(1955), Proceedings of the Second Symposium
    in Linear Programming, Washington, National Bureau of Standards,
    U.S. Department of Commerce.

Charnes, A and W.W. Cooper (1961), Management Models and Industrial
    Applications of Linear Programming, Part I and II, John Wiley,
    New York.

Charnes, A. and W.W. Cooper (1977), Goal Programming and Multiple
    Objective Optimizations - Part I, European Journal of Operational
    Research, Vol. 1/1, pp. 39-54.

Copeland, T.E. and J.F. Weston (1979), Financial Theory and Corpo-
    rate Policy, Addison-Wesley, Reading (Ma).

Cyert, R.M. and J.G. March (1963), A Behavioral Theory of the Firm,
    Prentice-Hall, Englewood Cliffs.

Hoffman, A.J. (1955), How to solve a Linear Programming Problem, in
    Antosiewicz [1955], pp. 397-424.

Keynes, J.M. (1926), The End of Laissez-Faire, Hogarth Press, London.

Koopmans, T.C. (1951), Analysis of Production as an Efficient
    Combination of Activities, in T.C. Koopmans (ed), Activity
    Analysis of Production and Allocation, Cowles Commission Monograph
    23, Wiley, New York.

Neumann, J. von and O. Morgenstern (1953), Theory of Games and
    Economic Behaviour, 3rd edition, Wiley, New York.

Nijkamp, P. (1979), Multidimensional Spatial Data and Decision Ana-
    lysis, Wiley, New York.

Simon, H.A. (1958), Administrative Behavior, MacMillan, New York.

Williamson, O.E. (1974), The Economics of Discretionary Behavior:
    Managerial Objectives in a Theory of the Firm, Kershaw, London.
    (2nd edition).

2. MULTIPLE GOALS IN CAPITAL BUDGETING AND FINANCIAL PLANNING

2.1. Introduction

In this study we consider capital budgeting and financial planning as decision problems involving multiple goals. In this chapter we will explain why. Among other things, we will argue that both the goal and the constraints used in the 'traditional' approaches to capital budgeting and financial planning should both be treated as goals, which can be traded off against each other. In the following chapters we will develop a normative framework for dealing with capital budgeting and financial planning models with multiple goals.

'*Capital budgeting* is concerned with the allocation of the firm's scarce resources among the available investment opportunities', (Philippatos [1973, p.66]). The evaluation of investment opportunities within the capital budgeting process involves the consideration of the immediate and future *cash flows* implied by the investments. Throughout this study we assume C_{ti}, the cash flow in period $t (t=1,...,T)$ associated with project $i (i=1,...,n)$, to be concentrated at the end of period t. Thus we assume discrete instead of continuous time. A positive sign of C_{ti} denotes a *cash inflow*, a negative sign a *cash outflow*. All cash flows are assumed to be determined according to the '*with-or-without*' principle, implying that the cash flows represent the incremental effects of the project on the quality of the owners' income over time. This is to take account of the possible interdependency between projects. Generally, a distinction is made between *economic* and *stochastic* dependence. *Economic dependence* occurs if the mere acceptance of one project influences the cash flows of another project. A special case is offered by mutually exclusive projects, which means that the acceptance of one project prohibits the other project's acceptance.

Two projects are said to be *stochastically dependent* if the covariance between their respective cash flows is non-zero. In reality, all conceivable combinations of economic with stochastic dependence may occur.

Given these definitions, the market value of a project can be expressed as a function of the cash flows (including the initial investment outlays) associated with the project. For example, the net present value of project i may be defined as

(2.1) $$b_i = \sum_{t=o}^{T} \gamma_{t_i} . c_{ti}$$

where γ_{ti} represents the net present value of one dollar of the cash flow c_{ti}.

Financial planning can be seen as an extended capital budgeting problem. In financial planning, the investment opportunities are considered simultaneously with the financing and dividend options available to the firm (see e.g. Myers and Pogue [1974]).

An important assumption made in the literature on capital budgeting and financial planning is that the firm tries to maximize its owners' wealth. Because this wealth is co-determined by the risk-return charasteristics of the income streams generated by the firm, both 'risk' (bad: to be minimized) and 'expected return' (good: to be maximized) are often taken as separate goals in the evaluation of capital investment projects. Assuming an efficient capital market, these goals can be replaced by a single goal, i.e. the ' firm's market value' (to be maximized), which leaves a single criterion decision problem.

Goals however, other than those mentioned above, may also influence decisions concerning the selection of investment projects. As will be shown in this chapter, both the public and the private enterprise have to deal with a complex of multiple goals which

changes over time. It will not always be possible to bring these
multiple goals back to one single goal. In consequence, project
selection might be seen as a decision problem involving multiple
goals.

In spite of these possible arguments to treat capital budgeting
and financial planning as multiple criteria decision problems, they
are generally discussed in the literature as being single criterion
decision problems. However, the single criterion concerned (very
often the firm's market value) is optimized subject to a set of
constraints, part of which relates to managerial choices which might
just as well be considered as separate goals. Therefore, we will
discuss the nature of these constraints used in capital budgeting
and financial planning in more detail in the following section.
In this section, we will give a more precise meaning of the concepts
of 'goal' and 'constraint', as used in this study.

The word *goal* very often denotes a more or less detailed
description of a desired situation to be strived for by an individual
(or group of individuals), by (or for) whom this goal has been
formulated. Examples are the desire to 'maximize profits' and the
desire to 'maintain the current level of employment'. In our opinion,
one should distinguish between the *object* and the *nature* of a goal.
By the object of a goal we mean the entity that is being strived for.
Thus in the above examples the objects are 'profits' and the 'level
of employment' respectively. The object of a goal is a variable,
referred to as a *goal variable* (see also Section 3.1). The nature of
a goal indicates what the decision maker wants with the object at
hand, e.g. in the case of the goal variable 'profits', should it be
maximized, minimized, or should a certain minimum level be strived
for?
        If goals are to be mandatory for the determination of the action
to be chosen, a more or less clear relationship between the object of
the goal and the alternative actions should be definable (see Section
3.1). In our opinion, if such a relationship can (in principle) not

be defined, the goal has no practical meaning.

In this study, the term *constraint* (or *restriction*) is used in the usual sense. Thus a constraint is a condition (often stated in mathematical terms) imposed on the alternatives that might be conceived of. Alternatives which do not meet the stated condition have to be disregarded. They are, in other words, *infeasible* or *inadmissible alternatives*.

In common parlance, the difference between goals and constraints is rather vague. For instance, if we say that 'we do not accept any action which yields a lower profit than last year', we formulate the goal to attain a certain amount of profit as a constraint. On the other hand, constraints that are formulated in terms of rigid conditions may often be violated to some extent. If this is the case (which may occur e.g. with capacity constraints), the desire to not violate the constraints can be seen as goals.

In this study we will distinguish between goals and constraints according to the above definitions. However, in order to take account of 'goals formulated as constraints' and of 'constraints formulated as goals' we will introduce an additional concept, viz. *goal constraints*, which will be defined more precisely in Section 3.1.

2.2. Constraints in Capital Budgeting and Financial Planning

If the solution to a decision problem has to satisfy certain constraints, the nature and the exact formulation of these constraints should be clear to the decision maker. This is because the constraints co-determine which actions are feasible. Alternatively, constraints might be viewed as goals having top priority. Let us therefore have a closer look at the constraints in the capital budgeting and financial planning problems.

Both capital budgeting and financial planning deal with constraints on the required outlays for the projects in each of the time periods of the planning horizon. This phenomenon is commonly called capital rationing. A well-known mathematical programming formulation of the capital rationing problem has been provided by Weingartner [1961].

The model can be written as

$$\text{Max} \sum_{i=1}^{n} b_i \cdot x_i,$$

(2.2)

$$\text{s.t.} \sum_{i=1}^{n} e_{ti} \cdot x_i \leq E_t \qquad \text{for } t = 1, \ldots, T;$$

$$0 \leq x_i \leq 1 \qquad \text{for } i = 1, \ldots, n;$$

where b_i denotes the net present value of project i, and e_{ti} is the outlay required for project i in period t. The maximum permissable expenditure in period t is given by E_t. The fraction of project i accepted is given by x_i. This fraction can be required to be either zero or one, by which the linear programming problem turns into an integer programming problem. Both problems have been dealt with in detail by Weingartner [1961, 1963, 1966].

It should be noted that the term 'capital rationing' has not always been used in the same way in the literature. As was clearly shown by Weingartner [1977], various authors have made different assumptions about the phenomenon of capital rationing. Not surprisingly these differences have led to series of controversies regarding the discount rate that should be used in computing present values, what this rate actually stands for, and whether it does measure the firm's opportunity cost of capital properly. According to Weingartner [Ibid], most participants in the controversies have interpreted capital rationing as a market-imposed limitation on the expenditures a firm may make. Within this interpretation, which will be denoted by external capital rationing, a further subdivision can be made. One manifestation of external capital rationing is called pure (or hard), defining the situation in which neither the firm nor its owners have access to financial markets. More often, the firm is thought to exist apart from its (possibly) many owners. In this case only the firm is supposed to be rationed by the financial markets.

One may rightly wonder whether external capital rationing, in one form or another, exists for the private enterprise in reality.

One may argue that for any project offering a future and uncertain
income stream, some funds will be available. Indeed, a given option
on such an income stream is being valued by the capital market. For
this valuation, the expected returns and the riskiness of an option
constitute important determinants. If the expected returns are low
and/or the riskiness is high, the value of the option will be low,
but it will have a value. The value of such an option, at the time
of issuance, can be considered as the amount of funds the firm can
get in exchange for the option concerned. Seemingly, no discernable
reason exists for the market to deny the company any funds which
according to the market itself would contribute to the company's
market value. Obviously, given the market conditions, the option
'price' offered by the capital market may be too low to yield a
positive net present value for the project. In that case, the funds
are not acquired and the project is not undertaken. In our opinion,
the reason for not attracting funds is that the project does not
meet the market standards rather than that the firm is being rationed
by the market.

This brings us to another interpretation of rationing: the
so-called internal (or self-imposed) capital rationing. A firm may
refuse to attract additional funds, because it considers the conditions
offered by the market to be unfavourable. A factor causing this
refusal may be that there is an important disagreement between the
firm and the capital market with respect to the prospects of the firm.
Another reason for a firm to impose limits on its expenditures
may be that its current owners do not want to lose their control
over the firm.

Capital budgeting models incorporating capital rationing constraints can also be used in situations quite different from those
described above. Indeed, Weingartner [Ibid, p. 1404] states that his
'contributions have been directed at utilizing the informational
content of the programming formulation as an aid to decision making
and not as a positive theory of financial markets'. In the managerial
process of capital budgeting within firms, limits are frequently set

on plans for expenditures on capital account. According to Weingartner
[Ibid, p. 1428], this is done for planning and control purposes, and
consequently, is not a proper case of capital rationing. Because the
choice of these expenditure limits is subject to managerial choice,
it would be better not to treat them as constraints which have to be
met 'at any cost'. Instead, the decision maker should have the possibility to 'trade-off' these constraints against other goals. We will
return to this point later on in this study.

As with the expenditure limits, many other 'constraints' are
formulated in capital budgeting and financial planning problems.
Some examples are a) *operational constraints* like manpower, capacity
and liquidity constraints, b) *constraints to take account of the
capital market*, e.g. to limit the risk of financial failure, to
'smooth' dividends and earnings patterns over time and to limit the
amount of debt outstanding, c) *organizational constraints*, like
constraints on the percentage of total investments concerning new
products, constraints on employment, etc., and d) *external constraints*,
for instance to take account of the environmental effects of the
projects undertaken.

Clearly, many of these and other constraints are being used in
practice. Some reasons for this phenomenon will be discussed in the
following two sections.

2.3. The Goal of Market Value Maximization

As mentioned in the introductory section, the desirability of
(a set) of capital investment project(s) - as viewed by the firm's
owners - is determined by the project effects on the quality of the
owners' income over time. The quality of an income stream depends on
its height, riskiness, and timing. These quality effects can be
translated into one measure of the project's desirability, generally
called its *market value*. In most capital budgeting and financial
planning models, every project's market value is assumed to be a
point-estimate determined *a priori* by the decision maker. An example
is provided by the Weingartner model in (2.2), in which the value of

the i'th project is represented by the net present value of the
project (b_i).

The use of these *single* dimensional measures for a project's
desirability can be justified theoretically through the existence
of a price mechanism. The latter, being the capital market, determines
'prices' (i.e. discount factors, risk premiums, etc.) for lending
and borrowing money, subject to different risks. Below, we will go
into the theoretical justification of the use of a project's market
value as a measure of the project's desirability.

Most theories dealing with the appropriateness of the use of the
project's market value, assume *a priori* that the firm is trying to
maximize its owners' (stockholders') wealth. To reach an optimal
solution, both the firm and its owners can (and should) also consider
the exchange opportunities as offered by the capital market.

Assuming certainty, Hirshleifer [1958] has shown 'that the
present value rule for investment decisions is correct in a wide
variety of cases'. One of these cases occurs when investment
opportunities are independent and the capital market is 'perfect'
(a perfect capital market is one in which the lending rate equals
the borrowing rate, where this rate is independent of the amount of
borrowing or lending, and where no capital rationing exists).
However, if the lending rate is not equal to the borrowing rate, it
may happen that the present value rule is only correct in a formal
sense, because 'the discounting rate used is not an external opportunity but an internal shadow price which comes out of the analysis'
(Ibid). Unfortunately, there are also cases for which the present
value rule fails to give answers that are correct 'in the desired
sense of providing an objectively calculable criterion independent
of subjective preference considerations' (Hirshleifer [1970, p. 199]).
This may be the case if the capital market is no longer assumed to
be perfect: for example if the marginal borrowing rates increase as
the scale of borrowing is expanded.

In an <u>uncertain</u> world the analysis becomes even more complicated.
The main problem becomes the specification of the capital market
model, evaluating uncertain future income streams. Some authors have
tried to avoid the need for a detailed market equilibrium model (see
Modigliani and Miller [1958]). Others have used a very general uncertainty model, the time-state preference approach (see e.g.
Hirshleifer [1970]). For both approaches it is difficult to derive
meaningful decision rules for capital budgeting within the firm. An
intermediate approach is the capital asset pricing model (CAPM), as
developed by Sharpe, Lintner and Mossin. The CAPM, which essentially
is a one-period model [1], has produced results which have shown
empirically to be reasonably close approximations of the valuation
of uncertain income streams by capital markets. This theory says,
that in market equilibrium, the value of each uncertain income
stream $\tilde{X}$ is determined by the riskfree interest rate, $\tilde{X}$'s covariance
with the income generated by the total market and the so-called
market price of risk. Because investors have the possibility to
diversify their portfolios, the competitive capital market assigns
no value to the *unsystematic risk* of $\tilde{X}$, which is associated with the
part of $\tilde{X}$, which is stochastically independent of the market. The
same kind of reasoning can be applied to the valuation of the firm's
capital investment projects. Given an economically independent project,
and given the firm's objective to maximize its stockholders' wealth,
the firm neither has to worry about the unsystematic risk of
the projects nor about the stochastic dependencies between the
projects, because 'it is of no value to its owners'. Accordingly,
the discount factor to be used can be expressed in terms of the risk-
free interest rate, the market price of risk, and the project's

1) In order to make the CAPM-analysis suitable for multiple period
   capital budgeting, additional - rather restrictive and unrealistic
   - assumptions should be made. See e.g. Hamada [1969], Rubinstein
   [1973] and Stapleton [1971].

covariance with the market (its *systematic* risk) - (cf. Ballendux and Van Vliet [1978]). In consequence, different projects will require different discount factors.

So far we have dealt with the theoretical construction underlying the use of market values to measure a project's desirability. What about the fundaments, i.e. the assumptions, on which this theoretical construction itself has been built? Two very important assumptions have been made in the analysis:
(a) capital markets are efficient;
(b) firms are, and should be maximizing their owners' wealth.
As argued by Gordon [1980], the second assumption is already included in a similar but more limited assumption than (a), viz. that 'all markets - not just capital markets - are competitive'. We do not want to make this stronger assumption here. Instead we will deal with assumptions (a) and (b) separately; (a) will be discussed in the remainder of this section, and (b) will be discussed in Section 2.5.

Are capital markets efficient? Two distinct courses may be pursued to answer this question. First, the conditions indicated as being necessary for capital markets to be efficient can be verified (see Diepenhorst [1974]) for a set of conditions which is sufficient for efficiency. Secondly, the implications of the efficiency concept might be tested empirically. The latter line of thought has been followed among others by Haley and Schall [1973], stating with respect to capital market theory in general: '... *However, we are forced to make a number of fairly restrictive assumptions in developing the theory. The assumptions may not appear realistic; but if the implications of the theory are reasonable approximations to the facts we observe, the theory will be worth-while* ...'. From a methodological point of view, the latter 'justification' of the capital market theory is rather poor. The fact that theories, based on rather unrealistic assumptions, are not falsified by their implications is in itself not sufficient to accept these theories as being worthwhile.

It is hardly necessary to repeat the assumptions which are generally considered to be unrealistic. In the real world, taxes, transaction costs and bankruptcy costs do exist. Also, managers and owners often disagree about a firm's expected performance, partly due to the imperfect diffusion of information. As a matter of fact, all of these difficulties are extensively discussed in the finance literature. Many answers have been given, telling how certain assumptions might be relaxed, while indicating how the theories' implications might be affected by the relaxations. As yet, no such answer has been given while dropping or relaxing all unrealistic assumptions (cf. also Gordon [1980]).

What remains is a number of observations, being important for the analysis of capital budgeting and financial planning problems. First, the potential income generated by a quoted company is being valuated on the capital market. The value of an income stream is positively effected by its level, and negatively by its riskiness, although part of this risk can be diversified by the investors on the capital market. Thus if the influence of capital investments on the owners' wealth has to be accounted for, the market values of the investment projects should be included in the analysis. Obviously, the estimation of these market values will be a hazardous and difficult task. Secondly, there are several capital market imperfections that cannot be ignored. Notably in the evaluation of capital investment projects, taxes, transaction costs and the possible (economic) inter-dependencies between the projects should be accounted for. Further-more, situations may occur in which the managers of the firm and the investors do not have the same expectations with respect to the performance of the firm.

2.4. Assumptions with Respect to the Decision Maker and the Organization

As many empirical studies show, most spokesmen assert that in their firms, a multiplicity of goals is strived for. The goal of market value maximization is seldom mentioned. And if it is mentioned, it is generally not considered to be the only goal to be pursued (see for an overview of empirical studies of the goal(s) of the firm e.g. (Bethe [1975] and Petty and Scott [1980]). As observed by several authors, many of the goals appearing in empirical studies have clear relationships with the goal of market value maximization. Assuming that these relationships are indeed very clear, it is surprising that they are seldom dealt with in empirical studies. Notwithstanding the many difficulties connected with empirical studies of the goals of the firm [1], sufficient evidence exists to accept the result that the firm is striving for a multiplicity of goals. As a matter of fact, this is one of the main assumptions underlying this study. Below, we will describe in more detail which assumptions are made with respect to the decision maker and with respect to the organization in which he is operating.

Assumptions with respect to the decision maker

The exclusive use of market values to select capital investment projects explicitly assumes this is in optimal agreement with the desires of the firm's owners. Implicitly, it is assumed that the desires of the firm's other participants are translated as cost factors co-determining the market values, or as constraints co-determining the set of feasible projects. Furthermore, those engaged in selecting projects have the ability to make all necessary

---

1) One such difficulty concerns the question on which goals the study should be concentrated: personal goals (e.g. goals of individuals within the organization), organizational goals, or both? And what about the goals of groups of individuals? Furthermore, does the study address the goals the respondent thinks he is striving for, those he says he is striving for, those he is trying to strive for or even the goals he is in fact bringing nearer?

estimates and evaluations to calculate those projects which are
theoretically worthwhile. In fact, unbounded rational individuals
are assumed, who know exactly what they want, know the alternative
actions and their implications, and are able to translate this
information into optimal actions. What is wanted is the maximization
of the wealth of the firm's owners - and nothing else.

These assumptions, describing the 'economic man', who plays an
important part in many micro-economic theories, are generally not
considered to be useful for describing the behaviour of particular
decision makers. More realistic descriptions have been developed in
(social) psychology, sociology and organizational theory. Especially
the contributions of Simon, who studied human behaviour within
organizations (see e.g. Simon [1957,1960]), should be mentioned
here. Another useful framework has been provided by Yu [1980], who
summarizes a number of basic findings from psychology and sketches
the importance of these findings for normative decision methods.

In this study, we assume that man is not omniscient. Although
the human's information processing capacity is almost without limits,
the complexity of man's environment cannot be captured completely
by the human brain. Therefore, following Simon, we assume that man's
rationality is bounded.

This position has several implications. People neither know
exactly what their possibilities are, nor do they know exactly what
they want. Nevertheless, human beings have a set of motivational
needs. These needs may be assumed to be structured hierarchically,
although it should be noted that these structures of needs differ
from individual to individual and moreover, may change over time.
It may be postulated that people's choices depend on the state of
their socio-cultural environment (on the other hand, people's
choices may influence their environment). An important fact to be
stressed here is that human needs are certainly not unidimensional.

In order to satisfy their needs, people search for alternative
solutions. It appears that man is a learning and adaptive being,
reacting on new information, creating new thoughts and changing his

aspirations.

In the method developed in this study we assume that the decision maker has to choose a 'good' action from among the alternative
actions available. What makes an action 'good' depends on the decision maker's desires (goals) and on his evaluation of the conditions
that command the availability and outcomes of the actions (see also
Section 3.2).

We assume the decision maker to be capable of specifying which
goals (goal variables) are relevant in a particular decision situation, and furthermore, that he is capable of choosing between the
various alternatives proposed to him. However, we take account of
the possibility that the decision maker may change his mind.

Assumptions with respect to the organization

As already indicated in our discussion of the constraints used
in capital budgeting and financial planning, several organizational
aspects may influence the choice of capital investment projects.
Capital budgeting and financial planning are usually intended to
take account of at least some of these aspects. It is therefore important that we summarize a few results of organizational theory and
sociology (see among others Easton [1973], March and Simon [1958],
and Simon [1958].

Firms, as much as many other organizations, can be viewed as
open systems in which a number of *participants* can be distinguished.
We assume that people and other parties participate in organizations
because - and as long as - they can better satisfy their needs,
maybe with less risk, than without participation in the organization
concerned. The participants' needs are satisfied by 'rewards' (both
material and immaterial) received from the organization in exchange
for goods, money and services provided by the participants. As set
out above, the participants' needs depend on the individual's socio-
cultural environment. Part of this environment is the economic market

in which the participant operates. From the firm's point of view,
the contributions of the participants must justify the rewards to be
offered. What is justified depends on the alternatives available to
the firm. Thus the participants cooperate on the basis of more or less
complex exchange relationships. Both sides of these exchange relationships are subject to external influences such as socio-cultural
factors and market forces. All actions available to the firm are, of
course, co-determined by the contributions of the participants. The
contributions depend on the 'rewards' required by the participants,
by which these rewards can be viewed as indirectly co-determining
the available action. As such, these rewards can be viewed as goals
or goal variables, defined in the first part of this section. Because
the firm has to deal with a manifold of participants whose desired
rewards depend on external, and thus dynamic factors, the firm has
to deal with a *dynamic goal complex*.

The sketched picture of the firm may seem rather mechanistic.
However, it should be clear that we live in an uncertain world in
which the exchange relationships mentioned above are not always
very clear. Also, the co-operation between participants cannot be
assumed to be without friction. On the other hand, certain relations
may also contain some 'slack'.

At this point we have to mention an important organizational
assumption made in the remainder of this study, i.e. that decisions
can be treated as though they are made by a single decision maker,
deciding on basis of his view of the set of actions available and
of the dynamic goal complex. In reality, several decision makers may
take a decision together, either in a team as equivalent participants
or in some hierarchical organizational structure. Neither case is
irrelevant for capital budgeting and financial planning. Decisions
on capital investment projects are often taken step by step, thus
passing through several decision levels. Many of the decisions leading
to the final choice of projects are taken by teams of decision makers.
Nevertheless, we limit the scope of this study to the case in which
only one decision maker is involved, facing a multiplicity of goals.

2.5. The Firm's Market Value as One of the Elements in a Dynamic Goal Complex

As argued several times in this chapter, firms in reality have to deal with several goal variables. Two main questions can be raised: What is the role of the 'owner's wealth maximization' in this dynamic goal complex, and - for the purpose of financial management - can the firm be viewed as if maximizing its owners' wealth?

One of the 'plain observations' at the end of Section 2 was that the income streams generated by a firm are being valued by the capital market. The market value of these income streams does not depend *directly* on all of the goals strived for by the firm. Generally however, all of the goals may affect the income streams. In consequence, the market value depends indirectly on these goals.

From the other point of view, the realization of goals other than wealth maximization may depend on the firm's market value. For instance, if the firm is to attract new equity, the road to the capital market should be open - and the toll to follow this road should not be too high. Normally, the entrance to the capital market, and its price, is not independent of the market value of the firm's current stock. However, where the firm is planning a number of additional, or even new activities, for which the new equity is to be attracted, the capital market will certainly form expectations about the profitability and the risk of the planned activities. Furthermore, the market evaluates how the firm normally takes care of its stockholders' interests. Thus stockholder relations are at least partly reflected in the firm's current market value.

Another reason for the firm to support its market value is to avoid the risk of being taken over, which would certainly influence the interests of most of the firm's participants. The firm's top managers keep their eye on the firm's stock prices, so as to limit the risk of being fired by the stockholders. Notwithstanding this risk, there is usually some margin for the managers to strive for other goals besides the goal of maximizing market values.

Thus several reasons to keep up the market value exist. No reason has been given as to why the firm's market value should be <u>maxi-</u>
<u>mized</u>. In our opinion, market value maximization only makes sense
in the rather unrealistic situation in which all interests of all
participants run parallel to the goal of value maximization. Assuming that at least some participants want to allocate the firm's
means in directions other than necessary for value maximization,
and assuming they have the ability to co-determine the availability and to influence the allocation of these means, the goal of value
maximization has no satisfactory mathematical definition. The reason
is that the realization of this goal depends on the help of parti-
ipants whose goals deviate from market value maximization. The participants who strive for market value maximization thus cannot
control all of the variables determining the market value. Likewise,
the other participants cannot control all variables relevant for
their maximization problem. As argued by von Neumann and Morgenstern [1953, p.11], these kinds of problems cannot be described
as 'maximum problems, but rather as a peculiar and disconcerting
mixture of several conflicting maximum problems'.

For the purpose of financial management, one might treat the
firm <u>as if</u> maximizing its stockholders' wealth, either by ignoring
the desires of the other participants or by taking these desires as
given and fixed. The first, rather relentless approach by no means
guarantees 'good' values for the ignored goal variables. It may even
be possible that one or more of them are so poorly served that the
quality of the income streams produced by the firm is seriously
affected. Thus 'maximizing' the firm's market value without consideration of the other goal variables may result in surprisingly bad
market values.

The other often proposed procedure is to take the desires not
accounted for in the firm's market value, as given and fixed, i.e.
to treat them as cost factors or constraints to be considered <u>before</u>
considering market values. There are two main objections against

this approach. The decision maker has to determine the cost factors and the restrictions independently from the evaluation of the market values. Furthermore, goals that are dealt with implicity as cost factors or explicitly as constraints have pre-emptive priority over the maximization, subject to the constraints and given the cost factors of the market value. In reality, the decision making process is far less rigid. For instance, if the obtained maximum market value is not judged to be satisfactory, some of the restrictions may be relaxed. Likewise, if the obtainable market value appears to be very good, some of the constraints may be strengthened.

In our opinion it is better to treat all goals and constraints which are not completely fixed, as goal variables to be traded off against each other. The firm's market value could be one of these goal variables. The firm which considers capital budgeting and financial planning as decision problems with multiple goal variables should also consider the use of multiple criteria decision methods. This will be the subject of the following chapters.

References

Ballendux, F.J. and J.K. van Vliet (1978), 'Firm Effects and Project Values' Report 7815/F, Centre for Research in Business Economics, Erasmus University Rotterdam, Rotterdam.

Bethe, H.J. (1975), Ondernemings-Doelstellingen bij nader inzien, Stenfert Kroese, Leiden.

Crum, R. and F. Derkinderen (1980), Proceedings of the Conference on Financial Management of Corporate Resource Allocations, Martinus Resource Allocations, Martinus Nijhoff, Boston.

Diepenhorst, A.I. (1974), Enkele opmerkingen over de efficiënte markt, in Aspecten van Effecten, University Press, Rotterdam.

Easton, A. (1973), 'Complex Managerial Decisions Involving Multiple Objectives', Wiley, New York.

Fandel, G. and T. Gal (eds) (1980), Multiple Criteria Decision Making-Theory and Applications, Springer, Berlin.

Gordon, M.J. (1980), The Interest in a Corporation of its Management Workers, and, Country, in Crum, R. and F. Derkinderen [1980].

Haley, C.W. and L.D. Achall (1973), The Theory of Financial Decisions, McGraw-Hill, New York.

Hamada, R.S. (1969), 'Portfolio Analysis, Market Equilibrium and Corporation Finance', Journal of Finance, pp. 13-31.

Hirshleifer, J. (1958), 'On the Theory of Optimal Investment Decision', Journal of Political Economy, pp. 329-352.

Hirshleifer, J. (1970), Investment, Interest and Capital, Prentice-Hall, Englewood Cliffs.

Lorie, J.H. and L.J. Savage (1955), Three Problems in Rationing Capital, Journal of Business, Oct. 1955, pp. 229-239.

March, J.G. and H.A. Simon (1958), Organizations, MacMillan, New York.

Modigliani, M. and M.H. Miller (1958), The Cost of Capital, Corporation Finance, and the Theory of Investment, American Economic Review, pp. 261-297.

Myers, S.C. and G.A. Pogue (1974), A Programming Approach to Corporate
    Financial Management, Journal of Finance, Vol. XXIX/2, pp. 579-599.

Neumann, J. von, and O. Morgenstern (1953), Theory of Games and
    Economic Behaviour, 3rd edition, Wiley, New York.

Petty, J.W. and D.F. Scott, Capital Budgeting Practives in Large
    American Firms: A Retrospective Analysis and Update, in Crum R.
    and F. Derkinderen [1980].

Rubinstein, M.E. (1973), A Mean-Variance Synthesis of Corporate
    Financial Theory, Journal of Finance, pp. 167-181.

Simon, H.A. (1957), Models of Man, Wiley, New York.

Simon, H.A. (1958), Administrative Behaviour, MacMillan, New York.

Simon, H.A. (1960), The New Science of Management Decision, Wiley,
    Englewood Cliffs.

Stapleton, R.C. (1971), Portfolio Analysis, Stock Valuation and
    Capital Budgeting Decision Rules for Risky Projects, Journal of
    Finance, pp. 95-117.

Weingartner, H.M. (1963), Mathematical Programming and the Analysis
    of Capital Budgeting Problems, Prentice-Hall, Englewood Cliffs.

Weingartner, H.M. (1966), Capital Budgeting of Interrelated Projects:
    Survey and Synthesis, Management Science, Vol. 12/7, March 1966,
    pp. 213-244.

Weingartner, H.M. (1977), Capital Rationing: in Authors in Search
    of a Plot, Journal of Finance, Vol. XXXII/5, pp. 1403-1431.

Yu, P.L. (1980), Behaviour Bases and Habitual Domains of Human
    Decision/Behaviour --- Concepts and Applications, in Fandel, G.
    and T. Gal [1980,pp. 511-539].

3. A SURVEY OF MULTIPLE CRITERIA DECISION METHODS

In this chapter and in the three subsequent chapters, we deal mainly with Multiple Criteria Decision Methods (MCDM). In Chapter 6, this analysis results in a description of a new approach: Interactive Multiple Goal Programming (IMGP). Beforehand - in Chapters 4 and 5 - we describe the methods which constitute the basis for this new approach.

The present chapter is devoted to a survey of multiple criteria decision methods. In Section 3.1 we explain a number of important definitions and some basic concepts of multiple criteria decision making, which is followed in Section 3.2 by the description of a general framework used to show how these kinds of *methods* might help in practical decision *problems*. In order to know which method might be used beneficially in a particular decision problem, the analyst should first determine the most important characteristics of the problem. Therefore, before presenting an overview of methods, we list a number of characteristics of decision problems in Section 3.3. This is followed by a general overview of multiple criteria decision methods in Section 3.4. In Section 3.5 a more detailed discussion of the subclass of methods based on mathematical programming techniques is presented. Our main conclusions are given in Section 3.6.

3.1. Terminology and Basic Concepts

Ultimately, decision making involves choosing between alternative actions (policies, strategies, or simply alternatives). The set of alternative actions can either be described explicitly - by describing its elements one by one - or implicitly. In the latter case, every action is described by a vector $\underline{x}$ of values of the instrumental (policy, or decision) variables x_1, ..., x_n. The

set of alternative actions (set of admissable alternatives or
feasible region) is described indirectly by means of constraints
(restrictions) on the values of the instrumental variables.

From the set of alternative actions, one (or in some cases
more than one) alternative must be found which meets the decision
maker's preferences in an optimal (or sometimes if not optimal, at
least in a satisfactory) way. The decision maker's preferences
depend on certain properties (or attributes) of the alternative
actions. These preferences may be considered to be directly related
to the attribute values, or alternatively, as a function of certain
goal variables, which in their turn depend on the value(s) of one
or more attributes. In the case that the set of alternative actions
has been described implicitly, it is rather common to consider
the values of the instrumental variables in a given solution as
attribute values, and thus the goal variables as functions of the
instrumental variables. The preferences can then be considered to
depend either on the values of the goal variables or on the deviations from certain goal values (aspiration levels, targets) aspired
by the decision maker.

The term objective function will be reserved here exclusively
for the function in a mathematical model (describing a certain
decision situation), which is to be optimized. In general, the
objective function serves as a means to optimize the decision
maker's preference function. Depending on the problem formulation
at hand, the objective function may, but does not need to coincide
with the decision maker's preference function.

If some aspired goal value is formulated as a constraint, from
which one may deviate through the inclusion of deviational
variables (cf. Section 3.3 and Chapter 4), we will term such a constraint a goal constraint (restriction).

An alternative which is described by a set of instrument
values can clearly be represented as a vector in the instrument
value space. This alternative can of course also be represented
by the vector of goal values, attained for this alternative, in

the goal value space (often but less desirably called the 'objective function space'). A vector in the goal value space will be referred to as a solution.[1] Note that an element of the instrument value

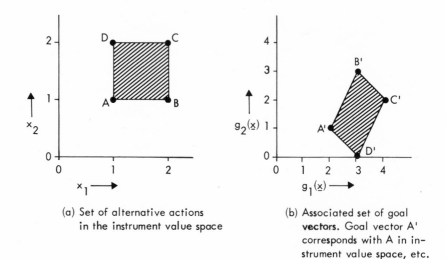

(a) Set of alternative actions in the instrument value space

(b) Associated set of goal vectors. Goal vector A' corresponds with A in instrument value space, etc.

Figure 3.1. A set of alternative actions in the instrument value space and the associated goal vectors in the goal value space

1) The term solution will be reserved exclusively for a vector in the goal value space. Note, however, that many authors in MCDM literature also use this term to indicate an element of the instrument value space. Here, an element of the instrument value space will be referred to as the action, i.e. vector of instruments $\underline{x}$, generating a solution $g(\underline{x}) = (g_1(\underline{x}), \ldots, g_m(\underline{x}))$.

In our opinion it is preferable to use different terms for the elements of these two different spaces.

space can always be mapped uniquely into the goal value space, but that the reverse does not necessarily apply. This is because different actions can result into the same solution. In Figure 3.1 we give an example of a (feasible) set of alternative actions and the associated set of goal vectors in the goal value space. We assume two instrumental variables, x_1 and x_2, and two goal variables, $g_1(\underline{x}) = x_1 + x_2$ and $g_2(\underline{x}) = 2x_1 - x_2$.

A very important concept in multiple criteria decision making is the notion of an efficient (non-inferior, non-dominated, or Pareto-optimal) solution. This is an element of the set of feasible solutions for which no other solution in the same set of feasible solutions can be found to have a better value for one or more of the goal variables without having worse values for one or more of the other goal variables. Returning to Figure 3.1 and assuming that both $g_1(\underline{x})$ and $g_2(\underline{x})$ are to be maximized, it is easily seen that (in the goal value space) both B' and C' and all vectors on the line connecting B' and C' are efficient. Gradually going from C' to B' gives a better value of $g_2(\underline{x})$, but at the price of worsening the value of $g_1(\underline{x})$. However, all feasible solutions below the line B'C' are non-efficient in this case. The problem to find all efficient solutions is generally referred to as the vector-maximum problem.

The concept of efficiency is very useful because it offers a generally powerful tool to reduce the number of alternatives to be evaluated by the decision maker. Nevertheless, one should be very careful with regard to the use of the efficiency concept for the reduction of the set of alternatives. That is, for a given set of alternatives and a given set of goal variables, the set of efficient solutions can, in principle, be calculated. If a new goal variable is added, the set of efficient solutions generally grows considerably. In that case the decision maker will not necessarily choose a solution which was already efficient before adding the new goal variable. Therefore if in a given problem formulation it is not certain that all the decision maker's goal variables have been

included, it may be undesirable to limit further analysis to the set
of efficient solutions.

Another important notion frequently used in multiple criteria
decision making is the concept of the ideal solution (see e.g.
Zeleny [1976]). The elements of the ideal solution are the maximum
values of the goal variables which are individually attainable
within the set of feasible actions. In most multiple criteria
decision problems these maxima cannot be attained simultaneously.
Then the term utopia solution (cf. Yu [1973]) better denotes the
true meaning of this concept. The importance of ideal (utopia)
solutions is that they can be used as 'points of reference' for
judging alternatives.

In the example underlying Figure 3.1, the ideal solution is
defined by $g_1(\underline{x}) = 4$ and $g_2(\underline{x}) = 3$. In this case a unique action
corresponds with the ideal solution. This action is found by
solving $g_1(\underline{x}) = x_1 + x_2 = 4$ and $g_2(\underline{x}) = 2x_1 - x_2 = 3$, which gives
$x_1 = 0.5$ and $x_2 = 3.5$. Clearly, both the ideal solution and the
corresponding action are infeasible.

As is the case with the set of efficient solutions, the ideal
solution can be found using no information about the decision
maker's preferences other than the knowledge on which goal variables are important and whether these should be maximized or
minimized.

Because generally not all individual maximum goal values can
be attained simultaneously, the decision maker will either have to
be content with a compromise solution or will have to enlarge the
set of feasible actions (by relaxing constraints or by introducing
new actions). In some multiple criteria decision procedures (see
Section 3.3 and Chapters 5 and 6), the decision maker is repeatedly
confronted with new compromise solutions, on which basis he has to
express his (local) preferences, which are then used to calculate
a new compromise solution, and so forth. These procedures are aimed

at finding a so-called <u>final (best) compromise solution.</u>

3.2. Decision Problems and Methods

Most methods dealt with in this study explicitly aim at helping
the decision maker (or the group of decision makers) in the decision
making process. As such, these and many other procedures developed
in economics, management science, and operations research are
normative by construction. *'If you accept our propositions, you are
better off to follow our instructions'* could be a general slogan
for these approaches. Clearly, the more these propositions correspond
to practical decision problems the higher the chance that a certain
method will be accepted in practice. This is, however, not the only
consideration in evaluating such a method. Many tools developed
for assisting decision making are very powerful and worthwhile
simply because of a number of basic simplifying assumptions (e.g.
the assumption of certainty, transitivity of preferences, etc.).
Thus, depending on the decision situation and the type of decision
assistance required, a balance between the above factors must be
strived for.

To be able to confront the features of these normative methods
with the needs in practice, we give, in Figure 3.2, a very simplified
scheme of the decision situation of a decision maker who wants to
rely on normative methods. The scheme is very simplified indeed.
The dynamic aspects of a decision process are not indicated; nor
are the organizational (e.g. power structures, hierarchical decision
levels, interactions and communication) and human (e.g. capabilities,
rationality, preference formation) aspects of decision making.
Nevertheless, this scheme helps to describe the character of these
normative approaches. As shown in Figure 3.2, we assume the decision
maker to be a part of a system (e.g. a firm) which produces (under
the influence of the decision maker, other actors participate in the
system, the environment, and so forth) a constant stream of <u>actions,</u>
which in their turn result in <u>outcomes</u> (e.g. profit, wages, pollution).
These outcomes are evaluated by the decision maker and other

36

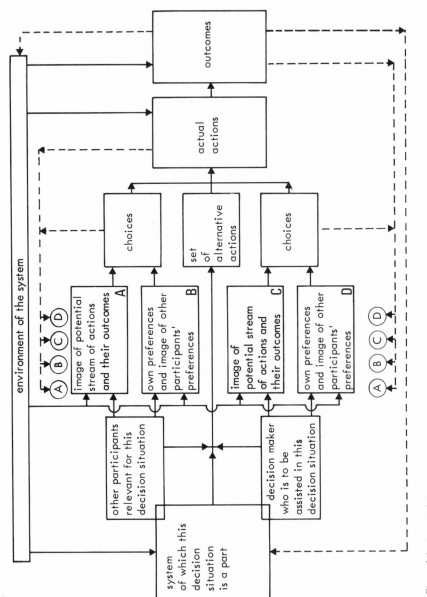

Figure 3.2. A typical decision situation

participants, and may thus give rise to pressures to change the
stream of actions in order to improve future outcomes. It then
becomes the decision maker's task to influence the stream of
actions in a way which will meet the desires of the decision
maker(s), other participants and the system's environment as good
as possible. The decision maker can influence the stream of actions
both directly and indirectly. Directly, by changing his own actions;
indirectly, by asking (if not instructing) other participants to
change their actions in a certain way. Clearly, as long as the
decision maker is not managing a show of puppets, he is not
always certain whether the stream of actions will change in the
indicated way, and if so, whether they will lead to the desired
outcomes. Of course, the decision maker tries to make an appropriate
decision. This will be based on his perception of the possible
streams of actions (and the outcomes implied), on the desires and
pressures of the other participants, and finally on the decision
maker's own preferences (see Figure 3.2).

In general, most normative approaches to decision making aim
at assisting the decision maker(s) in one or more of the following
ways:

(a) Improve the image of the set of alternative streams of actions

Examples are methods which help to find a feasible stream of
actions and methods which generate new streams of actions.

(b) Clarify the relationships between actions and outcomes

Many kinds of simulation models and econometric models can be
classified under this leading.

(c) Help to choose a (set of) suitable stream(s) of actions

A large part of economics and the main parts of operations
research and management science are aimed at providing 'optimal
solutions'. Recently, however, it has been stressed that a
normative procedure does not necessarily have to indicate a
unique, optimal solution (cf. Roy [1976, 1977]).

For instance, these methods may be used to eliminate a number of
apparently inferior solutions.

Clearly, there seem to be many perspectives for normative decision
methods. Nevertheless, many of the proposed normative methods have
been criticized and have encountered a lot of resistance. Why?
Several methods have evoked much criticism due to the advanced
theoretical nature of these methods which claimed 'to solve all
your problems'. On the other hand, methods have been condemned
completely because they were erratically used in situations for
which they were neither designed nor suited. Indeed, several
assumptions which are frequently made are rather strong and thus
hard to be met in reality. This has given rise to a lot of principal
questions. Is the relationship between means and ends always
quantifiable? If so, can it be represented by a rigid mathematical
expression? Can all outcomes be translated into a single measure?
What about the preferences of participants other than the decision
maker: can they be ignored, or should they be represented by
restrictions? Is it possible to model 'means' independently of
'ends'? Can preferences be represented by a mathematical function
(possibly in one dimension)? Should these methods help to find an
optimal solution, or rather help to improve the decision process?
Detailed discussions on these and related topics can be found e.g.
in Keen [1977], and Lindblom [1959].

Many developments in operations research and management science
look very promising. New methods are created and old methods are
refined and adapted in order to be suitable for decision situations
which were hitherto inaccessible. Also, there are clear tendencies
to pay more attention to the dynamic (including the psychological,
sociological, and organizational) aspects of decision making. One
of the features of these tendencies is the rapid and broad development of multiple criteria decision making theory. Due to their
greater correspondence with reality, multiple criteria decision
methods seem to be better suited for assisting the decision maker

than single criteria decision methods. However, no decision maker
can be replaced by any of these methods. No method can prescribe
the best solution in a particular situation. At best, a method can
assist the decision maker by strengthening the basis on which the
decisions are made and by improving the quality of the decision
process.

Obviously, for a particular decision problem an appropriate
method should be chosen. In order to facilitate this choice we will
next list a number of problem characteristics, followed by an
overview of available methods.

3.3. Some Characteristics of Decision Problems

Before presenting an overview of multiple criteria decision
methods, we list a number of characteristics of decision problems
by means of which these methods can be typified. Ideally, a
typology of methods should be problem-oriented. The method's
description should thus indicate for which decision situation(s)
the method might be used. Most multiple criteria decision methods
have not yet been described in such a way. The reason is that the
field is not only very rapidly growing, but also - and mainly -
that there is as yet no detailed and generally accepted overview
of the class of decision problems and situations in which multiple
criteria decision methods might possibly be used. Studies in this
direction have been initiated by Despontin and Spronk [1979] and
Moscarola [1979].

From the above it is clear that different decision situations
may require different methodologies, although some methods may be
useful in several situations. As shown in Figure 3.3, the class of
characteristics to be described can roughly be subdivided into
three subsets, describing the data, the information processing
system and the required output (cf. Despontin and Spronk [1979]
and Rietveld [1980]). Without pretending to be exhaustive (which is
clearly impossible), we will describe a number of charasteristics
for each of these subsets.

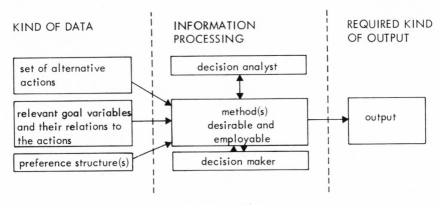

Figure 3.3. Some sets of characteristics of decision problems

        The relevant characteristics to typify the <u>kind of data</u>
which can be handled by a particular methodology concern the set
of alternative actions, the set of goal variables (including their
relationships with the set of actions) and the nature of the
preference structure(s) of the decision maker(s).

(a) <u>The set of alternative actions</u>

    - this set may be fixed or may change in the course of the
      decision process
    - an action may be defined as a single action or as a strategy,
      i.e. a series of coherent actions
    - the actions may be described explicitly (one by one) or
      implicitly by means of constraints
    - the feasibility of the actions may be certain or uncertain
    - the actions may be well-defined or may be stated in fuzzy
      terms

(b) <u>Relevant goal variables and their relationship to the actions</u>

    - this set may also be fixed or may change in the course of the
      decision process
    - the goal variables may be well-defined or may be stated in
      fuzzy terms

- the relations between goal variables and actions may be deterministic or stochastic
- the relations between goal variables and actions may be well-
  defined or fuzzy

(c) Nature of the preference structure(s)

- how detailed is the preference information required from the
  decision maker(s)?
- which kind of preference structure(s) can be handled?
- is the preference structure considered to be fixed, or can it
  change in the course of the decision process?
- are one or more decision makers involved?

To characterize the way in which the input data are transformed into answers and advice to the decision maker i.e. the
information processing (see Figure 3.3), the properties of the
method, the demands upon both decision maker and analyst as well
as their interrelationships are to be described next.

(d) Properties of the method (desirability/feasibility)

- is it a standard method or must it be adapted for each
  particular decision situation?
- is the method easy to use, or does it for example require
  that extensive models be built?
- what are the costs to employ the method?
- does the method converge to the desired type of output and
  if so, how fast?

(e) Demands on the decision maker(s)

- how many decision makers are involved?
- are there one or more hierarchical decision levels involved,
  and does such a level consist of one or several branches?
- is the method easy or difficult to understand?
- how much time does the method require from the decision
  maker(s)?

(f) Demands on the analyst(s)

- how many analysts are to be involved?
- how much of their time is needed?

- what kind of training do they need to be able to employ the
  method?

(g) Interrelationships (see also Section 5.2)

- how many and what kind of questions are to be answered by
  the decision maker(s)?
- what kind of information is provided to the decision maker(s)?
- what are the decision maker's options to control the solution
  process?
- when and how is the analyst involved?
- does the analyst have the possibility to manipulate the
  solution process?

Depending on the nature of the decision problem at hand, the
kind of output (see Figure 3.3) expected from a normative decision
method may vary considerably. For many years, most normative
decision methods were built with the aim to provide 'the optimal
solution' for a given decision problem. As pointed out by Roy
[1977], normative methods may also be aimed at reducing the set
of feasible actions (for instance by removing all inferior solutions)
or they may help to construct a preference ranking order of the
set of alternatives. As a purpose in itself, but usually as a
byproduct of serving the other purposes, a normative decision method
may help to structure the decision process and to clarify the
relationships between actions, goal variables and preferences.

In complete accordance with the possibilities listed under
(a) and (b), the action (or set of actions) selected with the help
of the decision method may be feasible with certainty or subject
to uncertainty, and may be well-defined or formulated in fuzzy
terms. The same possibilities hold for the goal values attained
through these actions. Consequently, also the output of a decision
method may be formulated as a random variable and/or may even be
stated in ill-defined terms. For instance, one method may deliver
the optimal solution with certainty (given the model of the decision situation), while another method shows a set of actions which
will 'very probably' be 'fairly good'.

As mentioned above, this list of characteristics is, and can not be, exhaustive. The closer one looks at particular decision situations, at the way decision makers solve their problems, and at the ways normative methods can be used within the solution process, the clearer it becomes that many situations have their own typical characteristics. The above list is intended to serve only as a general typology. In particular problems, other characteristics may also play a role. For instance, this is the case when we discuss interactive procedures (Chapter 5) and capital budgeting problems (Chapter 8).

3.4. A General Overview of Available Methods

Many overviews of available multiple criteria decision methods have been published (see e.g. Hwang and Masud [1979], MacCrimmon [1973], Nijkamp and Spronk [1979a,1980], Rietveld [1980], Roy [1971,1977], Starr and Zeleny [1977], and Zionts [1979]). With the aid of the list of problem characteristics described in the preceding section, the set of available methods may be subdivided in several ways. The general overview in this section (as well as the more specific overview in the next section) is based on the main operational options (see also Roy [1977]) which can be chosen by the analyst. These options are defined as the main approaches to transform the input data into the desired type of output. In a particular decision situation, the choice of such an option thus depends on the type of input data available and on the type of output desired by the decision maker. We will distinguish between the following options:

(1) Help to clarify and to structure the decision situation.
(2) Reduce the set of alternatives on basis of very obvious *a priori* information.
(3) Collect *a priori* information about the decision maker's preferences. Use this information to reduce and to (partially) order the set of alternatives. Accept the fact that the

decision maker may judge different actions as incomparable and that his preferences might be intransitive.

(4) Collect sufficient *a priori* information about the decision maker's preferences to be able to (completely) order the set of alternatives and to deduct an (optimal) final solution. Do not provide for incomparability and intransitivity.

(5) Confront successively the decision maker with compromise solutions. Collect the decision maker's (local) preferences with respect to such a compromise solution and use this information to calculate a new compromise solution. The decision maker thus progressively articulates part of his preferences while searching for a best compromise solution.

Several combinations of the above options do exist. To mention a few examples, (1) may come prior to any of the other options but it may also be integrated in and result from the other options; (2) and (5) are often integrated; and (5) may be used to reduce the number of alternative actions to be evaluated by means of attitude (4).

Within each operational option, one can, as in Section 3.3, distinguish between deterministic and stochastic methods dealing with explicitly or implicitly given constraints, etc. Below, we give a general description of each option, together with an indication of the kind of methods which are typical for these options.

(1) Clarification of the decision situation

In general, the proclaimed purpose of multiple criteria decision methods is to assist the decision maker in choosing a suitable action or set of actions. Nevertheless, these methods may also help the decision maker to clarify his perception of the decision situation. In close co-operation with the decision maker, the analyst tries to learn which alternative actions do exist, how the decision maker's preferences look, and how these preferences relate to the actions. All these questions improve the decision maker's understanding of the decision

problem. In this respect, multiple criteria decision methods are not
principally different from other normative methods. However, the
fact that multiple criteria decision methods explicitly take
account of multiple and mutually conflicting goal variables, defined
by one and sometimes more decision makers, raises some additional
problems. Decision makers do not necessarily know exactly what they
want, and even if so, they may not always be willing to express
their desires. If more decision makers and/or other participants
are involved, it may be very difficult to estimate the interpersonal
relationships which might influence the decision situation (cf.
Patton [1978, Chs. 6 and 7]). Thus far, the theory of multiple
criteria decision making has paid relatively little attention to
these problems. Although a wide body of literature on the psychological and organizational aspects of decision making does exist, many
of the reported results from these fields have never, or seldom
been used in normative multiple criteria decision methods. This
may be one reason why some of these - and other normative methods -
have never been, and probably never will be used in practice.
Fortunately, more and more attention is being paid to the psychological and organizational side of normative decision making (cf.
Moscarola [1979] and Roy [1977]).

Very few methods and procedures especially intended to help
clarify the decision maker's image of the decision situation exist
apart from the more general 'clarification methods' already mentioned
in Section 3.2. For example, one procedure is to give a spatial
representation of the alternative actions which may be useful e.g.
in location problems with multiple goals. This procedure was used
in a highway location problem. Alternative routes were proposed,
respectively characterized by minimum costs for construction,
maximum scenic attractiveness, minimum disruptiveness, and so forth.
These and the subsequent compromise locations were shown on trans-
parencies (see Manheim [1966]).

(2) Reduction of the set of alternatives

     In many decision situations at least some elementary
a priori information is available. Even if this information is
very simple, it can often be used beneficially in multiple
criteria decision situations. With the help of an everyday
example, we will show how simple information can be used to
reduce the number of alternatives to be evaluated by the decision
maker. Let us assume a decision maker, who has to select a new
truck. One example of very simple information may be that the
decision maker wants a truck of about the correct size, i.e.
(in his words) that its length should be 20 - 25 feet and 7 - 9
feet in width. Obviously, the set of available alternatives can
be reduced drastically by formulating constraints on the size
of the truck to be bought. In fact, formulating constraints
is one of the oldest and most straightforward ways to reduce
the number of alternatives to be evaluated by the decision
maker. Constraints may be of different types, i.e. they may
be conjunctive, which means that the alternatives have to satisfy
all constraints, as for example in linear programming, or they
may be disjunctive, which means that every alternative has to
meet at least one of a series of constraints: 'We generally
accept a proposal for an expansion investment if it has excellent
sales expectations or if it removes important bottlenecks in the
production process'. Continuing our earlier example, the decision
maker might have given the additional information, that his truck
must be as cheap and as powerful as possible. With the help of
this information, the efficiency-concept (cf. Section 3.1) may
help to reduce the number of alternatives to be evaluated in more
detail. Given a set of trucks which only differ with respect
to price and power, all trucks which are non-efficient, and
thus dominated by other trucks, do not have to be evaluated
further by our decision maker. The efficiency-concept has proved
to be extremely useful, especially in relation to multiple

objective programming methods (see for instance Gal [1977], and
Yu and Zeleny [1975]).

(3) Partial ordering of the set of alternatives

In this option, which has been developed and promoted by
a.o. Roy (see e.g. Roy [1977]), the analyst only models 'those
preferences he is capable of establishing objectively and with
sufficient reliability' (ibid, p. 200). In doing so, incomparability of alternatives and intransitivities of preference
relations are not excluded. Roy starts with the 'fundamental
partial comparability axiom', which states that the preferences
for every two potential actions α and α' can be modelled by
exactly one of the following relations: (a) indifference,which
is reflexive and symmetric, (b) strict preference, which is
irreflexive and antisymmetric, (c) large preference, which is
also irreflexive and antisymmetric, and (d) incomparability,
which is irreflexive and symmetric. Thus, in contrast to
utility theory (see option (4)), this approach explicitly
includes incomparability and large preference. The latter is
defined as the case in which one of two actions is not strictly
preferred to the other, although it is impossible to say whether
this other action is strictly preferable or whether indifference
holds. Given these concepts, Roy introduced the notion of
outranking relation. A potential action α' outranks the potential
action α if the analyst has enough reasons' ... to admit that in
the eyes of the decision maker α' is at least as good as α...'.
Action α' does not outrank α if'... the arguments in favor of the
outranking proposition are judged insufficient' (in this case
α is either incomparable with or preferred to α'). To include
the case in which the analyst hesitates to either accept or
reject an outranking relation, the latter notion can be extended
to that of a fuzzy outranking relation (see Roy [1977]), in
which the degree of

credibility of a certain outranking relation can be expressed
by means of a number $d(\alpha,\alpha')$, $0 \leq d \leq 1$. Several techniques to
establish the outranking relations are discussed by the same
author, who also shows how the relations can be used (a) to
help to choose a best action, (b) to subdivide the set of
actions in a subset of 'good' actions, a set of 'bad' actions,
and a set of actions which are to be examined in more detail
and (c) to help rank the actions in decreasing order of
preference. All of the procedures are operational (known by
the names ELECTRE I, II, III) and have found various applications,
especially in the French-speaking world (see Roy [Ibid] for
more references).

(4) Complete ordering of the set of alternatives

This option underlies most of the existing normative
decision methods. The usual way to proceed is (in very simply-
fied terms) to model the decision alternatives and the decision
maker's preferences first, and next to calculate the 'optimal'
solution. This 'classical' option has also been chosen in
several approaches to multiple criteria decision making. Given
the *a priori* information (or 'model') of the decision maker's
preferences, several ways to calculate the final solution exist.
One may calculate an index value of each alternative action, one
may maximize a preference function relating to the attributes
or goal variables, one may minimize a distance function (i.e.
a dispreference function) to an ideal point, or one may use
other procedures. A more fundamental difference between the
approaches of this class lies in the ways the decision maker's
preferences are modelled.

One approach to this modelling problem is to infer the
decision maker's preferences from past decisions. Provided that
the decision problem is sufficiently repetitive, data concerning
past decisions and the corresponding attribute values can be
used as inputs for an extrapolation procedure as for instance

linear regression and related techniques (see e.g. Dawes [1971] and Slovic and Lichtenstein [1971]). Surprisingly, even very simple models of the decision maker's preferences often give very good predictions of the decision maker's choices in new situations.

Another way to model the decision maker's preferences is based on direct questioning. For the case in which there is a number of explicitly given alternatives, the outcomes of which are random variables, the utility theory developed by von Neumann and Morgenstern [1953] has been extended explicitly to a 'multiple attribute utility theory'. Surveys and theoretical details are given a.o. by Farquhar [1977], Fishburn [1978], and Keeney and Raiffa [1976]. Once the probability distributions and the utility function have been assessed, the most preferred action can be calculated using the customary techniques. Consequently, most attention has been paid to the techniques of obtaining information about probabilities and utilities from the decision maker. The multiple attribute utility approach has a firm theoretical basis and is therefore very attractive. An important axiom underlying multiple attribute utility theory is that the decision maker's preferences with respect to any pair of potential actions α and α' can be modelled by means of the indifference or the strict preference relation mentioned under (3) above, which moreover are assumed to be transitivity relations. As argued by Roy [1977] a.o., these assumptions are rather strong. Since this approach is moreover very demanding for the decision maker, it can at best be used only in very important decisions, with a limited number of mutually comparable and well-defined decision alternatives playing a role.

(5) Sequential articulation of preferences

Instead of requiring all preference information from the decision maker prior to calculating the desired solution (or

set of solutions), many procedures gather this information in
a stepwise and iterative manner. As suggested by an overview
of 'sequential elimination methods' (cf. MacCrimmon [1973]),
decision makers in practice do often decide in a stepwise and
iterative way. This phenomenon has been formalized within the
so-called interactive procedures, which operate in an iterative
fashion from one solution (or set of solutions) to another,
guided by the local (i.e. given the current solution) preferences
of the decision maker. Compared with approaches (3) and (4), the
interactive procedures need much less *a priori* information on the
decision maker's preferences. Moreover, the decision maker
becomes more closely involved in the solution process which may
induce important learning effects. Interactive procedures have
been developed both for problems with explicitly and implicitly
given alternatives. Chapter 5 will be completely devoted to a
general discussion and overview of interactive procedures.

3.5. An Overview of Multiple Objective Programming Methods

In this section we present an overview of the class of multiple
criteria decision methods dealing with implicitly given alternatives
(see Section 3.3). These methods are generally based on mathematical
programming methods and are therefore often called multiple objective
programming methods. In the present study we limit ourselves to
this class of methods and to their applications in capital budgeting
and financial planning. Note that in case alternative capital
investment projects, budgets or financial plans have been described
explicitly, they can quite easily be adopted in a programming
framework. Nevertheless, if only a limited number of explicitly
given alternatives is relevant, the role of programming methods
may become less important.

Multiple objective programming methods can be classified along
the same lines as followed in the preceding section for the more
general classification of multiple criteria decision methods: i.e.

by means of the operational options chosen by the analyst, although one of them (the partial ordering approach) is not found in multiple objective programming. The other operational options exist in multiple objective programming and will be discussed next.

(1) Clarification of trade-offs

In single objective programming, the calculation of the optimal solution is generally not considered to be the only answer to be submitted by the analyst. A presumably more important question to be answered is what happens if the values of the instrumental variables differ slightly from their 'optimal' values, or what happens if the availability of resources changes. These questions are generally tackled by means of sensitivity analysis, for which many methods offer a well-developed analytical apparatus. As observed by several authors, this apparatus can be very helpful in clarifying multiple criteria decision situations. One straightforward way is to optimize only one goal variable, subject to constraints on the values of the goal variables which are not optimized. A subsequent sensitivity analysis can then be used to clarify the trade-offs between the various goal variables. For the linear case, this line of thought has been elaborated by Gal [1979] and Gal and Nemoda [1972].

(2) Reduction of the set of alternatives on the basis of elementary a priori information

Obviously, if threshold values of certain goal variables are stated a priori, these can be formalized quite easily by means of 'hard' constraints in multiple objective programming models. Because these constraints co-determine the feasible region, one should verify whether the decision maker is certain about the goal values which are formulated as 'hard' constraints. That is, goal values which are formulated as 'hard' constraints, have absolute priority over all the other goal variables. Therefore, it is often preferable to formulate desired goal values as goal constraints (see Section 3.1).

As mentioned in the preceding section, the efficiency concept has proved to be very useful in multiple objective programming methods. The body of literature relating to the properties of the efficient set under different assumptions about the feasible region and the nature of the goal variables is rapidly growing. Moreover, for different problems, procedures have been developed to find all elements of the efficient set or to find a well-defined subset of this efficient set.

(3) Reduction of the set of alternatives by means of (partial) orderings

Thus far, this operational option has not been pursued in multiple objective programming methods, although some starting points might be found in the 'fuzzy multiple objective programming techniques' discussed by Zimmerman [1978], in which goal variables and constraints are characterized by their membership functions.

(4) Collection of sufficient *a priori* information to reach an optimal solution

Many multiple objective programming methods assume the availability of sufficient *a priori* preference information to reach an optimal solution, given the set of feasible actions. They do not deal as such with the collection of this information, but rather with using it to calculate the optimal solution given the preference information. The calculation of the optimal solution can be accomplished along one of the following lines:

(a) *Maximization of a preference function.*

In this case it is assumed that the whole vector of relevant goal variables can be translated into an unambiguous scalar-valued preference function by means of a weighing procedure. The most straightforward weighing procedure is the linear one, i.e. the preference function is a linear combination of the (possibly standardized) goal variables.

(b) *Minimization of deviations from targets.*

Here it is assumed that the decision maker has specified certain aspiration or target values of the goal variables. Discrepancies between the actual goal values and the target values are penalized by a dispreference or penalty function which is also to be specified by the decision maker. Well-known examples are the quadratic penalty function approach (see among others Theil [1968]) and goal programming. Both approaches are attractive because of the use of aspiration levels which are not uncommon in practice (cf. Chapter 2). Among these two methods, goal programming is most attractive because it is more flexible than the other approach with respect to the nature of the preference functions that can be incorporated, and moreover is much easier to use. We return to these approaches in greater detail in Chapter 4.

(c) *Minimization of deviations from ideal solution(s).*

In this third approach, an ideal point (as defined in Section 3.1) is calculated after which a dispreference function (again to be specified by the decision maker) is minimized. This approach is often imbedded in interactive approaches. We will return to them later.

(5) Sequential articulation of preferences

This option can also be adopted within a multiple objective programming framework. Especially, many interactive procedures have been developed. Chapter 5 will be devoted to these inter-active multiple objective programming methods because, in our view, they constitute very promising tools for solving multiple

objective programming problems. In Chapter 6 we present our own
interactive multiple objective programming method.

3.6. Conclusion

Normative decision methods are not only useful in helping the
decision maker to choose a suitable action but may also improve his
way of viewing the decision situation. Normative decision methods
may be better accepted by the decision maker if the underlying
assumptions do not go too far beyond the decision maker's reality.
For this reason we seek methods that are able to include multiple,
conflicting goal variables. Many multiple criteria decision methods
have been developed for many kinds of decision situations. With
the set of characteristics described in Section 3.3 one might check
for which decision situation(s) a particular method is suited. In
our opinion, five different (although not mutually exclusive)
operational options for the multiple criteria decision problem can
be distinguished. These options are described in Section 3.4.

In the remainder of this study we restrict ourselves to those
decision problems which can be translated as multiple objective
programming methods. Within this class we attempt to combine the
advantages of goal programming (see Chapter 4), with the advantages
of interactive procedures (see Chapter 5). Goal programming closely
corresponds with decision making in practice, but requires a fair
amount of *a priori* information about the decision maker's preferences. By means of interactive procedures, the decision maker becomes
more closely involved in the solution process while demanding
relatively little *a priori* information.

The new method, Interactive Multiple Goal Programming, is
described in Chapter 6 and illustrated in Chapter 7. Its merits
for capital budgeting and financial planning with multiple goals
are discussed and illustrated in Chapters 8 and 9.

References

Cochrane, J.L. and M. Zeleny (1973), Multiple Criteria Decision Making, University of South Carolina Press, Columbia (SC).

Dawes, R.M. (1971), A Case Study of Graduate Admissions, American Psychologist, pp. 180-188.

Despontin, M and J. Spronk (1979), Comparison and Evaluation of Multiple Criteria Decision Models, Report 7923/A, Centre for Research in Business Economics, Erasmus University Rotterdam, Rotterdam.

Farquhar, P.H. (1977), A Survey of Multiattribute Utility Theory and Applications, in Starr, M.K. and M. Zeleny [1977, pp. 59-89].

Fishburn, P.C. (1978), A Survey of Multiattribute/Multicriterion Evaluation Theories, in Zionts, S., [1978, pp. 181-224].

Gal, T. (1977), A General Method for Determining the Set of All Efficient Solutions to a Linear Vectormaximum Problem, European Journal of Operational Research, Vol. 1/5, pp. 307-322.

Gal, T. and J. Nemoda (1972), Multiparametric Linear Programming, Management Science, Vol. 18/7, pp. 406-421.

Gal, T. (1979), Postoptimal Analyses, Parametric Programming, and Related Topics, McGraw-Hill, New York.

Hwang, C.L. and A.S.M. Masud (1979), Multiple Objective Decision Making - Methods and Applications, Springer, Berlin.

Keen, P.G.W., (1977), The Evolving Concept of Optimality, in Starr, M.K. and M. Zeleny, [1977, pp.31-58].

Keeney, R.L. and H. Raiffa, (1976), Decisions with Multiple Objectives: Preferences and Value Tradeoffs, Wiley, New York.

Lindblom, C.E. (1959), The Science of Muddling Through, Public Administration Review, Vol. 19, pp. 79-88.

MacCrimmon, K.R. (1973), An Overview of Multiple Objective Decision Making, in Cochrane, J.L. and M. Zeleny, [1973, pp. 18-44].

Manheim, M.L. (1966), Hierarchical Structure: A Model of Design and Planning Processes, M.I.T. Press, Cambridge (Ma).

Moscarola, J.S. (1979), Recherche Opérationelle, Processus de
    Décision et Aide à la Décision, Université de Paris-Dauphine,
    U.E.R. Sciences des Organisations, cahier no. 68.

Neumann, J. von and O. Morgenstern (1953), Theory of Games and
    Economic Behaviour, 3th edition, Princeton University Press.

Nijkamp, P. and J. Spronk (1979b), Goal Programming for Decision
    Making, Ricerca Operativa, Vol. 12, pp. 3-49.

Nijkamp, P. and J. Spronk (1979a), Analysis of Production and
    Location Decisions by Means of Multi-Criteria Analysis,
    Engineering and Process Economics, Vol. 4.

Nijkamp, P. and J. Spronk (eds) (1980), Multicriteria Analysis:
    Practical Methods, Gower Press Inc., London.

Patton, M.Q. (1978), Utilization Focused Evaluation, Sage, Beverly
    Hills/London.

Rietveld, P. (1980), Multiple Objective Decision Making and Regional
    Planning, North-Holland Publ. Co., Amsterdam.

Roy, B.(1971), Problems and Methods with Multiple Objective
    Functions, Mathematical Programming, Vol. 1, pp. 239-266.

Roy, B.(1976), From Optimization to Multi-Criteria Decision Aid:
    Three Main Operational Attitudes, in Thiriez, H. and S. Zionts,
    [1976, pp. 1-34].

Roy, B. (1977), A Conceptual Framework for a Prescriptive Theory of
    Decision-Aids, in Starr, M.K. and M. Zeleny, [1977, pp. 179-210].

Slovic, P. and S. Lichtenstein (1971), Comparison of Bayesian and
    Regression Approaches to the Study of Information Processing in
    Judgement, Organizational Behaviour and Human Performance,
    pp. 651-730.

Starr, M.K. and M. Zeleny (1977), MCDM - State and Future of the Arts,
    in Starr, M.K. and M. Zeleny (eds), [1977, pp. 5-30].

Starr, M.K. and M. Zeleny (eds) (1977), Multiple Criteria Decision
    Making, Vol. 6 in the TIMS Studies in the Management Sciences
    Series, North-Holland, Amsterdam.

Theil, H. (1968), Optimal Decision Rules for Government and
    Industry, North-Holland, Amsterdam.

Thiriez, H. and S. Zionts (eds) (1976), Multiple Criteria Decision Making, Jouy-en-Josas, France 1975, Springer Verlag, Berlin.

Yu, P.L. (1973), A Class of Solutions for Group Decision Problems, Management Science, Vol. 19/8, pp. 936-946.

Yu, P.L. and M. Zeleny (1975), The Set of All Nondominated Solutions in Linear Cases and a Multicriteria Simplex Method, Journal of Mathematical Analysis and Application, Vol. 49, pp. 430-468.

Zeleny, M. (1976), The Theory of the Displaced Ideal, in Zeleny, M. (ed.) [1976, pp. 153-206].

Zeleny, M. (ed.)(1976), Multiple Criteria Decision Making Kyoto 1975, Springer Berlin.

Zimmermann, H.J. (1978), Fuzzy Programming and Linear Programming with Several Objective Functions, Fuzzy Sets and Systems, Vol. 1/1, pp. 45-55.

Zionts, S. (1979), Methods for Solving Management Problems Involving Multiple Objectives, Working Paper No. 400, School of Management, State University of New York at Buffalo.

4. GOAL PROGRAMMING

Goal programming, an approach developed mainly by Charnes and Cooper, Ijiri, Lee, and Ignizio, is one of the earliest practical techniques in multiple criteria decision making. In our opinion, goal programming is one of the stronger methods available, especially for capital budgeting and financial planning with multiple goals. Its use of aspiration levels and pre-emptive priorities closely corresponds to decision making in practice. Furthermore, goal programming possesses a number of attractive technical properties.

Several empirical findings from decision making practice are indeed rather convincing in demonstrating the practical usefulness of goal programming. As mentioned by several authors, the method corresponds quite well to the results of the behavioral theory of the firm. In practice, decision makers are aiming at various goals, formulated as aspiration levels. The intensity with which the goals are strived for may vary for each goal, in other words, different 'weights' may be assigned to different goals. The use of aspiration levels in decision making is also reported by scientists from other fields, for instance, psychology (see for a short overview Monarchi et al. [1976]). In the same way, pre-emptive priorities are also known in real life problems. Support for this essentially lexico-graphic viewpoint is provided a.o. by Fishburn [1974] and Monarchi et al. [1976]. A more concrete example of the correspondence of goal programming and practice is provided by Ijiri [1965], who regards goal programming as an extension of break even analysis, which is widely used in business practice.

The above plea for goal programming is of a somewhat theoretical nature. However, the operational usefulness of goal programming has also been recognized in practice, as shown by the many applications which have been reported in literature (see Nijkamp and Spronk [1979] for an overview).

58

One of the technical advantages of goal programming is that it always provides a solution, even if none of the goals are realizable, provided the feasible region is non-empty. This is due to the inclusion of deviational variables, which show whether the goals are attained or not. In the latter case they measure the distance between the realized and aspired goal levels. Another advantage of goal programming is that it does not require very sophisticated solution procedures. Especially the linear goal programming problems can be solved by easily available linear programming routines.

4.1. General Formulation

In problems involving multiple goals a number (say m) of goal variables, depending on a number of instrumental variables $x_1, x_2, \ldots, x_n$ (in vector notation $\underline{x}$), can be identified. From the set of admissable values of the instrumental variables $\underline{x}$, an element (or set of elements) must be selected, resulting in certain aspired levels of the goal variables. If such instrument vectors do exist, they are solutions of

$$\underline{b} = \underline{g}(\underline{x})$$
(4.1)
$$\underline{x} \in R, \text{ where } R = \{\underline{x} | \underline{h}(\underline{x}) \leq \underline{h}\},$$

and $\underline{b}$ is the m x 1 vector of aspired levels of the goal variables $g_j(\underline{x})$, $j = 1, \ldots, m$; and R denotes the feasible region, being the set of admissable values of the instrumental variables $\underline{x}$, given the k x 1 vector of available resources, $\underline{h}$. In this section we assume both $\underline{g}(\underline{x})$ and $\underline{h}(\underline{x})$ to be linear in $\underline{x}$. Then, the problem can be formalized as finding the set of vectors $\underline{x}$, for which

$$\underline{b} = \underline{g}(\underline{x}) = A.\underline{x}$$
(4.2)
$$\underline{x} \in R, \text{ where } R = \{\underline{x} | \underline{h}(\underline{x}) = B.\underline{x} \leq \underline{h}\},$$

A is a matrix of order m x n, and B is a matrix of order k x n.

Due to the possible incompatibility of goals - at least within
the feasible region R - we have to account for deviations of the
goal variables from the aspired levels b_1, b_2, ..., b_m. This can
be done by introducing the m x 1 vectors $\underline{y}^+$ en $\underline{y}^-$ which measure
respectively the over- and underachievements of the stated goals.
Because over- and underachievement of a given goal cannot take place
at the same time, we impose the conditions $y_i^+ \cdot y_i^- = 0$ for
i = 1,2, ..., m; $\underline{y}^+ \geq 0$ and $\underline{y}^- \geq 0$. Assuming that a <u>dispreference</u>
<u>function</u> $f(\underline{y}^+, \underline{y}^-)$ can be specified which reflects the undesirability
of the deviations properly, the problem becomes

$$\text{Min } f(\underline{y}^+, \underline{y}^-) \text{ , s.t.}$$

$$A.\underline{x} - \underline{y}^+ + \underline{y}^- = \underline{b} \text{ ,}$$

(4.3)

$$y_i^+ \cdot y_i^- = 0 \text{ for } i = 1, \ldots, m;$$

$$\underline{x} \in R, \text{ and } \underline{y}^+, \underline{y}^- \geq \underline{0}$$

In goal programming, this formulation is often extended as follows.
First, divide the m goals in p (p < m) classes C_t, t = 1, ..., p; in
such a way that the goals in the first class have a preemptive
priority above the goals in the second class and so forth. In this
essentially lexicographic approach (see also Fishburn [1974]), the
goals in a certain priority class must be satisfied 'as well as
possible' before paying attention to the goals of subsequent classes.
Defining b_{ts} as the s'th goal of the t'th priority class and

m_t ($\sum_{t=1}^{p} m_t = m$) as the number of goals in class C_t, we can formulate

this sequential problem as

First:

$$\text{Min } f_1(\underline{y}^+, \underline{y}^-) = f(y_{11}^+, y_{12}^+, \ldots, y_{1m_1}^+, \ y_{11}^-, y_{12}^-, \ldots, y_{1m_1}^-) \ , \ \text{s.t.}$$

$$A.\underline{x} - \underline{y}^+ + \underline{y}^- = \underline{b},$$

$$y_i^+ \cdot y_i^- = 0 \text{ for } i = 1, \ldots, m;$$

$$\underline{x} \in R, \text{ and } \underline{y}^+, \underline{y}^- \geq \underline{0}$$

If this problem has only one optimal $\underline{x}$ vector, stop.

Otherwise:

$$\text{Min } f_2(\underline{y}^+, \underline{y}^-) = f(y_{21}^+, y_{22}^+, \ldots, y_{2m_2}^+, y_{21}^-, y_{22}^-, \ldots, y_{2m_2}^-) \ , \ \text{s.t.}$$

$$f_1(\underline{y}^+, \underline{y}^-) = \text{Min}\{f_1(\underline{y}^+, \underline{y}^-)\},$$

$$A.\underline{x} - \underline{y}^+ + \underline{y}^- = \underline{b}$$

$$y_i^+ \cdot y_i^- = 0 \text{ for } i = 1, \ldots, m;$$

$$\underline{x} \in R, \text{ and } \underline{y}^+, \underline{y}^- \geq \underline{0}$$

(4.4)   If this problem has only one optimal $\underline{x}$ vector, stop.

Otherwise:

.   .   .

.   .   .

.   .

If this problem has only one optimal $\underline{x}$ vector, stop.

Otherwise:

$$\text{Min } f_p(\underline{y}^+, \underline{y}^-) = f(y_{p1}^+, y_{p2}^+, \ldots, y_{pm_p}^+, y_{p1}^-, y_{p2}^-, \ldots, y_{pm_p}^-) \ , \ \text{s.t.}$$

$$f_i(\underline{y}^+, \underline{y}^-) = \text{Min}\{f_i(\underline{y}^+, \underline{y}^-)\} \text{ for } i = 1, 2, \ldots, p-1.$$

$$A.\underline{x} - \underline{y}^+ + \underline{y}^- = \underline{b} \ ,$$

$$y_i^+ \cdot y_i^- = 0 \text{ for } i = 1, \ldots, m;$$

$$\underline{x} \in R, \text{ and } \underline{y}^+, \underline{y}^- \geq \underline{0}$$

In general, each step of the minimization in (4.4) reduces the feasible region remaining for the fulfilment of the lower priority goals. Let C_t be the first class in the priority ordering where not all goals can be fulfilled simultaneously (thus for

$t' < t$ all goals in C_t are attainable). Then we need to specify
the dispreference function $f_t(\underline{y}^+,\underline{y}^-)$ in order to choose among the
goals within C_t with goal levels $b_{t1}, b_{t2}, \ldots, b_{tm_t}$. By definition,
this dispreference function is a function of the deviations from
the aspired goal levels, and can thus be regarded as a distance
function requiring some distance measure.

A number of alternative specifications of such distance functions can be derived from the general Minkovski metric, used among
others in welfare economics (cf. Bartels and Nijkamp [1976]). As
a welfare criterion, the Minkovski metric can be specified as
follows

$$(4.5) \qquad \text{Min } f = \{ \sum_{i=1}^{m} \left| \frac{z_i - \bar{z}}{\bar{z}} \right|^p \}^{1/p}$$

where $\bar{z}_i$ is the average income (or some other appropriate welfare
indicator) in class $i(i=1,\ldots,m)$ and $\bar{z}$ is the overall average
income. More generally, the term in the inner brackets can be
interpreted as a standardized distance from a predetermined norm.
Realizing there is not a single norm (as $\bar{z}$ in (4.5)) in (4.3) and
(4.4), we can adapt (4.5) in terms of the multiple goal problem
(4.3) to

$$(4.6) \qquad \text{Min } f = \{ \sum_{i=1}^{m} \left| \frac{a(i).\underline{x} - b_i}{b_i} \right|^p \}^{1/p}$$

where $\underline{a(i)}$ is the i'th row of A. Unfortunately, this form does not
discriminate between positive and negative deviations from the
stated goal levels $b_i, i, = 1, \ldots, m$. In order to bridge this gap
note that (cf. Charnes and Cooper [1977 ,p.9])

$$(4.7a) \qquad y_i^+ = \frac{|a(i).\underline{x} - b_i| + (a(i).\underline{x} - b_i)}{2} \quad \text{for } i = 1, \ldots, m;$$

represents the positive deviations, and

(4.7b) $\bar{y}_i = \dfrac{|a(i).\underline{x}-b_i| - (a(i).\underline{x}-b_i)}{2}$ for i = 1, ..., m ;

represents the negative deviations. Substracting (4.7b) from (4.7a) gives

(4.8) $y_i^+ - y_i^- = \underline{a(i)}.\underline{x} - b_i$ for i = 1, ..., m;

which exactly equals the goal restrictions in (4.3). Adding (4.7a) and (4.7b) gives

(4.9) $y_i^+ + y_i^- = |\underline{a(i)}.\underline{x} - b_i|$

which can be substituted in (4.6), to get $f(y^+,y^-)$ as a function of the standardized deviations from the aspired goal levels:

(4.10) $\text{Min } f = f(\underline{y}^+,\underline{y}^-) = \left\{ \displaystyle\sum_{i=1}^{m} \left(\dfrac{y_i^+ + y_i^-}{|b_i|}\right)^p \right\}^{1/p}$

Then of course, to exclude the possibility of y_i^+ and y_i^- being both positive at the same time, $y_i^+ \cdot y_i^- = 0$ must hold for i = 1, ..., m. Assuming $b_i > 0$, this condition permits us[1] to write (4.10) as

(4.11) $\text{Min } f(\underline{y}^+,\underline{y}^-) = \left\{ \displaystyle\sum_{i=1}^{m} \left(\dfrac{y_i^+}{b_i}\right)^p + \displaystyle\sum_{i=1}^{m} \left(\dfrac{y_i^-}{b_i}\right)^p \right\}^{1/p}$

This form is preferable to (4.10) if not all deviations are valued

---

1) Since $y_i^+ \cdot y_i^- = 0$, either $y_i^+ = 0$ or $y_i^- = 0$ or $y_i^+ = y_i^- = 0$. Assume $y_i^+ = 0$. Then:

$$\left(\frac{y_i^+ + y_i^-}{b_i}\right)^p = \left(\frac{y_i^-}{b_i}\right)^p = \left(\frac{y_i^-}{b_i}\right)^p + \left(\frac{0}{b_i}\right)^p = \left(\frac{y_i^-}{b_i}\right)^p + \left(\frac{y_i^+}{b_i}\right)^p. \qquad \text{q.e.d.}$$

For either $y_i^- = 0$ or $y_i^+ = y_i^- = 0$ the proof is similar.

equally by the decision maker. In that case (4.11) permits different
weights for the positive and negative deviations from the same aspiration level whereas (4.10) does not. The specification of the weights
in (4.11) may be given by

$$(4.12) \qquad \text{Min } f(\underline{y}^+, \underline{y}^-) = \left\{ \sum_{i=1}^{m} \alpha_i^+ \cdot \left(\frac{y_i^+}{b_i} \right)^p + \sum_{i=1}^{m} \alpha_i^- \cdot \left(\frac{y_i^-}{b_i} \right)^p \right\}^{1/p}$$

Obviously both (4.10) and (4.11) or their weighted forms, may serve
as the (generally non-linear) dispreference function $f(\underline{y}^+, \underline{y}^-)$ in (4.3)

It is easily seen that both (4.10) and (4.11) include some very
popular metrics. That is, for $p = 1$ we get an absolute value metric
and for $p = 2$ we get a Euclidean metric, while for $p \to \infty$ a Chebychev
metric results which in turn shows close resemblance to the minimax
criterion (cf. also Charnes and Cooper [1961, app. A] and Lane
[1970]). Of course different metrics will usually generate different
results. As was pointed out by Ijiri [1965, p.56], this means, that
apart from the determination of the weights α_i, the prescription of
the metric constitutes a problem of managerial choice. One may wish
to simulate this choice by extrapolating from managerial actions
in the past. In that case an *ex post* estimation of the p value in
(4.6) or (4.12) must be made. For a further discussion on the sensitivity of the results for the p value used, we refer to Nijkamp and
Rietveld [1977].

Under special circumstances, (4.12) can be used in another way.
That is, if $p = 1$ it can be used as an index of goal attainment.
For the sake of simplicity let us assume that only the y^- variables
are opportune, and furthermore that

(4.13) $\sum\limits_{i=1}^{n} \alpha_i^- = 1$, $A\underline{x} \geq \underline{0}$, and $b_i > 0$ for all i

Instead of (4.11) we then get

(4.14) $$f^*(\underline{y}^-) = \sum\limits_{i=1}^{n} \alpha_i^- \cdot \frac{y_i^-}{b_i}$$

where all terms $\dfrac{y_i^-}{b_i}$ must lie in the closed interval [0,1]. If the
aspiration level b_i is completely reached the term is zero and if
the underattainment is at maximum we have $y_i^- \leq b_i$ so that
$\dfrac{y_i^-}{b_i} \leq 1$. Obviously (4.14) is at its maximum value (which is 1 by
virtue of the condition that the weights α_i add up to 1) when all
aspiration levels are maximally underattained and is at its
minimum level (which is 0) when all goals are simultaneously
attained. Such an index might be used in the evaluation and
comparison of algorithms designed for the multiple goal problem.

4.2. The Objective Function

Goal programming is often used to model some kind of satisficing behaviour. Nevertheless, the class of objective functions which
can be incorporated within the goal programming framework, provides
the possibility to represent other kinds of behaviour. In this section, we shall give an outline of this class of objective functions
for the case that p = 1, i.e. for linear goal programming.

In general, the objective function is a function of the deviations from certain aspired goal levels. Goal programs may include
aspired goal levels of one goal variable only or, alternatively,
they may include goal levels of several distinct goal variables.
Consequently, the objective functions may relate either to one or
to several goal variables. These two classes of objective functions
will be discussed below.

We will pay special attention to the *'one-sided goal programming'* formulation, in which the objective function includes only one deviation variable for each aspired goal level. It appears that many objective functions can be effectively translated in this 'one-sided' way. One of the advantages is an easier access to the techniques developed for solving the linear goal program and its dual. Furthermore, such a formulation has some advantages within the interactive approach to goal programming which will be described in Chapter 6.

Objective Functions Relating to One Goal Variable Only

If only one goal variable has been defined, the decision maker may have formulated either one or several aspired goal levels. We will first consider the case in which <u>only one aspiration level</u> (say b) has been defined. Then, the objective function becomes

(4.15) $\text{Min}\{\alpha^+.y^+/b + \bar{\alpha}.y^-/b\}$

For the sake of simplicity we assume b > 0 to be incorporated in α^+ and α^-, by which we can write

(4.16) $\text{Min}\{\alpha^+.y^+ + \bar{\alpha}.y^-\}$

The factors α^+ and α^- are not 'weights' in the usual sense, simply because $y^+.y^- = 0$ by which y^+ and y^- cannot be 'traded-off' against each other. However, both α^+ and α^- can be given values $-1,1$ or zero in order to indicate whether the deviation in question must be maximized, minimized, or is not relevant for the decision maker's preferences. In Table 4.1 we combine these possibilities (cf. Ijiri [1965]) Furthermore, we show the effect of these functionals being minimized without explicitly taking account of the condition $y^+.y^- = 0$.

Table 4.1. The effect of different functionals $\alpha^+.y^+ + \alpha^-.y^-$ being minimized

| | | value of α^+ | | |
		−1	0	1
value of α^-	−1	infinite solution	infinite solution	minimum goal variable
	0	infinite solution		minimum over-attainment
	1	maximum goal variable	minimal under-attainment	exact attainment

The infinite solutions occur because both y^+ and y^- can be made arbitrarily large without violating the goal constraint

(4.17) $A.\underline{x} - y^+ + y^- = b,$

where A in this case is a (n x 1) vector. The functionals in the lower left and upper right corners of Table 4.1. bring about maximization and minimization of the goal variable concerned. In general, these functionals do not produce unique values for y^+ and y^-.[1] Of course, other methods can be used to minimize or maximize a single goal variable. One possibility is to directly

1) See also Ijiri [1965, p.40 ff.]. If the simplex procedure is used, a unique solution can be guaranteed (see p.83).

minimize or maximize the goal variable without using the
deviational variables. Otherwise one can keep in line with the
goal programming formulation by defining an aspiration level that
is known to be unattainable and then minimizing the relevant
deviational variable. In this way the only three functionals of
importance are those within the marked lines of Table 4.1. This
means that introduction of two deviational variables in the
objective function is strictly necessary only in the razor - edge
case of exact attainment of the aspiration level. The other finite
cases are one-sided goal programming problems.

Even in the case when only one goal variable, say $g(\underline{x})$, has been
defined, it may be desirable to use several aspiration levels,
say $\underline{b} = b_1, \ldots, b_v$; for this single goal variable. In this case,
the most general form for the objective function becomes

(4.18) $\text{Min}\{ \sum_{u=1}^{v} (\alpha_u^+ \cdot y_u^+ + \alpha_u^- \cdot y_u^-) \}$,

which may be specified in several ways. First, a goal variable may
be a piecewise linear function of the instrumental variables. Such
a functional form may be defined in its own right (see Ijiri [1965])
or as an approximation of a continuous function (see e.g. Goodman
[1974] and Laurent [1976]). We will deal with the 'kinks' in the
piecewise linear function as if they are aspiration levels. In Figure 4.1 we give an example of a goal variable which is a piecewise
linear function of one instrumental variable. In this example, the
goal variable represents a one-product firm's total revenue, being
a function of the firm's volume of sales. Here the β_u, $u = 1, \ldots, v$;
are activity levels, for which the marginal contribution of the activity level x to the value of the goal variable $g(x)$ changes. Furthermore, if $\beta_1 < x < \beta_v$ where $\beta_1 = 0$ and c_u is defined as the marginal
contribution to the goal variable for activity levels between β_u
and β_{u+1}, then according to Ijiri (Ibid) the function $g(x)$ can be
written in a linear form

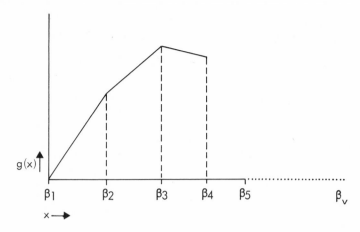

Figure 4.1. A goal variable being a piecewise linear function of one instrumental variable

as

$$g(x) = \sum_{u=1}^{v} (c_u - c_{u-1}) \cdot z_u^+,$$

(4.19) $x - z_u^+ + z_u^- = \beta_u,$ for u = 1, ..., v.

$$z_u^+ \cdot z_u^- = 0 \text{ and } x, z_u^+, z_u^- \geq 0$$

Assume next that the decision maker has defined the aspiration level g^* of $g(x)$. Then, introducing two additional variables to measure the deviation from this aspired goal level, a goal restriction can be formulated, as well as an objective function (see Table 4.1) in terms of the previously added deviational variables.

If, in contrast with the situation in Figure 4.1. $g(x)$ is monotone non-decreasing or monotone non-increasing in x, it is not always necessary to include the two additional deviational variables. Let $g(x)$ be monotone non-decreasing. Its value in the points β_u are then given by

(4.20)

$$g(b_1) = 0 \text{ and}$$

$$g(b_u) = \sum_{w=1}^{u-1} c_w \cdot (\beta_{w+1} - \beta_w) \quad \text{for } u = 2, \ldots, v.$$

Given these values it is easy to trace the interval $[\beta_k, \beta_{k+1}]$ containing the activity level x^* for which $g(x^*) = g^*$, the aspired level of $g(x)$. This is done by determining the first $k, k = 1, \ldots, v-1$ for which

(4.21) $$g(\beta_k) \leq g^* \leq g(\beta_{k+1})$$

holds. Next define $g_u(x)$, $u = 1, \ldots, v-1$ as the linear functions which for $\beta_u \leq x \leq \beta_{u+1}$ coincide with $g(x)$. Clearly $g_u(x)$ can be defined as:

(4.22) $$g_1(x) = c_1 \cdot x \text{ for } \beta_1 \leq x \leq \beta_2, \text{ and}$$

$$g_u(x) = \sum_{w=1}^{u-1} c_w \cdot (\beta_{w+1} - \beta_w) + c_u(x - \beta_u)$$

$$u = 2, \ldots, v-1.$$

$$\text{for } \beta_u \leq x \leq \beta_{u+1}$$

We then consider $g_u(x)$, $u = 1, \ldots, k$ (k being the index of the interval containing x^*) as goal variables and $g_u(\beta_{u+1}) = g(\beta_{u+1})$ as their respective aspiration levels. The goal restrictions become

(4.23) $g_u(x) - y_u^+ + y_u^- = g(\beta_{u+1})$ for $u = 1, \ldots, k$,

which after substitution of (4.20) and (4.22) can be reduced to

(4.24) $c_u \cdot x - y_u^+ + y_u^- = c_u \cdot \beta_{u+1}$ for $u = 1, \ldots, k$.

The distance to the aspired level g* can then be minimized by

(4.25) $\text{Min } \{ \sum_{u=1}^{k} M_u \cdot y_u \}$,

where $M_u > M_{u+1}$ are factors used to represent the pre-emptive priority of the minimization of y_u over the minimization of y_{u+1}.[1]
Thus this problem is also written in the one-sided way.
In recent years, several authors (see e.g. Collomb [1971], Charnes
and Cooper [1977] and Charnes, Cooper, Klingman and Niehaus [1979])
have extended the capacity of goal programming to deal with piecewise linear functions. This has resulted in a new technique known
as 'goal interval programming'.

    A second reason for more than one aspiration level being de-
fined for the same goal variable occurs when the aspiration level
g* of g(x) has been replaced by a range of aspiration levels, which
we shall describe by $[g_L^*, g_U^*]$. In this case the decision maker prefers values of g(x) within this interval to values $g(x) < g_L^*$ or
values $g(x) > g_U^*$. Examples in practice can easily be found. Enter-
prises may wish to hold their inventories of goods and cash within
certain limits. In financial planning it may be desirable that
growth should not be too high or too low. (It will be clear from
these examples that the arguments for the determination of the lower
bound aspiration level g_L^* may differ from those for the upper bound

1) See also (4.4) and p.84.

aspiration level g_U^*). In this case the goal programming problem is

$$\text{Min } \{f = \alpha_L^- \cdot y_L^- + \alpha_U^+ \cdot y_U^+\}, \text{ s.t.}$$

$$g(x) - y_L^+ + y_L^- = g_L^*,$$

(4.26) $$g(x) - y_U^+ + y_L^- = g_U^*,$$

$$y_L^+ \cdot y_L^- = y_U^+ \cdot y_U^- = 0$$

$x \in R$, and all variables non-negative.

The weights α_L^- and α_U^+ can be used to represent the relative preference of y_L^- and y_U^+ with respect to other goal variables, if introduced. Note that no trade-off can occur between y_L^- and y_U^+ ($y_U^+ > 0$ implies $y_L^+ > 0$ and $y_L^- = 0$ by $y_L^+ \cdot y_L^- = 0$). Problems may arise when $g(x)$ itself is a piecewise linear function. As shown in Figure 4.2a, there may be two mutual exclusive subsets of the domain (here $[x_1,x_2]$ and $[x_3,x_4]$) for which $g(x) \in [g_L^*,g_U^*]$. This means that the function f to be minimized in (4.26) is not convex in x for all functional forms of $g(x)$. To illustrate this point we have depicted f in (4.26) as a function of the $g(x)$ in Figure 4.2a (whereby $\alpha_L^- = \alpha_U^\tau = 2$). Consequently, f(x) can be expressed as a function of x, as shown in Figure 4.2b.

Objective Functions Relating to Several Goal Variables

When the objective function refers to two or more goal variables, the relative and pre-emptive priorities between the goal variables must be elucidated and expressed in mathematical form. To illustrate the flexibility of goal programming with respect to

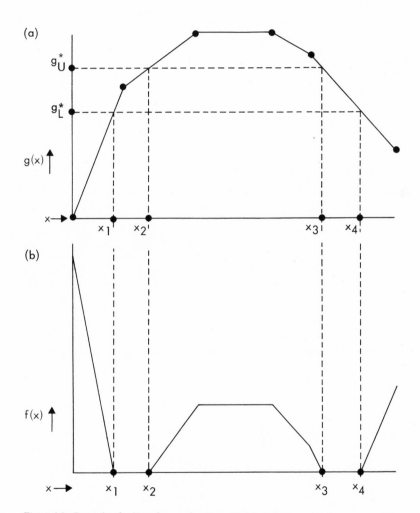

Figure 4.2. Example of a dispreference function which is not convex in x

this kind of objective functions, we give the following example.
Assume an enterprise's management has two goal variables, viz.
sales represented by $g_S(\underline{x})$ and profit represented by $g_p(\underline{x})$. Next
consider the following linear goal programming formulation.

$$\text{Min } \{f = 3.y_p^- - 2.y_p^+ + 1.y_S^- - 0.75y_S^+\}, \text{ s.t.}$$

(4.27)
$$g_p(\underline{x}) - y_p^+ + y_p^- = g_p^*,$$

$$g_S(\underline{x}) - y_S^+ + y_S^- = g_S^*,$$

$$\underline{x} \in R$$

By this formulation the feasible region R has been subdivided into
four different regions. Each subregion has its own trade-off between profit and sales, as shown in Table 4.2.

Table 4.2. Example of possible trade-offs between profit and sales

	$g_p(\underline{x}) \leq g_p^*$	$g_p(\underline{x}) > g_p^*$
$g_S(\underline{x}) \leq g_S^*$	$3/1 = 3$	$2/1 = 2$
$g_S(\underline{x}) > g_S^*$	$3/.75 = 4$	$2/.75 = 2.66$

Remark: the trade-offs are given in terms of goal variables
and not in terms of the deviations.

Of course, the trade-off between two goal variables may change at
more goal levels than in the above example. This situation can be
handled by translating each of these 'critical' goal levels as a

goal constraint (which has been defined in Section 3.1 as a constraint including deviational variables).

Furthermore, note that the objective function f can be written as the sum of 2 piecewise linear functions f_i, one for each
of the two goal variables.

$$f = f_1 + f_2, \text{ with}$$

(4.28)
$$f_1 = 3.y_p^- - 2.y_p^+,$$

$$f_2 = 1.y_S^- - 0.75y_S^+$$

Because f_i is a piecewise linear function of the goal variable
g_i, which itself is a linear or piecewise linear function of the
instrumental variables $\underline{x}$, f_i also becomes a piecewise linear function in $\underline{x}$, which can be handled by the methods described earlier
in this section (see (4.18) - (4.25)). This not only holds for the
example, but also in the more general case in which there are
several goal variables and a more complex trade-off pattern.

In general, if all f_i are monotone non-increasing[1] (or all
are monotone non-decreasing) in $\underline{x}$ and thus f is of the same type,
the problem can be formulated as a one-sided goal programming
problem. Consider $g_i(\underline{x})$ with 'kinks' in its dispreference function
f_i for $g_i(\underline{x}) = g_{ij}^*$, $j = 1,2,\ldots,$ m-1 and let $g_{im}^* = \max\{g_i(\underline{x}) \mid \underline{x} \in R\}$.
The problem can then be written as

---

1) Note that functions that do not meet this condition (as f in
   (4.26)) can sometimes be written as the sum of two linear or
   piecewise linear functions.

$$\text{Min } \{ \sum_{j=1}^{m} \alpha_{ij}^- \cdot y_{ij}^- \}, \text{ s.t.}$$

(4.29) $g_i(\underline{x}) - y_{ij}^+ + y_{ij}^- = g_{ij}^*$ for $j = 1, \ldots, m$;

and $\underline{x} \in R$

In this formulation the weights α_{ij}^- do not represent the slope of the dispreference function f_i because $y_{ij}^- > 0$ implies $y_{ik}^- > 0$ for $k = j+1, \ldots, m$. This means that the dispreference for some point $g^* \in [g_{ij-1}, g_{ij}]$ is given by $\sum_{k=j}^{m} \alpha_{ik}^- \cdot y_{ik}^-$.

It has been shown in this section (for $p = 1$) that different kinds of objective functions can be incorporated within goal programming. Furthermore, it appeared that many linear goal problems can be written in the 'one-sided' way. Such a formulation gives an easier access to the interactive approach to goal programming which is described in Chapter 6.

We next turn to a number of solution procedures for goal programming.

4.3. Solution Procedures

In minimizing the distance function (4.11), good approximations of the minimum function value may be obtained by means of mathematical programming techniques, as shown for example by Barrodale and Roberts [1970]. For certain values of the parameter p in the distance function, even an exact solution can be obtained. In this section we will discuss the cases in which $p \to \infty$, $p = 2$ and $p = 1$ respectively. In the next section the latter case will be elaborated further.

The Case in which $p \to \infty$

If p should approach infinity, it can be shown (cf. Beckenbach and Bellman [1961]) that (4.11) is equivalent to

$$(4.30) \qquad \text{Min Max } \{\alpha^+ \cdot (y_i^+/b_i), \alpha_i^- \cdot (y_i^-/b_i)\}.$$

According to Charnes and Cooper [1977], Lane [1970] and Zukhovitsky and Avdeyeva [1966] this can be put into a linear programming format as

$$\text{Min } \{\lambda\}, \text{ s.t.}$$

$$(4.31) \qquad (\alpha_i^+/b_i) \cdot (-b_i + \underline{a(i)} \cdot \underline{x}) \leq \lambda \qquad \text{for } i = 1, \ldots, m;$$

$$(\alpha_i^-/b_i) \cdot (b_i - \underline{a(i)} \cdot \underline{x}) \leq \lambda \qquad \text{for } i = 1, \ldots, m;$$

$$\underline{x} \in R,$$

where $\underline{a(i)}$ is the i'th row of matrix A. This in fact minimaxing metric has been employed a.o. in the STEP-method of Benayoun et al. [1974] and in an interactive approach by Nijkamp and Rietveld [1976].

The Case in which $p = 2$

In discussing this case, we at first do not discriminate between positive and negative deviations from the goal levels[1], so

---

1) With the help of (4.7a) and (4.7b) it is straightforward to discriminate between positive and negative deviations from the goal levels

that by refering to (4.3) and (4.6) the problem can be stated
as

$$(4.32) \qquad \text{Min } Q = \left\{ \sum_{i=1}^{m} \left| \frac{a(i) \cdot \underline{x} - b_i}{b_i} \right|^2 \right\}^{\frac{1}{2}}$$

$$\text{s.t. } \underline{x} \in R,$$

which closely resembles a quadratic programming format[1]. In fact,
a unique solution to (4.32) can be found by solving

$$(4.33) \qquad \text{Min } W = \underline{x}'.B'.B.\underline{x} - 2b'.B.\underline{x}$$

$$\text{s.t. } \underline{x} \in R$$

where B is an (m x n) matrix which results when A is premultiplied
by the (m x m) diagonal matrix whose elements are equal to $1/b_i$
for i = 1, ..., m, provided B'B and therefore A'A are positive
definite. In order to meet this condition, A must have full column
rank, which is of course not always the case. For instance the
number of instruments n may exceed the number of goals m. In that
case other methods can be used to solve the problem. For instance,
Charnes and Cooper [1961] show that a positive semidefinite matrix
A'.A can be reduced to a positive definite one by perturbing it
to A'.A + ε.I for any $\varepsilon > 0$. Ijiri [1970] suggested another solution
procedure which will next be described.

　　　Ijiri promotes the idea of using the generalized inverse of a
matrix for solving the multiple goal problem (4.3), no matter
whether m < n, m = n or m > n. Here we summarize his results in

1) See again (4.7a) and (4.7b).

broad lines only. Every matrix A – not necessarily being a non-singular, square or non-zero matrix – has its own unique generalized inverse, A^+, which is defined as

(4.32) $A^+ = (A'.A)^{-1}.A'$,

where A' is the transpose of A. Important features of the generalized inverse are 'its least squares property' (see below) and the fact that the generalized inverse of a non-singular square matrix is identical to its ordinary inverse.

The use of the generalized inverse can be shown when we take from (4.2) the set of goals

(4.33) $A.\underline{x} = \underline{b}$

Let us assume the existence of at least one $\underline{x}$ satisfying all the goals b_i, i = 1, ..., m. Then the complete set of solutions is given by

(4.34) $\underline{x} = A^+.\underline{b} + (I-A^+.A).\underline{z}$

where I is the (nxn) identity matrix and $\underline{z}$ is an arbitrary (nx1) vector. The matrix $(I-A^+A)$ maps $\underline{z}$ into the null space of A. If this null space contains only $\underline{0}$, $\underline{x}$ is unique. Otherwise, there is a set of solutions (given by (4.34)) all satisfying (4.33) which contains more than one element (in general it has an infinite number of elements because $\underline{z}$ may be freely chosen). Within this set of solutions, goals not included in $\underline{b}$ may be strived for.

As stated in (4.2) the choice of the instrumental variables $\underline{x}$ may be subject to constraints. These can be translated into constraints on the choice of the vectors $\underline{z}$. For instance, we can substitute (4.34) in the set of restrictions

(4.35) $B.\underline{x} \leq \underline{h},$

which results in

(4.36) $B.(I-A^{+}.A).\underline{z} \leq \underline{h} - B.A.\underline{b},$

by which $\underline{x}$ is indirectly restrained to (4.35).

Before formulating (4.34) we assumed the existence of at least
one $\underline{x}$ satisfying all goals b_i. In the absence of such a solution it
can be shown (Ibid, p.59 and p.161) that the least squares property
of A^{+} is equivalent to the fact that $\underline{x} = A^{+}.b$ minimizes the ℓ_2 metric

(4.37) $\left\{ \sum_{i=1}^{m} (\underline{a(i)}\underline{x} - b_i)^2 \right\}^{\frac{1}{2}},$

where $\underline{a(i)}$ is the i'th row of A. Of course this metric can be
modified in order to incorporate the subjective weights α_i,
$i = 1, \ldots, m$ to be assigned to the deviations. This yields

(4.38) $\left\{ \sum_{i=1}^{m} \alpha_i.(\underline{a(i)}\underline{x}-b_i)^2 \right\}^{\frac{1}{2}},$

which is minimized by $\underline{x} = (I_\alpha.A)^{+}. I_\alpha.\underline{b}$, where I_α is the diagonal
matrix of order m with diagonal elements $\sqrt{\alpha_i}$.

As was indicated in Section 4.1, goals are not always
commensurable. The suggested approach there was to divide the set
of m goals into the pre-emptive priority classes C_t, $t = 1, \ldots, p$.
Then the goals of class C_t had to be fulfilled before those of $C_{t'}$
if and only if $t < t'$. The problem of incommensurability is thus
restrained to the first priority class in which not all goals can
be satisfied simultaneously. The same approach is applicable when

generalized inverses are used (Ibid.,pp.57-62). In that case (4.33) has to be partitioned into

$$(4.39) \qquad A_t \cdot \underline{x} = \underline{b}_t \quad \text{for } t = 1, \ldots, p;$$

where A_t is the matrix of the coefficients of the goal variables that are in the t'th priority class C_t and $\underline{b}_t$ is the vector of aspiration levels for these goal variables. The set of solutions (if not empty) which satisfy the goals of the first priority class can now be found by

$$(4.40) \qquad \underline{x} = A_1^+ \cdot \underline{b}_1 + (I - A_1^+ \cdot \underline{a(1)}) \cdot \underline{z}.$$

Within this set of solutions - denoted by R_1 - the goals of the second priority class must be met. The problem is then to find the solutions of

$$(4.41) \qquad A_2 \cdot \underline{x} = \underline{b}_2 \quad \text{s.t.}$$

$$\underline{x} \in R_1$$

If the solution set R_2 of (4.41) is not empty one can proceed by determining the set of solutions that satisfy the goals of the third priority class. This procedure continues until a priority class C_k is found of which not all goals can be reached simultaneously. Accordingly we have to find the solution in R_{k-1} which has minimum distance to the goals of class C_k, being $b_{k1}, \ldots, b_{km_k}$. If this distance is measured by the ℓ_2 metric, then by virtue of (4.38) and (4.41) the problem is to find the solution of

$$(4.42) \qquad I_{\alpha m_k} \cdot A_k \cdot \underline{x} = I_{\alpha m_k} \cdot \underline{b}_k,$$

$$\underline{x} \in R_{k-1},$$

where $I_{\alpha m_k}$ is a diagonal matrix of order $(m_k x m_k)$, with diagonal
elements $\sqrt{\alpha_{ks}}$, $s = 1, \ldots, m_k$ - being the square roots of the
weights assigned to the m_k goals of the k'th priority class C_i.
In practice a unique least squares solution to (4.42) can be found
by the procedure described in (4.33) through (4.36). However, one
serious drawback of this procedure should be stressed. That is, first
the set of unconstrained least squares solutions is calculated. Then
this set is intersected with the set of solutions being feasible
(in this case R_{k-1}) in order to form the final solution set (here
R_k). Thus, it is tacitly assumed there _is_ a non-empty intersection.
However, this assumption may not be satisfied. In that case the
problem remains to find a least squares solution _within_ the region
R_{k-1}.

    To summarize, the solution of the stated problem by means of
generalized inverses is not a simple task. It becomes even worse
when the instrumental variables $\underline{x}$ are subject to exogenous constraints
as stated in (4.35). Furthermore, under- and overachievement of the
stated goals b_i, $i = 1, \ldots, m$; were assumed to be equally undesirable. If this assumption is relaxed so as to include goals where
under- and overachievement are being valued differently, the approach
using generalized inverses becomes unclear. Fortunately, much research has been recently carried out and will surely be carried
out in the near future, not at least because of its applicability
in constrained regression (see e.g. Ben-Israel and Greville [1974]
and Theil [1971]). Therefore, efficient procedures for this kind of
multiple goal problems may be developed soon.

The Case in which p = 1

    Next, we will discuss a number of solution procedures for the

ℓ_1 specification of the objective function. Moreover we conjecture that m goals are to be ordered in $p(1 \leq p \leq m)$ pre-emptive priority classes. Charnes and Cooper [1961] and Ijiri [1965] paid a lot of attention to the ℓ_1 specification of the multiple goal problem; in fact they developed the linear programming formulation of this problem, which is now known as linear goal programming. By reference to (4.3) and (4.11), their formulation can be written in the standardized form by

(4.43)
$$\text{Min} \left\{ \sum_{i=1}^{m} \alpha_i^+ . y_i^+ / b_i + \sum_{i=1}^{m} \alpha_i^- . y_i^- / b_i \right\}$$

$$\text{s.t. } A.\underline{x} - I.\underline{y}^+ + I.\underline{y}^- = \underline{b}$$

and $\underline{x} \in R$,

where I is the $m \times m$ identity matrix and all other symbols have been defined as before. In this linear programming format there is of course no place for the non-linear constraints $y_i^+ . y_i^- = 0$, $(i=1,\ldots,m)$. However, the latter are automatically fulfilled when the simplex method of linear programming is used. Then the y_i^+ and y_i^- vectors are linearly dependent, and hence they cannot appear together in the same basic solution (cf. Charnes et al. [1955]). Strictly speaking, the non-linear conditions need only be met at the optimum (cf. Charnes and Cooper [1977]). If the weights α_i^+ and α_i^- are non-negative these conditions are fulfilled as a consequence of the minimization process. This means that in this case methods other than the simplex routine can also be used. For the sake of illustration consider

(4.44)
$$\text{Min}\{\alpha^+ . y^+ + \alpha^- . y^-\}, \text{ with } \alpha^+, \alpha^- \geq 0,$$

$$\text{s.t. } \underline{a}'.\underline{x} - y^+ + y^- = b$$

and $\underline{x} \in R$

where $\underline{a}$ is a (nx1) vector and b is a scalar. Assume a solution
exists with $y^+ = t > 0$, $y^- = u > 0$ and $t > u$. This solution is not
optimal because the value of the objective function declines when
both y^+ and y^- are reduced by the same amount. Thus define
$y^+ = t - \delta$ and $y^- = u - \delta$, which gives

$$f = \alpha^+.y^+ + \alpha^-.y^- =$$

(4.45) $$= \alpha^+.(t-\delta) + \alpha^-.(u-\delta) =$$

$$= (\alpha^+.t+\alpha^-.u) - (\alpha^++\alpha^-).\delta,$$

where the first term represents the value of the first solution
and the second term its possible reduction. This reduction is an
increasing function of δ, which , however, is restricted by the
non-negativity restrictions on y^+ and y^-. The latter can be stated
as $t-\delta \geq 0$ and $u-\delta \geq 0$. Since we assumed $t > u$, the maximal value
of δ (and consequently the minimal value of f) is reached for
$\delta = u$. Finally, the goal restriction in (4.44) remains unaffected
because both y^+ and y^- are reduced by the same amount.

In order to handle the pre-emptive priorities discussed in
Section 4.1, the deviations must be weighted by the non-Archimedean
values M_t. For instance, if goal t has pre-emptive priority above
goal t', the weights M_t and $M_{t'}$ are chosen such that

(4.46) $$M_t > > M_{t'},$$

which means that no real number γ - however large - can give

(4.47) $$\gamma M_{t'} = M_t$$

By this procedure a lexicographic ordering is obtained because no
trade-offs between goals of different priority classes are possible.
Within standard linear programming these preemptive priorities
raise special problems to which we shall return below.

Another possibility is to give one goal absolute priority above another. This can be done by constraints on the deviational variables. For instance

(4.48) $$y_i^+ + y_j^+ \leq \delta$$

to insure that the sum of two positive deviations under no circumstances exceeds the given value δ. These restrictions may only be used if they do not violate the non-linear constraints $y_i^+ . y_i^- = 0$.

In principle, the goal problem (4.43) can be solved by the usual linear programming techniques. However, introduction of the non-Archimedean factors M_t calls for a different approach. This stems from the fact there is no foolproof method which translates the non-Archimedean factors M_t *a priori* in real-valued weights μ_t, which can then be used within a linear programming format. One might consider replacing the M_t by real numbers μ_t having the property that μ_1, belonging to the most important priority class, is 'much bigger' than μ_2, the next important priority class and so on, where 'much bigger' is defined in an arbitrary way. Such procedures are of course *ad hoc* and lack proof of correctness.

Kornbluth [1973] and Salkin and Kornbluth [1973] use a straightforward procedure to handle pre-emptive priorities. Analogous to the approach using generalized inverses ((4.40) – (4.42)), they first determine the part of the feasible region, R_1, in which the goals of the first priority class are met. Given R_1, they try to fulfil the goals of the second priority class, and so. By reformulating (4.43) including pre-emptive priorities, we get

$$\text{Min } D = \sum_{t=1}^{p} M_t (\sum_{s=1}^{m_t} \alpha_{ts}^+ \cdot y_{ts}^+ / b_{ts} + \alpha_{ts}^- \cdot y_{ts}^- / b_{ts}) ,$$

(4.49)   s.t. $A.\underline{x} - \underline{y}^+ + \underline{y}^- = \underline{b}$,

          and $\underline{x} \in R$,

where $M_1 \gg M_2 \gg ... \gg M_p$ and $\sum_{t=1}^{p} m_t = m$, while the other elements
are defined as before. This problem is solved through the following
sequential optimization process (Salkin and Kornbluth [1973]):

(i)   Set $t = 1$;

(ii)   Minimize $D_t = \sum_{s=1}^{m_t} \alpha_{ts}^+ \cdot y_{ts}^+ / b_{ts} + \alpha_{ts}^- \cdot y_{ts}^- / b_{ts}$;

        subject to the constraints in (4.49). Let the minimum be D_t^*;

(iii)   If the solution is unique (non-degenerate), stop; otherwise
(iv)   Flag out variables which are not part of the alternative
        bases of (ii) and add the constraint

$$D_t^* = \sum_{s=1}^{m_t} \alpha_{ts}^+ \cdot y_{ts}^+ / b_{ts} + \alpha_{ts}^- \cdot y_{ts}^- / b_{ts};$$

(v)   If all goals have been considered, stop;
        otherwise put $t = t + 1$ and go to (ii).

It will be clear that this procedure guarantees an optimal solution
within a number of $p' \leq p$ runs of the standard linear programming
problem (ii). Nevertheless it is possible to solve the problem in
one run by using an adapted version of the simplex procedure, as
proposed by Mao [1969] and Lee [1972]. This will be dealt with in
the next section.

4.4. An Adapted Simplex Procedure

In this section we describe an adapted simplex procedure presented by Lee [1972]. The notation used may be clarified with the help of the initial standard simplex tableau in Table 4.3.

Table 4.3. The initial standard simplex tableau

c_j			c_1				c_n				
	V	B	x_1				x_n	s_n			s_m
	s_1	b_1	a_{11}				a_{1n}	$I_{m \times m} =$			
	.	.	.				.				
	.	.	.				.	Identity Matrix			
	.	.	.				.				
	s_m	b_m	a_{m1}				a_{mn}				
$z_j - c_j$		0	$-c_1$				$-c_n$				

In this tableau the instrumental variables are $x_1 \ldots x_n$ and the slack variables $s_1 \ldots s_m$. The column headed V represents the vector of variables chosen in the basis. In this initial tableau the basis consists of the slack variables only. The values of the basic variables are given in the column headed B. The top row shows the variables' contribution to the value of the objective function. These values are duplicated in the lefthand column for the variables that are chosen into the basis. The bottom row gives the value of the objective function for the basis at hand. It also gives the negatives of the net changes in the value of the objective function ($z_j - c_j$) induced by the introduction of the respective non-basic variables into the basis (where the changes are measured per unit of the entering variable).

Procedure

The following elaboration of the adapted simplex method departs from the general formulation (4.49). For the sake of simplicity, we assume all constraints to have been formulated as goal constraints. The initial tableau for this minimization problem contains no slack variables since their role can be played by the deviational variables y_{ts}^-. Because we now have to deal with p preemptive priority classes, one single $z_j - c_j$ row is not enough. Instead, p rows are introduced (one for each priority class) which are labeled $(z_j-c_j)^1$ up to and including $(z_j-c_j)^p$. The format of the initial tableau is shown in Table 4.4. The value of the objective function to be minimized is equal to $\sum_{t=1}^{p} z_t$, where z_t has been defined as the weighted sum of the deviations from the goals is in the tth preemptive priority class, so that in the initial solution

$$(4.50) \qquad z_t = \sum_{s=1}^{m_t} M_t \cdot \alpha_{ts} \cdot y_{ts}^-$$

In the adapted simplex tableau all z_j's are shown separately. Accordingly the (z_j-c_j) row has been replaced by a matrix, consisting of the rows $(z_j-c_j)^p$ through $(z_j-c_j)^1$. The tth row of this matrix, $(z_j-c_j)^t$, gives the net influences on the value of z_t by entering the respective non-basic variables into the basis. The net influence on the objective function as a whole by introducing some non-basic variable is then found by summing up the elements of its column in the (Z-C) matrix.

With the construction of the initial tableau we have established the first step of the adapted simplex algorithm. The second step consists of the identification of the new entering variable. To that end we find the highest pre-emptive priority class that has not been completely attained. This is the first class k whose corresponding

Table 4.4. The initial adapted simplex tableau

c_j	V	B	$x_1 \cdots x_n$	$M_1\alpha_{11}^- \cdots M_1\alpha_{m_1 1}^- \cdots\cdots M_p\alpha_{1p}^- \cdots M_p\alpha_{m_p p}^-$	$M_1\alpha_{11}^+ \cdots M_1\alpha_{m_1 1}^+ \cdots\cdots M_p\alpha_{1p}^+ \cdots M_p\alpha_{m_p p}^+$
				$y_{11}^- \cdots\ y_{m_1 1}^- \cdots\cdots\ y_{1p}^- \cdots\ y_{m_p p}^-$	$y_{11}^+ \cdots\ y_{m_1 1}^+ \cdots\cdots\ y_{1p}^+ \cdots\ y_{m_p p}^+$
$M_1\cdot\alpha_{11}^-$	y_{11}^-	b_1	$a_{11} \cdots a_{1n}$		
$M_1\cdot\alpha_{m_1 1}^-$	$y_{m_1 1}^-$			In the initial tableau this is the (m x m) identity matrix	In the initial tableau this is the (m x m) identity matrix
$M_p\cdot\alpha_{1p}^-$	y_{1p}^-				
$M_p\alpha_{m_p p}^-$	$y_{m_p p}^-$	b_m	$a_{m1} \cdots a_{mn}$		
$(z_j-c_j)^p$ $\cdots$ $(z_j-c_j)^1$		z_p $\cdots$ z_1	In the initial tableau $(z_j-c_j)=$ $M_1\left(\sum_{u=1}^{m_1}\alpha_{u1}\cdot a_{u1}\right)$	In the initial tableau this is the (p x m) null matrix	In the initial tableau the southwest-northeast diagonal of this matrix consists of the elements $M_1(\alpha_{11}^- - \alpha_{11}^+)$ through $M_p(\alpha_{m_p p}^- - \alpha_{m_p p}^+)$. All other elements are zero.

89

z_k value is positive. We then proceed to identifying the variable with the largest positive $(z_j-c_j)^k$ value. This will enter the basis in the next iteration. If two non-basic variables both have the maximum $(z_j-c_j)^k$ value, the tie may be broken by inspecting their respective $(z_j-c_j)^{k+1}$ values. The variable with the greater $(z_j-c_j)^{k+1}$ is then chosen.

In the <u>third step</u> the pivot row is found. This is the row which has minimum positive or zero value of the right hand constant divided by the coefficients in the pivot column. The associated variable leaves the basis in the next iteration. If there are two variables with minimum value remove the variable with the higher priority factor.

The new basic feasible solution is determined in the <u>fourth step</u>. First, the pivot row is divided by the pivot element. Secondly the new basic variable is eliminated from all other rows in the tableau.

The <u>fifth step</u> treats the optimality check. If $z_t = 0$ for $t = 1, \ldots, p$; all goals have been attained. If there exists a positive value of z_t, say z_k, examine the positive elements of $(z_j-c_j)^k$. In the case that such a positive element does not exist without its column containing a negative element in the higher priority rows $(z_j-c_j)^t$, $t = 1, \ldots, k-1$, the optimal solution has been reached. In other cases return to the second step.

The adapted simplex procedure is not very different from the 'standard' simplex procedure. The main difference is the pivot selection, which in the adapted procedure has to deal with non-Archimedean pivot elements. For a more detailed discussion of the adapted simplex procedure we refer to Lee [1972].

Sensitivity Analysis and Duality

The adapted simplex procedure has been developed in order to handle the pre-emptive priority factors M_t within a single simplex program. Both sensitivity analysis and duality are influenced by the character of the priority structure. Below, we shall discuss the two major differences as compared with 'standard' procedures (cf. also Ignizio [1976]). First, old questions receive new answers. Notably, changes in weighting factors, right-hand side constants and technological coefficients may affect more than one priority level of the final solution. Consequently, these influences must be shown and analyzed separately. Secondly, the nature of the priority structure raises new questions. For instance, the influence of a reordening of priority levels or of the addition of a new goal may be investigated.

Within an unchanged pre-emptive priority structure we can study the influence of changes in the weighting factors α_{ts}. When the variable weighted by α_{ts} is non-basic in the final solution, a change in α_{ts} only results in a direct change of its corresponding element in the t'th row of the (Z-C) matrix. Whether the new tableau remains optimal is checked by the fifth step of the adapted simplex procedure. A change in the weighting factor α_{ts} of a basic variable can affect all elements of the t'th row of the (Z-C) matrix as well as the achievement value z_t of the t'th priority level. Again a new optimality check is necessary.

Changes in the right-hand side constants vector $\underline{b}$ result in a modified column vector $\underline{b}$ in the final tableau and in changes of the achievement levels z_t, $t = 1, \ldots, p$. If the new solution remains feasible, it too is optimal because the elements of the (Z-C) matrix are unaffected by changes in $\underline{b}$. An infeasible solution occurs if

at least one of the elements of the vector $\underline{b}$ in the final solution
is negative. In that case the optimal solution can be found by using
the 'dual adapted simplex method' developed by Ignizio (Ibid).

A modification of the technological coefficients α_{ts} yields
no problems as long as non-basic variables are concerned. An initial
change in the column vector of technological coefficients of the
non-basic variable x_j affects no other elements of the final tableau
but the elements of x_j itself and its accompanying column in the
(Z-C) matrix (the latter being the multidimensional opportunity
loss associated with the introduction of x_j). Again an optimality
check becomes necessary. The introduction of a new activity is
easily handled by considering it as a set of changes in an old
activity of which all technological coefficients are equal to zero.
The analysis of changes in technological coefficients of basic
variables is not straightforward and involves a simultaneous consideration of both the primal and the dual problem.

The addition of a new goal involves the introduction in the
final tableau of both a goal restriction and at least one weighting
factor (associated with the positive or negative deviational variable of this new goal). After eliminating the basic variables from the
new row, the achievement levels Z_t, $t = 1, \ldots, p$; and the matrix
(Z-C) can be recalculated. Again, an optimality check is necessary.
Furthermore, the right-hand side constant of the new goal constraint
may have become negative. This can be handled by the dual adapted
simplex method mentioned above. To study the effect of reordering
pre-emptive priority levels the same method is available. This
implies a recalculation of the achievement levels Z_j and the (Z-C)
matrix, followed by the optimality check.

Effects of Changing the Goal Levels

We next consider changes in the goal levels b_i for the case that all goals have the same pre-emptive priority. Consider the primal problem written as

$$\text{Max}\{-(\underline{\alpha}^+)'.\underline{y}^+ - (\underline{\alpha}^-)'.\underline{y}^-\}, \text{ s.t.}$$

$$A.\underline{x} - \underline{y}^+ + \underline{y}^- = \underline{b}$$

(4.51)

$$B.\underline{x} \leq \underline{h}, \text{ and}$$

$$\underline{x}, \underline{y}^+, \underline{y}^- \geq \underline{0}, \text{ where}$$

$\underline{\alpha}^+$ and $\underline{\alpha}^-$ are m dimensional vectors of weighting factors. The dual problem can then be formulated as

$$\text{Min } \{\underline{b}'.\underline{u} + \underline{h}'.\underline{v}\}$$

$$A'.\underline{u} + B'.\underline{v} \geq \underline{0}$$

(4.52)

$$\underline{\alpha}^+ \geq \underline{u} \geq -\underline{\alpha}^-, \text{ and}$$

$$\underline{v} \geq \underline{0}, \underline{u} \text{ unrestricted in sign}$$

The Kuhn-Tucker conditions connecting problems (4.51) and (4.52) are given by

$$\underline{u}'.(\underline{y}^+ - \underline{y}^-) = 0, \text{ and}$$

(4.53)

$$\underline{v}'.(\underline{h} - B.\underline{x}) = 0$$

By defining $\underline{u} = \underline{u}^- - \underline{u}^+$, where $\underline{u}^-, \underline{u}^+ \geq 0$, we can reformulate (4.52) as

$$\text{Min}\{b'.(-\underline{u}^+ + \underline{u}^-) + h'.\underline{v}\}, \text{ s.t.}$$

$$A'.(-\underline{u}^+ + \underline{u}^-) + B'.\underline{v} \geq 0,$$

(4.53)
$$\underline{u}^- \leq \underline{\alpha}^+,$$

$$\underline{u}^+ \leq \underline{\alpha}^-, \text{ and}$$

$$\underline{u}^+, \underline{u}^-, v \geq 0$$

The variables u_i^+, u_i^- and $(u_i^+ - u_i^-)$ can be interpreted as the decrease in the value of the objective function when the right-hand side constant b_i is augmented by one unit (provided the solution remains feasible and optimal, which we shall assume hereafter). Such a shift in b_i causes one out of two possible effects. Either y_i^+ grows by one unit or y_i^- declines by one unit (a negative shift of b_i causes the opposite effects). This is shown in Figure 4.3 where the effects on y_i^+ and y_i^- are shown for a negative shift in the aspiration level b_i of a given goal variable $g_i(\underline{x})$ and a given solution $g_i(\underline{x}) = S$.

The increase of the objective function caused by a negative shift of b_i is given by $u_i = -u_i^+ + u_i^-$. Obviously $-u_i^+$ represents the effect of a decrease in y_i^-, whereas u_i^- represents the effect of a possible increase of y_i^-. The effect on the objective function of a unit increase of y_i^+ and of a unit decrease of y_i^- must be equal to the weights of these variables in the objective function of the primal problem. These effects are thus α_i^+ and $-\alpha_i^-$ respectively. Because these effects are not exactly the same when b_i is shifted upwards, we list all possibilities in (4.54).

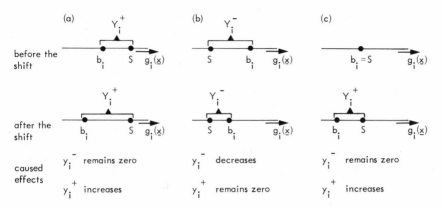

Figure 4.3. The effects of a negative shift of the aspiration level b_i on the deviational variables y_i^+ and y_i^-

$$u_i^+ = \alpha_i^- \text{ for } y_i^+ = 0 \text{ and } y_i^- > 0$$

$$= \alpha_i^- \text{ for } y_i^+ = y^- = 0 \text{ and when } b_i \text{ is raised}$$

$$(4.54) \qquad = 0 \text{ in all other cases}$$

$$u_i^- = \alpha_i^+ \text{ for } y_i^- = 0 \text{ and } y_i^+ > 0$$

$$= \alpha_i^+ \text{ for } y_i^+ = y_i^- = 0 \text{ and when } b_i \text{ is lowered.}$$

$$= 0 \text{ in all other cases.}$$

4.5. Concluding Remarks

Goal programming has been extended in various ways. From several possible extensions we only discussed the inclusion of piecewise linear functions in the goal programming model. Kornbluth [1973] paid special attention to ratio form goals as 'return on assets', 'profit to sales', etc. (see also Chapter 8). In some cases these

goals may induce computational obstacles, which according to Charnes
and Cooper [1977] can be circumvented if the Chebychev metric (see
p.64) is used. Ignizio [1976] proposes a method to include integer
conditions within the goal programming framework. Discussions about
the extension towards stochastic goal programming can be found in
Charnes and Cooper [1963] and Contini [1968].

In addition to the use of goal programming for multiple
criteria decision making, this technique is suitable for other areas
of application. According to Charnes and Cooper [1977] goal programming was developed (in 1952) to obtain constrained regression
estimates for an executive compensation formula which would conform
to management policies (cf. Charnes et al. [1955]). The use of goal
programming in econometrics has been studied further (see Charnes
and Cooper [1975]) and has been advocated for other application
areas. For instance, Spivey and Tamura [1970] present goal programming as an alternative to simultaneous equation models for use in
macro economic decision making. For them, important advantages of
goal programming are its access to sensitivity analysis, its
flexibility in formulating the preference function, and its ability
to deal with political and institutional variables explicitly.

An important drawback of goal programming is its need for fairly
detailed *a priori* information on the decision maker's preferences.
Goal programming requires definition of aspiration levels,
partitioning of the set of goals into pre-emptive priority classes
and assessment of weights within these classes. A problem not to be
overlooked is the critical role of the aspiration levels and the
pre-emptive priorities defined by the decision maker. Once a goal
obtains pre-emptive priority above another, no trade-off between
these goals is admitted anymore. In other words first order priority
goals determine the solution space for goals of less important
priority classes. This means that the definition of the goal levels
must be completely reliable or that some kind of bargaining about

these levels must remain possible.

Clearly, the elucidation of the decision maker's preferences in this 'direct' way is not a sinecure. We do agree with the scholars advocating interactive methods, which neither require an explicit representation or specification of the decision maker's preference function nor an explicit quantitative representation of trade-offs among conflicting goal variables.

Unfortunately, most of the usual interactive approaches lack some of the advantages of 'traditional' goal programming, such as for instance the possibility to include pre-emptive priorities. Furthermore, in contrast with most existing interactive methods, goal programming is particularly suitable in situations of satisficing behaviour. Together, these advantages of goal programming justify the effort to seek an interactive variant of the traditional approach. One such effort is described in the following chapters.

References

Barrodale, I. and F.D.K. Roberts (1970), Applications of Mathematical
    Programming to ℓ Approximation, in Rosen et al. [1970].

Bartels, C.P.A. and P. Nijkamp (1976), An Empirical Welfare Approach
    to Regional Income Distributions, Socio-Economic Planning Sciences,
    p. 117 ff.

Beckenbach, E. and R. Bellman (1961), An Introduction to Inequalities,
    Random House.

Benayoun, R., J. de Montgolfier, J. Tergny and O. Laritchev (1974),
    Linear Programming with Multiple Objective Functions: Step Method
    (STEM), Mathematical Programming, p. 366.

Ben-Israel, A. and T.N. Greville (1974), Generalized Inverses, Wiley.

Charnes, A., W.W. Cooper and R.O. Ferguson (1955), Optimal Estimation
    of Executive Compensation by Linear Programming, Management
    Science, p. 138 ff.

Charnes, A. and W.W. Cooper (1961), Management Models and Industrial
    Applications of Linear Programming, Part I and II, John Wiley,
    New York.

Charnes, A. and W.W. Cooper (1963), Deterministic Equivalents for
    Optimizing and Satisfying under Chance Constraints, Operations
    Research, p. 18 ff.

Charnes, A. and W.W. Cooper (1975), Goal Programming and Constrained
    Regression - A Comment, Omega, p. 403 ff.

Charnes, A. and W.W. Cooper (1977), Goal Programming and Multiple
    Objective Optimizations, Part I, European Journal of Operational
    Research, p. 39 ff.

Charnes, A., W.W. Cooper, D. Klingman and R.J. Niehaus (1979), Expli-
    cit Solutions in Convex Goal Programming, Management Science.

Collomb, B.P. (1971), Goal Interval Approaches to Intertemporal
    Analysis and Decentralization in Management, Ph. D. Thesis,
    University of Texas, Austin.

Contini, B. (1968), A Stochastic Approach to Goal Programming,
   Operations Research, p. 576 ff.

Fishburn, P.C. (1974), Lexicographic Orders; Utilities and Decision
   Rules: A Survey, Management Science, p. 1442 ff.

Goodman, D.A. (1974), A Goal Programming Approach to Aggregate
   Planning of Production and Work Force, Management Science,
   p. 1569 ff.

Ignizio, J.P. (1976), Goal Programming and Extensions, Lexington.

Ijiri, Y. (1965), Management Goals and Accounting for Control,
   North-Holland.

Kornbluth, J.S.H. (1973), A Survey of Goal Programming, Omega,
   p. 193 ff.

Lane, M.N. (1970), Goal Programming and Satisficing Models in
   Economic Analysis, Ph. D. thesis, University of Texas.

Laurent, G. (1976), A Note on Range Programming, Management Science,
   p. 713 ff.

Lee, S.M. (1972), Goal Programming for Decision Analysis, Auerbach.

Mao, J.C.T. (1969), Quantitative Analysis of Financial Decisions,
   McMillan.

Monarchi, D.E., J.E. Weber and L. Duckstein (1976), An Interactive
   Multiple Objective Decision-Making Aid Using Non-Linear Goal
   Programming, in Zeleny, [1976], pp. 235-253.

Nijkamp, P. and P. Rietveld (1976), Multi-Objective Programming
   Models; New Ways in Regional Decision-Making, Regional Science
   and Urban Economics, p. 253 ff.

Nijkamp, P. and P. Rietveld (1977), Impact Analysis, Spatial
   Externalities and Policy Choices, North-East Regional Science
   Review, Vol. 8.

Nijkamp, P. and J. Spronk (1979), Goal Programming for Decision
   Making, An Overview and a Discussion, Ricerca Operativa, pp. 3-49.

Rosen, J., O. Mangasarian and K. Ritter (eds)(1970), Non-Linear
   Programming, Academic Press.

Salkin, G.R. and J.S.H. Kornbluth (1973), Linear Programming
   in Financial Planning, Haymarket.

Spivey, W.A. and H. Tamura (1970), Goal Programming in Econometrics, Naval Research Logistics Quarterly, p. 183 ff.

Theil, H. (1971), Principles of Econometrics, Wiley.

Zeleny, M.(ed.)(1976), Multiple Criteria Decision-Making, Springer, Berlin.

Zukhovitsky, S.I. and L.I. Avdeyeva (1966), Linear and Convex Programming, Philadelphia Saunders.

5. INTERACTIVE MULTIPLE OBJECTIVE PROGRAMMING METHODS

Each time a new method is proposed, one has to judge its contribution to the set of already existing comparable methods. Because we are advocating a new interactive variant of goal programming in our study, we have to expose its relationships both with other interactive methods and with goal programming. As mentioned in Chapter 4, interactive methods may circumvent the considerable information requirements that make goal programming sometimes less valuable. A characterization, together with an overview of the main features of interactive methods is given in Section 5.2. A more detailed typology of interactive methods (based on the framework sketched in Chapter 3), is presented in Section 5.3. Because the majority of the existing interactive methods lack some important advantages of goal programming, it is worthwhile seeking an interactive variant of goal programming. In Section 5.4 we discuss a sample of such interactive variants of goal programming. Our main conclusions can be found in Section 5.5.

5.1. Features of an Interactive Approach

If in a decision situation involving multiple goals, the set of alternative solutions has been clearly described, and if the preferences of the decision maker have been expressed explicitly in terms of the instrumental variables, the multiple criteria decision problem can be reduced to an exclusively mathematical (optimization) problem. Very often, however, and especially if the number of decision alternatives increases, a situation arises in which the decision maker is unable or unwilling to provide all required *a priori* preference information. In such cases, interactive procedures might offer much help.

The interactive approach assumes that the decision maker is at least capable of defining which goal variables influence his preferences. Furthermore, it assumes that the decision maker is able to provide <u>local</u> preference information, i.e. information with respect to a given solution (or a given set of solutions) which is known to exist and to be feasible. The kind of local preference . information required varies for each interactive procedure. In some methods the decision maker has to give his local trade-offs with respect to the goal levels of the solution concerned. In other methods, the decision maker has to indicate whether a given solution is acceptable or not, and if not which of the goal values should be changed.

Typically, in the interactive approach, the decision maker has to express his local preferences with respect to a series of solutions, which are presented to him in a stepwise manner and are partly the result of his previous answers. This process of presenting solutions and expressing the local preferences with respect to these solutions is embedded in an interactive framework. The interaction takes place between the decision maker, an analyst and a (computer) model of the decision problem. The model (designed by the analyst in consultation with the decision maker) describes the set of feasible decision alternatives, the set of goal variables and the relationships between decision alternatives and goal variables. In most interactive procedures, the analyst (using the model) proposes a starting solution to the decision maker. The latter gives his preference information with respect to this solution to the analyst, who transforms this information into a new solution, again using the model and guided by the requirements of the interactive procedure at hand. This new solution is presented to the decision maker, who expresses his preferences, and so on, until a final solution is reached which is judged satisfactory. In consideration of errors and learning effects, the decision maker may obviously wish to repeat the whole process. Moreover, because of new insights obtained, it may become necessary to revise the model. In Figure 5.1 a sketch of the interactive approach is given.

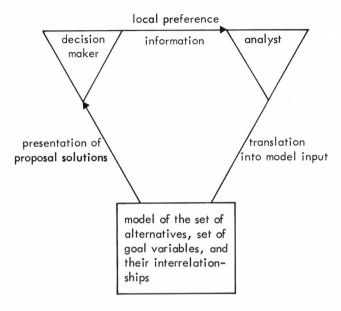

Figure 5.1. The interactive approach

Generally, the role of the analyst during the interactive process is more passive than in the preparatory phase. This is because the translation from the decision maker's preference information into a new solution can mostly be computerized in a straightforward manner. Nevertheless, the analyst still has to be involved in the interactive process: to instruct and reinstruct the decision maker about the properties of the interactive procedure at hand, to help analyze the model results and if necessary to prepare possible model revisions.

Advantages and Disadvantages of the Interactive Approach

An obvious advantage of the interactive approach is the limited amount of preference information required from the decision maker, as compared to methods in which the decision maker has to give his

preference information on an *a priori* basis. In the latter case,
the decision maker has to consider all kinds of choices and trade-
off questions which might be relevant. However, because this
articulation of preferences takes place before knowing whether the
alternatives influenced by these preferences are feasible or not,
and if feasible, whether they are dominated, this kind of preference
information may clearly be redundant. Furthermore, this preference
information can only be obtained by means of hypothetical questions
such as 'What would you prefer if you could choose between alternatives A and B?' This is in contrast with the interactive approach,
in which the decision maker has to express his preferences based on
a well-defined solution which is known to exist and to be feasible.
Questions to be answered now become quite concrete, such as 'Do you
accept this solution or not?', and 'Which goal value of the given
solution is too low?'.

The assumptions related to the preference structure of the
decision maker are less restrictive in the interactive approach than
in procedures aiming at the *a priori* articulation of preferences.
Also, because the decision maker is closely involved in the solution
process, the solution finally chosen has a better chance of being
implemented (cf. also Hwang and Masud [1979]).

By means of interactive decision procedures the decision maker
may become more closely involved in the process of solving his
decision problem, thus obtaining more insight into the trade-offs
among different goal variables. The feed-back process inherent in
interactive decision procedures leads to a closer cooperation between
decision maker and analyst. In a sense, the interactive approach
can be regarded as an operational application of learning theory
(cf. also Atkinson et al. [1965], Golledge [1969], and Hilgard and
Bower [1969]). One of the learning effects induced by the interactive
approach may be that the decision maker's perception of the decision
situation changes during the interactive process. This in turn may
necessitate restructuring the model describing the decision problem,
e.g. by changing a goal variable or by adding an instrumental

variable. In addition, the decision maker's preferences may change because of new insights into the decision situation. In addition, one should take the occurrence of possible errors made by the decision maker into account. Therefore, it is wise to repeat the whole interactive process several times to ensure that a final solution is found which is as close to the 'optimum' as possible.

Of course, the characteristics of the learning process started by the interactive approach depend among other things on the very interactive procedure chosen, and - given a particular procedure - on the starting point. It is virtually impossible to test the influences of different interactive procedures and different starting points on the learning process empirically. This makes the choice of a particular procedure and of a particular starting solution somewhat arbitrary, although on theoretical grounds several criteria can be formulated which may influence the choice of such a procedure (cf. Section 5.2).

Traditionally, the entrepreneurial preference structure was considered by such academic fields as economics, operations research and management science to be a given. As described in Chapter 2, this given mostly consisted of some profit maximization or cost minimization assumption. Given the recognition of the existence of multiple goals, no straightforward assumption on the decision maker's preference structure can, in a general sense, be made. The only solution is to model the decision maker's preferences in a more direct way, e.g. by interviewing techniques (cf. also Chapter 3).

In interviewing techniques the same phenomenon may arise as in interactive procedures. The very way of interviewing may also induce a learning process. As long as this is clear to the decision maker, there are no objections to this situation.

To summarize, we can state that the interactive approach offers a powerful tool in decision situations in which the decision maker's preferences are not known *a priori*. It is able to include and to benefit from learning effects, it involves a closer co-operation of the decision maker in the solution process and moreover, the

information to be given by the decision maker concerns real
instead of hypothetical choices. In the next section we list a
number of elements which might be useful for evaluating interactive
procedures.

5.2. Elements of Interactive Methods

In the preceding section we argued that interactive methods
may be regarded as a learning process in which the decision maker
reacts upon the questions posed to him. From this viewpoint, the
specific method of obtaining information from a decision maker may
influence his answers. Therefore, one should pay heed to the
behavioural assumptions made in a particular interactive method.

The convergence of a particular interactive method might often
be accelerated by adding a few behavioural assumptions. This,
however, would in turn affect the class of problems which can be
tackled by this method.

These points show that the evaluation of an interactive
decision method itself can be regarded as a multiple criteria
problem. In order to illustrate this statement, we shall propose
a set of elements which may be important in evaluating interactive
decision methods. Some of these elements have been adopted from
studies of Cohon and Marks [1975], Roy [1971,1976ab], Wallenius
[1975] and Wallenius and Zionts [1976].

Because we have already (in Section 3.2) listed a number of
characteristics of decision problems to be used for the evaluation
of multiple criteria decision methods in general, we limit ourselves
here to the more specific elements of interactive methods, subdivided
into the following groups:

I.   The communication process between decision maker and decision
     model

II. Technical properties of the interactive process
These features will be described in more detail below.

The Communication Process between Decision Maker and Decision Model

Clearly, the way in which the process of interaction between decision maker and model (possibly guided by an analyst) has been structured is of crucial importance for the acceptance of the interactive method by the decision maker. For instance, when only limited information is provided to the decision maker, he may feel that some information is being withheld from him. Likewise, he will require some freedom to influence the direction of the interactive process.

To characterize the communication process, we suggest the following qualifications.

a. The questions posed to the decision maker

- Is he requested to answer 'zero-one' questions (e.g., 'Do you prefer this solution to the preceding one?') or does he have to specify cardinal information (e.g., the specification of a marginal rate of substitution between two goal variables)?

- Is he requested to answer these questions with respect to weights, with respect to achievement levels attached to the goal variables, or both?

- How many questions are to be answered at each iteration and in total?

To stress the importance of including these qualifications, we quote Cohon and Marks [1975, p. 209]: 'It is futile, and antithetical to the essence of planning, to complicate the analysis with all sorts of esoteric terms and terminology. Yet, some of the multiobjective techniques rely on the collection of abstruse, sometimes exotic data from the decision maker, thereby producing meaningless results'.

b. The information for the decision maker

- Is the decision maker confronted with a fixed amount of information or does he have some options to select from the available information those items which he believes to be interesting?

- Does the model allow for the possibility of sensitivity analysis; at each stage of the problem?
- Is the decision maker given one or more solutions at a time?
c. Options available to the decision maker to control the interactive process
    - What are the decision maker's degrees of freedom to change the
      direction of the search process for a consecutive solution?
    - If the decision maker changes his mind during the interactive
      procedure, can he return to an earlier solution?
d. Perception of the method by the decision maker

The evaluation of an interactive method also presupposes some
idea of how the method is perceived by the decision maker. Wallenius
[1975] carried out a laboratory experiment in order to compare the
performance of three interactive methods from a human decision maker's point of view. From this experiment we adopt the following
measures, which are obviously of a more subjective nature than the
preceding ones.
- The decision maker's confidence in the best compromise.
- The ease of using the method.
- The ease of understanding the logic of the method.
- The use of the information provided to aid the decision maker.
- The claim on the decision maker's time.
In the next section we will briefly describe some of the experimen-
tal results with respect to the decision maker's perception of in-
teractive methods.

Technical Properties of Interactive Methods

Interactive methods vary from very simple rules of thumb to
sophisticated mathematical programming methods. We therefore list
some technical characteristics:
a. The specific solution (optimization) procedure(s) which have to
   be used in the computational phases of the process

b. Computer time per iteration

This is not only important for the acceptance of the method by
the decision maker (see I.d), but also as a cost factor. Of course,
this measure depends on the problem to be solved, the solution
(optimization) procedure chosen, the efficiency of the computer
program and last but not least, the type of computer used.

c. Convergency properties

- Does the procedure converge to a final solution?
- What are the minimum and maximum number of iterations needed to
  approach such a final solution close enough? (This depends on
  the accuracy chosen, but also on the number of goal variables,
  the preference structure and the properties of the set of
  possible actions).
- If the procedure converges, is there a unique final solution
  or not?

Many of the elements of interactive methods mentioned in this
section, as well as some of the characteristics described in Section 3.2 will be discussed further in the following sections, in
which we will give a classification of interactive methods.

5.3. The Need of an Interactive Variant of Goal Programming

During the last decade, the number of multiple objective programming methods grew considerably. Besides, a wide variety of literature on the efficiency concept and on vector maximization has
emerged. Goal programming techniques, methods that maximize one
goal variable subject to *a priori* fixed levels of the other goal
variables, and methods which generate all efficient solutions (see
for instance Gal [1977]) have been proposed to deal with the multiple objective programming problem. The first two procedures need a
considerable amount of *a priori* information on the decision maker's
preferences (cf. Chapter 4). An important disadvantage of the third
kind of methods is that they often generate a very large number of

efficient solutions. Although preselection of efficient solutions seems to simplify the decision problem, the efficient set is normally practically unmanagable for the decision maker.

Many interactive procedures have been designed to overcome the above-mentioned difficulties. Recent overviews are given a.o. by Cohon [1978], Hwang and Masud [1979], Isermann [1979], and Winkels [1979]. All interactive procedures progress from one solution (or set of solutions) to another, guided by the desires of the decision maker, which must also be expressed iteratively, i.e. each time a new (set of) solution(s) is defined. With respect to the nature of the preference information to be given at each iteration by the decision maker, the set of available interactive procedures can be subdivided as follows.

(a) Methods in which the decision maker has to determine trade-offs among the goal variables at each iteration, given the goal values in the current solution.

(b) Methods in which the decision maker has to choose the 'best' solution from a limited (discrete) set of (generally efficient) solutions at each iteration.

(c) Methods in which the decision maker at each iteration has to define minimum or maximum values for one or more of the goal variables, which in most methods are translated into restrictions reducing the feasible region.

The union of type (a), (b) and (c) methods will be denoted hereafter as the class of 'interactive multiple objective programming' methods. Methods of type (c) will be classified as 'interactive goal programming' procedures. This classification of interactive programming methods is illustrated in Figure 5.2 (see p. 124). The methods in each class differ with respect to the accuracy required from the decision maker expressing his preferences. Some methods need 'exact' weights to be assigned to the goal variables, other merely require a range of weights (or present a series of weights from which the decision maker can choose). In some methods only the best one from a set of solutions must be selected, in others it suffices to select

a couple of 'best and 'near best' solutions. Similarly, certain
methods need the exact amount of maximally tolerable relaxation of
a goal value (given some proposal solution), others only need a
lower goal value which does not necessarily need to be exact.

Below, we will give a very short description and evaluation of
type (a) and type (b) methods, followed in Section 5.4 by a more
detailed description of type (c) methods.

Type (a) Methods

Type (a) methods provide a mechanism to find trade-offs among
the goal variables by interacting with the decision maker. A well-
known method of this type is described by Geoffrion et al. [1972],
who assume that the decision maker's preferences can be described
by a concave and differentiable utility function. The utility function as such is unknown to the decision maker, but he is assumed to
be able to provide information on all possible trade-offs among the
goal variables. The optimization procedure used, in this case the
Frank-Wolfe algorithm (cf. Frank and Wolfe [1956]), determines
the kind of information required. This algorithm proceeds from
solution to solution via the 'steepest ascent' direction, i.e.
the direction with maximum marginal increase in the overall utility
function. It also requires knowledge about the maximum allowable
step size in this direction. Both kind of data are to be fixed with
the help of the decision maker. Dyer [1972] links the above procedure to the one-sided goal programming model (cf. Chapter 4), thus
presenting the first interactive multiple objective programming
procedure based on goal programming. Because in Dyer's method the
goal levels themselves are considered to be determined *a priori*
by the decision maker, this method does not fall within our
definition of interactive goal programming. Contrary to Dyer, we
doubt whether the goal levels may be considered as given and fixed.
Goals are being formulated in practice, but this does not necessarily
mean that the decision maker is capable of formulating *a priori* any
goal that seems to be relevant in a particular decision problem.

Furthermore, goals formulated by the decision maker may change
during the process of formulating and solving the problem. The decision maker may change his mind because of information obtained
during the process. We believe that goals *a priori* defined by the
decision maker may form a rich source of information on his preference structure. However, the decision maker should have the explicit option to change these goals during the interactive process.

This type of approach is very intriguing, because it relates
interactive procedures to gradient methods. Moreover, in the linear
case, this approach only generates extreme points (cf. Hwang and
Masud [1979, p.121]), where an extreme point is a vector in the
feasible set R which cannot be expressed as a linear combination
of two other, mutually different vectors of the feasible set.
Furthermore, the precise nature of the interactions with the decision maker is rather obscure.

Type (b) Methods

For the class of type (b) methods a very attractive procedure
has been provided by Zionts and Wallenius [1976]. They also assume
an implicit utility function, on the basis of which the decision
maker gives his answers. Given a starting solution, which is
(arbitrarily) chosen from the efficient set, together with a set
of neighbouring efficient (corner) solutions, the decision maker
has to compare his preference for the starting solution with his
preference for each of its neighbours. From this preference information, a new solution is derived, which again with its neighbours
is presented to the decision maker, and so forth.

In this method, the demand on the decision maker's ability to
express his preferences is rather small, which is of course a very
important advantage. On the other hand, the method may sometimes
need a considerable amount of iterations. Also, there is a possibility of suboptimization if a certain proposal solution is surrounded
by efficient corner solutions with approximately the same preference
level as the proposal solution. The fact that only corner solutions

are generated may in itself be a disadvantage. Nevertheless, we consider this procedure to be one of the most promising and viable interactive procedures.

Another interesting representative of this type of methods is given by Steuer [1977]. At each iteration the decision maker is confronted with a limited set of efficient corner solutions, from which he has to select the 'best'. Given his choice, a new set is calculated and presented to the decision maker. This procedure has a number of attractive properties, e.g. the kind of answers needed from the decision maker does not seem to be very difficult, and it converges within a finite number of steps. A problem with this procedure is that the set of efficient corner solutions is often very large. Therefore, it is necessary to obtain at least some *a priori* information about the decision maker's preferences. For this reason, Steuer (Ibid.) asks the decision maker to specify lower and upper bounds on the 'weights' of the individual goal variables.

An approach which only generates efficient extreme points might sometimes be inconvenient (cf. Vincke [1976]). This is also valid in cases where the number of efficient corner solutions is few. Then the appproximation of an optimal (non-corner) solution by a neighbouring corner solution may be too inaccurate.

In the next section, we will present a sample of type (c) procedures which are rather well suited for the kind of problems we are dealing with in this study. Therefore, and for reasons which will become clear in the next section, we dismiss the methods of types (a) and (b). It should be noted, however, that other decision problems may exist, in which type (a) and type (b) methods should be preferred to those of type (c).

What do the decision makers themselves say about the types of methods that can be used to express their preferences? Some empirical evidence exists. Dyer [1973] asked a number of students to compare the Geoffrion approach (see above) with a trial-and-error procedure. All students found the trial-and-error procedure equally or more

difficult than the Geoffrion approach. Moreover, the students'
confidence in the results provided by the latter approach, was as
high as the confidence in the results obtained by trial-and-error.
Wallenius [1975] experimented with the help of business students
and managers. He compared the STEP-method, the Geoffrion approach,
and also a trial-and-error procedure and found that the first two
procedures were not judged to be better - and in some cases even
worse - than the trial-and-error procedure. To make the empirical
evidence even more inconclusive, Benson [1975] found that type (c)
methods are generally preferred to the other types.

        In our opinion, a more detailed comparative study of inter-
active procedures is highly necessary. Such a project has been
recently proposed by Despontin and Spronk [1979].

5.4. Interactive Goal Programming Methods

        In this section the interactive multiple objective programming
methods which we labeled 'interactive goal programming' (type (c))
methods in the preceding section are considered in more detail.
One broad subclass of interactive goal programming methods which
we have found in literature (type (c1)) is based on the calculation
of a compromise solution which has a minimum distance (given a
particular distance measure) to the ideal solution. Given such a
compromise, the decision maker has to define a set of goal levels
(or relaxations of the levels in the compromise solution), which
are then translated into restrictions and added to the underlying
programming model. Next a new ideal and a new compromise solution
are calculated, and so forth. Another subclass of interactive goal
programming methods found, type (c2), consists of procedures which
first find an 'optimal' value for one goal variable. Then, given
this optimal value (which is formulated as a restriction), an optimal
value for the second goal variable is strived for, and so on. As will
become clear in this and the next section, there are several reasons
to look for an interactive goal programming procedure outside these
two subclasses (see Figure 5.2).

Successive Relaxation of Compromise Goal Values: Type (c1) Methods

Quite a number of interactive procedures are based on the STEM procedure developed by Benayoun et al. [1971]. This procedure consists of a calculation phase and a decision phase. Given the goal variables $g_j(\underline{x})$, $j = 1, \ldots, m$; the ideal solution is calculated (as defined in Chapter 3), yielding goal-values

(5.1) $g_j^* = \text{Max}\{g_j(\underline{x}) \mid \underline{x} \in R\}$ for $j = 1, \ldots, m$.

Then, the distance to this ideal point is minimized by using the following minimax formulation (cf. also Section 4.3).

Min v, s.t.

(5.2) $v \geq w_j(g_j^* - g_j(\underline{x}))$ for $j = 1, \ldots, m$;

$v \geq 0$, and

$\underline{x} \in R$

The relative weights w_j are calculated in a rather mechanical way by means of

(5.3) $w_j = \dfrac{p_j}{\sum\limits_{j'=1}^{m} p_{j'}}$ and $p_j = \dfrac{g_j^* - g_j^{min}}{g_j^*} \Big/ \Big\{ \sum\limits_{i=1}^{m} (c_i^j)^2 \Big\}^{\frac{1}{2}}$,

where g_j^{min} is the minimum feasible value of $g_j(\underline{x})$ during the successive optimizations of all m separate goal variables, and c_i^j denotes the coefficient of the instrumental variable x_i in $g_j(\underline{x})$.

The compromise solutions g_j^o of (5.2) are proposed to the decision maker. If some g_j^o values are satisfactory and others not, the decision maker has to accept (and to define) a certain amount of relaxation Δg_k for goal variables k, the value of which is already satisfactory. Then the restrictions

(5.4)

$$g_k(\underline{x}) \geq g_k^0 - \Delta g_k, \text{ and}$$

$$g_\ell(\underline{x}) \geq g_\ell^0$$

where ℓ refers to the set of goal variables of which the value was judged to be unsatisfactory are introduced in the next calculatory phase and so on.

Instead of this rather straightforward way of determining the weights w_j, other procedures can be followed. Fandel [1972] and Nijkamp and Rietveld [1976] aimed at identifying an optimal solution while taking account of trade-offs between goal variables. The essential idea of their methods is that each efficient solution is associated with a set of weights for the set of goal variables (cf. Nijkamp and Rietveld [1976, p.7]). As in STEM, they then calculate efficient compromise solutions on the basis of which the decision maker has to determine a set of relaxations as in (5.4). Basically they use the same 'pay-off' information as in (5.1). From such a pay-off table, a vector of weights can be derived which links the solutions in this table to a parametric program. These weights are then used to calculate a new compromise solution.

Fichefet [1976] proposes a combination of STEM and goal programming, which he labeled GPSTEM, to deal with the situation in which there are m decision makers, each having formulated one goal variable. In the first step of GPSTEM, each decision maker has to specify in advance a satisfactory level $\bar{g}_j$ for the goal variable with which he is concerned. In order to find an initial compromise, the following program is solved.

(5.5)

$$\text{Min } v = \sum_{j=1}^{m} (z_j^+ + z_j^-), \text{ s.t.}$$

$$\underline{x} \in R$$

$$g_j(\underline{x}) - z^+ + z^- = \bar{g}_j \qquad \text{for } j = 1, \ldots, m;$$

$$\text{and } z_j^+ \cdot z_j^- = 0 \qquad \text{for } j = 1, \ldots, m.$$

On the basis of the solution of this program a set of parametric
programs is solved (one for each decision maker). The solutions are
used to construct a goal value matrix B which is confronted in a
bimatrix game with the usual STEM-type pay-off matrix A (see (5.1)).
The equilibrium solutions of this game are finally used to derive
an efficient compromise solution, on the basis of which the decision
makers have to determine a set of relaxations as in (5.4).

The essence of the STEM-type methods is that by using the
pay-off table information, an efficient compromise solution is
calculated on the basis of which the decision maker has to define
a set of relaxations. Although these methods are rather elegant, it
is not clear why they use such fairly mechanical and even complicated
procedures to calculate the compromise solutions, which only serve
as a point of reference for the decision maker, i.e. to help him to
formulate his set of relaxations. Moreover, the decision maker has
no opportunity to revise the relaxations if he does not like the
consequences, other than by repeating the entire interactive procedure.

The concept of ideal solutions is obviously very valuable. A
number of very interesting contributions to the 'theory of ideal
solutions' has been delivered by Yu and Zeleny (see e.g. Yu [1973]
and Zeleny [1976]). The latter proposes an interactive procedure
based on the adaptive displacement of ideal solutions, which is in
fact an interactive multiple objective programming procedure of
type (a), as discussed in the preceding section.

Sequential Optimization: Type (c2) Methods

Several methods proceed by searching for an 'optimal' value
for one goal variable. Then, with the former optimal goal value
imposed as a constraint, an 'optimal' value for the second goal
variable is found, and so on.

Van Delft and Nijkamp [1977] discuss hierarchical optimization
methods which are based on the assumption that the set of goal
variables can be ranked in an ordinal way as 'most important',

'next most important', etc. After such a hierarchical rank order
has been established, a series of constrained programming problems
has to be solved. First, the most important goal variable, $g_1(\underline{x})$
is maximized by

(5.6a)   Max $g_1(\underline{x})$

                                s.t. $\underline{x} \in R$

Then, given the optimal value, g_1^*, a tolerance limit is defined,
which is formulated as an inequality constraint added to the already
existing set of constraints. Then, the next most important goal
variable $g_2(\underline{x})$, is maximized, subject to the new set of constraints
by

                                Max $g_2(\underline{x})$

(5.6b)   s.t. $\underline{x} \in R$, and

                                $g_1(\underline{x}) \geq \beta_1 \cdot g_1^*$,

where $\beta_1 (0 \leq \beta_1 \leq 1)$ is the tolerance parameter associated with g_1^*.
For the derived maximum g_2^*, the tolerance parameter β_2 is defined,
which is followed by the constrained maximization of $g_3(\underline{x})$, as
described below.

                                Max $g_3(\underline{x})$

                                s.t. $\underline{x} \in R$,

(5.6c)
                                $g_1(\underline{x}) \geq \beta_1 \cdot g_1^*$, and

                                $g_2(\underline{x}) \geq \beta_2 \cdot g_2^*$

This procedure continues up to the point where all goal variables
have been dealt with. If all tolerance parameters are set equal to
1, the procedure is quite similar to the sequential method described
by (4.4).

An unambiguous ranking of the goal variables is necessary to have the procedure work properly. In our opinion, it is very hard if not impossible to obtain an appropriate ranking. Is one goal variable considered more important than another if (a) the first goal variable 'should be handled first', or (b) if the first goal variable has pre-emptive priority over the other (why then tolerance parameters?), or (c) if the first goal variable has a higher 'weight' than the second? In order to use these hierarchical methods properly, one should be sure about the decision maker's notion of 'one goal variable being more important than another'.

Another problem is the assessment of the tolerance parameters β_j, $j = 1, \ldots, m$. As shown in van Delft and Nijkamp [1977], the parameters can be assessed by means of an interactive procedure, in which the 'optimal' values of the tolerance parameters are calculated one by one, in hierarchical order. Such a procedure implicitly assumes the decision maker to be able to define trade-offs between more and less important goal variables, which must be valid in the optimal solution, although the optimal solution is unknown at the time of defining these trade-offs. Obviously, in the case of two goal variables, this problem does not exist because then the tolerance limit of the most important goal variable can be traded-off directly against the value of the less important goal variable, again in an interactive way.

Benson [1975] proposes a procedure which starts by asking the decision maker to specify a set of minimally acceptable goal levels. Next, the decision maker is asked to identify which of the specified goal levels is the least satisfactory. Then the goal variable concerned is maximized subject to the constraints on the other goal variables. If this maximum value is judged to be unsatisfactory, some of the goal levels specified for the other goal variables must be relaxed. If satisfactory, the obtained solution is either optimal or the value of the former least satisfactory goal variable is now too high. In the latter case, the decision maker is asked to specify the maximal amount of relaxation which is acceptable for this goal variable. Then the procedure is repeated by again asking the decision maker what is now the least satisfactory goal value, and so on.

Also in this method, it is hard to specify an 'optimal' value for one goal variable without knowing the optimal values for the others. Besides, there is very little help available to the decision maker to specify the optimal value (i.e. the allowable relaxation) of the formerly least satisfactory goal variable. The notion of a set of minimum goal levels to start with is very attractive, although in this case, by letting the decision maker specify these minimum levels, it may be hard and time consuming to find an initial set which is feasible. Also, these minimum values may have to be adapted in a downward direction during later stages of the procedure. These problems can be circumvented by defining (and specifying) these minimum goal values in a slightly different way (cf. Chapter 6). A clear advantage of this method is that, in principle at least, it can also solve non-linear models.

Monarchi et al. [1973] developed a procedure in which for every goal variable $g_j(\underline{x})$, $j = 1, \ldots, m$; an aspiration level $\bar{g}_j$, $j = 1, \ldots, m$; is defined by the decision maker. The aspiration levels may be desired upper bounds, lower bounds, razor-edge targets (cf. Chapter 4), or bounds of intervals within which the most preferred values of the goal variable concerned are contained, or, alternatively are not contained. For each goal defined in this way, a dimensionless indicator of attainment d_j is defined, which in general is a non-linear function of a goal variable which in its turn may be non-linear in the instrumental variables. At each iteration, one principal problem and m_i auxiliary problems are solved, where m_i is the number of goal variables the value of which has not yet been restricted in earlier iterations ($m_1 = m$, $m_2 = m-1$, $m_3 = m-2, \ldots$). At the first iteration, the principal problem is to

(5.7)
$$\text{Min} \sum_{j=1}^{m} d_j$$

$$\text{s.t. } \underline{x} \in R,$$

and the auxiliary problems are

$$\text{Min} \sum_{\substack{j=1 \\ j \neq j'}}^{m} d_j$$

(5.8)   s.t. $\underline{x} \in R$, and

$$g_{j'}(\underline{x}) \geq \bar{g}_{j'},$$

for $j' = 1, \ldots, m$. These problems are solved by means of a non-linear goal programming routine. The results are presented to the decision maker, who, on the basis of this information, revises one of the aspiration levels, which is then added as a constraint to problems (5.7) and (5.8). After dropping the indicator $d_{j'}$ (which belongs to the restricted goal variable) from the objective functions, these problems are solved again. On the basis of the results, the decision maker again adds a restriction to the problems, and so forth.

The method described has the attractive properties that it can incorporate goal variables which neither have to be maximized nor minimized, and that it can solve non-linear problems. Disadvantages are that linear problems are translated into non-linear problems (which demand a lot of computer time), the difficulty to specify aspiration levels on the basis of the data generated by the method, and the possibility of finding inconsistent constraint sets when solving auxiliary problems (cf. also Hwang and Masud [1979]).

As is evident from the above overview, there are quite a few interactive goal programming methods available. All of them share the advantage that the decision maker can express his preferences in terms of goal values. This seems to offer a close correspondence to everyday practice, in which decision makers are accustomed to thinking in terms of 'goals' and 'targets' (cf. also Chapters 2 and 4).

Interactive goal programming methods are not limited to efficient extreme points, which was one of the disadvantages of the procedures

described in the preceding section. Moreover, aspired levels of goal
variables which are non-linear in the instruments can be formulated
in a straightforward manner by introducing restrictions (e.g. goal
chance constraints or target ratio values,(cf. also Chapter 8).

Another advantage of interactive goal programming methods is
that the feasible region is reduced step by step. This may simplify
the computational efforts (which in themselves are not very cumber-
some in these types of methods)[1]. Moreover, each iteration reduces
the size of the decision problem, i.e. the number of alternatives
still to be evaluated. In general, this is not true for the interactive procedures of types (a) and (b).

There are two sides to every coin. Methods of type (c) also
have their disadvantages. In the case of the STEM-based methods it
is not clear why more or less complicated procedures are used for
the calculation of successive compromise solutions, which only serve
as a point of reference for the decision maker. Moreover, the decision
maker has complete freedom in defining the goal level relaxations
which are required at each iteration. This seems attractive, but may
in fact lead to inconsistencies, even more so as the relaxations
cannot be revised after they have been formulated. As will be shown
in the next chapter it is possible to guide the decision maker in his
choice of the aspired goal levels without affecting his freedom of
choice. The main disadvantages of the sequential optimization methods
are again the lack of assistance for the decision maker determining
aspired values of the goal variables, and the fact that the optimal
value of one goal variable must be determined without knowing
(often not even approximately) what the values of the other goal
variables will be. Interactive Multiple Goal Programming (IMGP),

_____

1) For instance because some of the constraints become redundant
   if certain goal levels have to be met (see Spronk and Telgen
   [1979] and Telgen [1979]). On the other hand, the introduction
   of goal levels as constraints increases the computational efforts.

the method described in Chapter 6, tries to circumvent this problem
by starting with a set of minimum goal levels which are satisfied
by a whole set of alternatives. The decision maker is then asked
to raise these goal values step by step, whereby it is not necessary
to first drive one goal variable to its optimum, then the next, and
so on. It is not necessary to define 'razor-edge' goal values.
Instead minimum values are to be given for which (in the decision
maker's opinion) it is certain that they do not exclude the optimal
solution. In defining these values the decision maker can use several
sources of information, such as the displacement of the ideal solution
resulting from the definition of new minimum goal values. The latter
may even be revised in later iterations.

5.5. Conclusion

In this chapter we have shown that interactive procedures may
be helpful in cases where it is too difficult or too costly to
obtain all the *a priori* information necessary to solve a given
multiple objective programming problem. We have divided these interactive multiple objective programming methods into three types,
depending on the kind of information to be delivered by the decision
maker:

(a) determination of trade-offs among the goal variables, given a
    particular solution
(b) determination of the *subset of 'best'* from among a given set of
    efficient solutions
(c) specification of aspired *goal values*, given a particular solu-
    tion.

Within each type, methods differ a.o. with respect to the required
accuracy of the information to be given by the decision maker.

In our opinion, each of the three types of methods has a right
of existence, given the fact that different decision situations may
need different methods. On rather theoretical grounds, we have made
a plea for type (c) methods. This type can be further subdivided,
for instance, into methods which successively relax the goal values

in subsequent compromise solutions, and into sequential optimization
methods. Our classification of interactive programming methods has
been illustrated in Figure 5.2. In the next chapter we describe a
new method, which tries to avoid the disadvantages and to combine
the advantages of the already available interactive goal programming
methods.

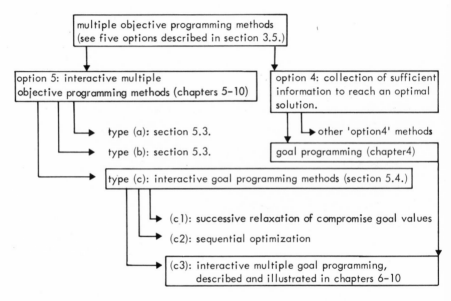

Figure 5.2. Classification of interactive multiple objective programming methods

References

Atkinson, R.C., G.H. Bower and E.J. Clothers (1965), An Introduction to Mathematical Learning Theory, Wiley, New York.

Benson, R.G. (1975), Interactive Multiple Criteria Optimization Using Satisfactory Goals, Ph. D. Thesis, University of Iowa.

Charnes, A. and W.W. Cooper (1977), Goal Programming and Multiple Objective Optimization, Part I, European Journal of Operational Research, pp. 39-54.

Cohon, J.L. (1978), Multiobjective Programming and Planning, Academic Press, New York.

Cohon, J.L. and D.H. Marks (1975), A Review and Evaluation of Multi-objective Programming Techniques, Water Resources Research, pp. 208-220.

Delft, A. van and P. Nijkamp (1977), Multi-Criteria Analysis and Regional Decision-Making, Martinus Nijhoff, Leiden/The Hague.

Despontin, M. and J. Spronk (1979), Comparison and Evaluation of Multiple Criteria Decision Methods, Report 7923/A, Centre for Research in Business Economics, Erasmus University, Rotterdam.

Dyer, J.S. (1972), Interactive Goal Programming, Management Science, Vol. 19/1, pp. 62-70.

Dyer, J.S. (1973), An Empirical Investigation of a Man-Machine Interactive Approach to the Solution of the Multiple Criteria Problem, in Cochrane, J. and M. Zeleny (eds), Multiple Criteria Decision Making, Univ. of South Carolina Press, Columbia, pp. 202-216.

Fandel, G. (1972), Optimale Entscheidung bei mehrfacher Zielsetzung, Springer, Berlin.

Fichefet, J. (1976), GPSTEM - An Interactive Multi-Objective Optimization Method, in A. Prékopa (ed), Progress in Operations Research, Vol.1, North-Holland, Amsterdam, pp. 317-332.

Frank, M. and P. Wolfe (1956), An Algorithm for Quadratic Programming, Naval Research Logistics Quarterly, Vol. 3, pp. 95-110.

Gal, T. (1977), A General Method for Determining the Set of All Efficient Solutions to a Linear Vectormaximum Problem, European Journal of Operational Research, pp. 307-322.

Geoffrion, A.M., J.S. Dyer and A. Feinberg (1972), An Interactive Approach for Multi-Criterion Optimization, with an Application to the Operation of an Academic Department, Management Science, Vol. 19/4, pp. 357-368.

Golledge, R.G. (1969), The Geographical Relevance of Some Learning Theories, Behavioral Problems in Geography (K.R. Cox and R.G. Golledge, eds), Northwestern University Studies in Geography, Illinois, no.17, pp. 101-145.

Hilgard, E.R. and G.H. Bower (1966), Theories of Learning, Appleton-Century-Crofts, New York.

Hwang, C.L. and A.S.M. Masud (1979), Multiple Objective Decision Making - Methods and Applications, Springer, Berlin.

Isermann, H. (1979), Strukturierung von Entscheidungsprozessen bei mehrfacher Zielsetzung, OR Spektrum, Vol 1/1, pp. 3-26.

Monarchi, D.E., C.C. Kisiel and L. Duckstein (1973), Interactive Multiobjective Programming in Water Resources: A Case Study, Water Resources Research, Vol. 9/4, pp. 837-850.

Monarchi, D.E., J.E. Weber and L. Duckstein (1976), An Interactive Multiple Objective Decision-Making Aid Using Non-Linear Goal Programming, in Zeleny, pp. 235-253.

Nijkamp, P. (1972), Planning of Industrial Complexes by Means of Geometric Programming, Rotterdam University Press, Rotterdam.

Nijkamp, P. and P. Rietveld (1976), Multi-Objective Programming Models: New Ways in Regional Decision-Making, Regional Science and Urban Economics, p. 253 ff.

Price, W.L. (1976), An Interactive Objective Function Generator for Goal Programming, in Thiriez and Zionts, pp. 147-158.

Roy, B. (1971), Problems and Methods with Multiple Objective Functions, Mathematical Programming, pp. 239-266.

Roy, B. (1976), From Optimization to Multi-Criteria Decision Aid: Three Main Operational Attitudes, in Thiriez and Zionts [1976].

Roy, B. (1977), A Conceptual Framework for a Normative Theory of Decision-Aid, in Starr and Zeleny [1977].

Spronk, J. and J. Telgen (1979), A note on Multiple Objective Programming and Redundancy, Report 7906/A, Centre for Research in Business Economics, Erasmus University Rotterdam, Rotterdam.

Starr, M.K. and M. Zeleny (eds) (1977), Multiple Criteria Decision Making, TIMS Studies in Management Sciences, Vol. 6, North-Holland

Steuer, R.E. (1977), An Interactive Multiple Objective Linear Programming Procedure, in Starr and Zeleny [1977, pp. 225-239].

Telgen, J. (1979) ,Redundancy and Linear Programs, Mathematical Centre, Amsterdam.

Thiriez, H. and S. Zionts (eds) (1976), Multiple Criteria Decision Making, Springer, Berlin.

Vincke, P. (1976), A New Approach to Multiple Criteria Decision-Making, in Thiriez, H. and S. Zionts [1976, pp. 341-350].

Wallenius, J. (1975), Comparative Evaluation of Some Interactive Approaches to Multicriterion Optimization, Management Science, pp. 1387-1396.

Wallenius, J. and S. Zionts (1976), Some Tests of an Interactive Programming Method for Multicriterion Optimization and an Attempt at Implementation, in Thiriez and Zionts [1976].

Winkels, H.M. (1979), Interaktive Lösungsverfahren für Lineare Probleme mit Mehrfacher Zielsetzung, in Stähly, P. and B. Schips, Quantitative Wirtschafts- und Unternehmensforschung, Springer, Berlin.

Yu, P.L. (1973), A Class of Solutions for Group Decision Problems, Management Science, Vol. 19/8, pp. 936-946.

Zeleny, M (ed.)(1976), Multiple Criteria Decision-Making, Springer, Berlin,

Zeleny, M. (1976), The Theory of the Displaced Ideal, in Zeleny (ed.) [1976], pp.153-206.

Zionts, S. and J. Wallenius (1976), An Interactive Programming
    Method for Solving the Multiple Criteria Problem, Management
    Science, Vol. 22/6, pp. 652-663.

6. INTERACTIVE MULTIPLE GOAL PROGRAMMING

6.1. Definitions and Assumptions

Interactive Multiple Goal Programming (IMGP) starts from the assumption that the decision maker has defined a number of goal variables $g_1(\underline{x}), \ldots, g_m(\underline{x})$, these being concave functions of the instrumental variables $x_1, \ldots, x_n$ ($\underline{x}$ in vector notation).

The decision maker's preferences with respect to the possible solutions can be modelled, at least in principle, by means of a *preference relation* which is *reflexive, transitive* and *complete*. These properties can be defined as follows.[1] Consider α, α' and α'' as elements of the set A of feasible solutions. Furthermore, let us introduce the preference relation $\alpha \geq \alpha'$ for any pair of elements α and α' in A, having the linguistic interpretation that α' is not preferred to α. Reflexivity means that for all elements α in A, $\alpha \geq \alpha$. The relation is transitive, if $\alpha \geq \alpha'$ and $\alpha' \geq \alpha''$ imply $\alpha \geq \alpha''$. The completeness property holds if for any pair α, α' in A with $\alpha \neq \alpha'$, either $\alpha \geq \alpha'$ or $\alpha' \geq \alpha$. If a preference relation possesses these three properties (i.e. reflexivity, transitivity and completeness), it is called a *total quasi ordering* (cf. Rietveld [1980] and Takayama [1974]). IMGP is not intended to model the total quasi ordering for all elements of A. Instead, it aims at finding the most preferred element (or subset of most preferred elements) of A. A crucial assumption is that such a subset exists and can be specified in terms of the goal variables.

---

[1] We refer to Rietveld [1980] for a more detailed discussion on preference relations in the framework of multiple objective programming.

Obviously, A corresponds to the image in goal value space of the set R of feasible instrumental values in instrumental value space. The feasible region R is assumed to be convex, bounded and closed.

IMGP is less restrictive than most other, comparable interactive methods (we will return to this point later on). We will discuss some of the kinds of preference relations that may give rise to successful application of IMGP.

First, the preference relation may be a *lexicographic ordering* (see Chapter 4). This ordering may either be based on a hierarchical ranking of the goal variables or on a hierarchical ranking of the deviational variables going with a series of aspired goal levels.[1] Assume that for a goal variable (or deviational variable) of given priority rank, alternative α yields a better value than does alternative α'. Assume furthermore that for the more important goal variables (deviational variables), alternative α does not yield worse values than does alternative α'. In this case, alternative α is preferred to alternative α', without regard to the performance of alternative α' for lower priority goals.

A total quasi ordering can also be tackled by means of IMGP if the ordering is *weakly convex*. A preference ordering is weakly convex if for any pair of alternatives α, α' in A, $\alpha \overset{>}{\ominus} \alpha'$ implies $t\alpha + (1-t)\alpha' \overset{>}{\ominus} \alpha'$, $0 < t < 1$, where $\alpha \neq \alpha'$. If a preference ordering is representable by a real-valued preference function (see below),

---

1) As explained in Chapter 4, the maximization (minimization) of a goal variable can also be represented as the minimization of the deviation from an unattainable aspiration level of this goal variable.

then the *quasi-concavity* of the preference function[1] corresponds
to the weak convexity of the preference ordering. The condition of
weakly convex preference orderings ensures that the subset of most
preferred alternatives in the convex set A is connected (see
Takayama [1974]).

As illustrated below for preference relations represented by
a real-valued preference function, the assumption of weakly convexity
allows for a great variety of different preference structures.

As shown by Debreu [1959], a total quasi ordering for all
elements of A can be represented by means of a real-valued continuous
preference function, if the set A is connected and the total quasi
ordering is *continuous*. In general, a preference relation is
continuous if given an alternative α' which is preferred to an
alternative α, all alternatives α'' which are very close to alternative α' are also preferred to α (see Rietveld [1980] for further
details).

In the remainder of this and in the following section it is con-
venient to assume preference relations that can be represented, in
principle, by means of a concave preference function. From the above
exposition it should be clear that we consider this assumption as a
sufficient but not as a necessary condition for the intended use of
IMGP (see also Section 6.4).

Given the concavity of the preference function f, quite a few
different preference patterns can be incorporated. A number of examples are given in Figure 6.1, where f is a function of one goal
variable $g(\underline{x})$ only. Because f is generally not a known function of
$g(\underline{x})$, it is very helpful if we know that f is either monotone increasing (Figure 6.1a) or monotone decreasing (Figure 6.1b). In these

---

1) A real-valued function defined over a convex set $A \subset R^n$ is quasi-
   concave if $f(\alpha) \geq f(\alpha')$ implies $f[t\alpha+(1-t)\alpha'] \geq f(\alpha')$ for all
   pairs α,α' in A and $0 \leq t \leq 1$.

cases, the maximization of f can be accomplished by means of the
maximization (respectively, minimization) of $g(\underline{x})$ subject to $\underline{x} \in R$.
In the cases sketched in Figures 6.1c - 6.1f, the solution procedure

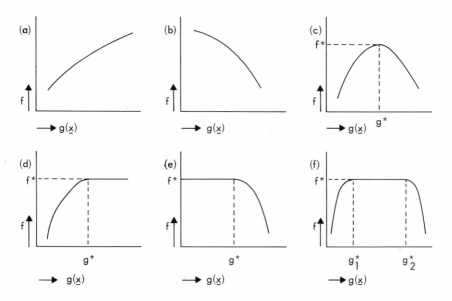

Figure 6.1. The preference function f as a function of one goal variable only

is less straightforward, since f is neither monotone increasing
nor monotone decreasing in $g(\underline{x})$. A natural idea is to split the
goal variable $g(\underline{x})$ into two other goal variables, one to be maximized
$(g_1(\underline{x}))$, the other to be minimized $(g_2(\underline{x}))$. For the example in
Figure 6.1c, this would give (assuming that g^* is known)

$$\text{Max}\{g_1(\underline{x}) = g(\underline{x})\} \quad \text{s.t.} \quad \underline{x} \in R \text{ and } g(\underline{x}) \leq g^*$$

(6.1)   and

$$\text{Min}\{g_2(x) = g(\underline{x})\} \quad \text{s.t.} \quad \underline{x} \in R \text{ and } g(x) \geq g^*$$

In this way, the problem is divided into two problems. However, as shown in Chapter 4, this formulation can be simplified by using the two-sided goal programming formulation. In this case, we would get

$$\text{Min}\{y^+ + y^-\}, \quad \text{s.t.}$$

(6.2)
$$\underline{x} \in R,$$
$$g(\underline{x}) - y^+ + y^- = g^* \text{ , and}$$
$$y^+ \cdot y^- = 0$$

In the same way, the problem in Figure 6.1d can be solved by minimizing y^-, whereas the problem in Figure 6.1e can be solved by minimizing y^+. The problem in Figure 6.1f is a little more complicated because there two 'threshold values', i.e. g_1^* and g_2^*, occur. In this case, two goal restrictions should be formulated. Then the objective function to be minimized includes the deviational variable y_1^- associated with g_1^*, and the variable y_2^+ associated with g_2^*.

The above analysis assumes that the threshold values g^*, g_1^* and g_2^* are known. If this is not the case, some complications arise (cf. Nijkamp and Spronk [1978] for a discussion).

Interactive multiple goal programming needs no more *a priori* information on the decision maker's preferences than other interactive multiple objective programming methods. However, although accurate *a priori* information about the decision maker's preferences may be difficult to obtain, there is usually some information contained in most decision situations. It would be a pity to let this information be unused. On the other hand, it must be realized that the *a priori* information is not always fool-proof. Furthermore, the decision maker may change his mind while dealing with the problem. Interactive multiple goal programming tries to use the *a priori* information in a fruitful manner, by offering the decision maker the opportunity during the interactive process to reconsider his *a priori* information. The *a priori* information used in this method mainly consists of aspiration levels, but relative and pre-emptive priority factors can also be incorporated within the procedure.

In IMGP, the decision maker has to provide information about his
preferences on the basis of a solution and a potency matrix presented
to him. A solution is a vector of (minimum) values for the respective
goal variables. The potency matrix consists of two vectors, representing the ideal and the pessimistic solution, respectively. The
ideal solution shows the maximum value for each of the goal variables
separately, given the goal values of the pessimistic solution concerned. The pessimistic solution lists a lower value for each of the
goal variables separately, either defined directly by the decision
maker or, in some cases in which this is possible and useful, derived
mathematically from known properties of his preference structure and
the set of alternatives. The decision maker merely has to indicate
whether or not a solution is satisfactory, and if not, which of the
pessimistic goal values should be raised. He does not have to specify how much these goal values should be raised. Nor is there any need
to specify weighting factors. (However, if he is able to specify
this kind of information, it can be used within the procedure). Then
a new solution is presented to him together with a new potency matrix.
The decision maker has to indicate whether the shifts in the solution
are outweighed by the shifts in the potency matrix. If not, a new
solution is calculated and so forth.

At this point it may be useful to pay more attention to the
definition of 'solution', as introduced above. Note that a 'solution'
has been defined as a vector of goal values, thus being a vector in
the goal value space (cf. Chapter 3). Obviously, a solution is not
necessarily feasible, i.e. there may be no vector x in the feasible
region of the space of instruments, which corresponds with this
solution (for instance, the ideal solution as defined above). In
IMGP, the goal values of a given solution are formulated as restrictions in the space of instruments, which are thus added to the set
of restrictions R, describing the region of feasible instrument
values.

In the example shown in Figure 6.2a, $g_1(\underline{x}) = x_1$ and $g_2(\underline{x}) = x_2$
(which are both to be maximized), so that the instrument value
space and the goal value space are equivalent. It is easily seen
that the solution S is infeasible, i.e. there is no $\underline{x}$ in ABCDE for
which S can be obtained. However, in this case, if the goal values
of S are formulated as inequality constaints in the instrument value
space (ES and SC respectively), there is an infinite number of
$\underline{x}$-vectors yielding a better solution than S.

In Figure 6.2b, the two spaces are not equivalent. We have de-
fined $g_1(\underline{x}) = x_1$ and $g_2(\underline{x}) = -x_1$, which are both to be maximized.
The worst value for $g_1(\underline{x})$ is reached in point G, whereas the worst
value for $g_2(\underline{x})$ is reached in point I. If we want to combine these
two worst values in a solution S, this can be represented in the
goal value space, although the solution as such is infeasible.
However, in the space of instruments, no $\underline{x}$-vector exists - whether

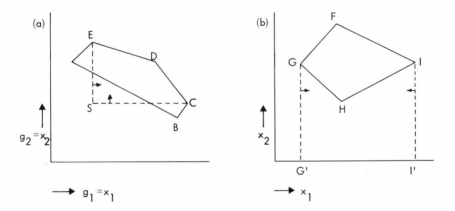

Figure 6.2. The relationship between solutions in the goal value space and in the instrument value
           space

feasible or not - which yields this solution. Again, formulating
these goal values as constraints added to the feasible region leaves
an infinite number of $\underline{x}$-vectors which offer better solutions than
S (in this case, the set of these $\underline{x}$-vectors is obviously equal to
the feasible region FGHI).

6.2. Description of the Procedure

At each iteration of Interactive Multiple Goal Programming
(IMGP), a new solution (as defined in Section 6.1) is proposed by
changing one or more elements of a former solution. The consequences
of these changes are then calculated. To simplify the explanation,
we first describe the method while assuming that at each iteration,
one and only one element of the solution will undergo a change. Next,
we will discuss a number of possible modifications of the method,
including the case in which more elements can change during the
same iteration.

Step 0 - Given the requirements described in the preceding section, identify the goal variables $g_i(\underline{x}), i = 1, \ldots, m$; as
functions of $\underline{x}$, the vector of instrumental variables
$x_1, x_2, \ldots, x_n$. Then specify the feasible set R within which
an optimal solution must be found. If the decision maker's
preferences could be described by a real-valued preference
function f (note, however, that we do not make any attempt
in this direction), this function should be a concave
function of both $g_i(\underline{x})$, $i = 1, \ldots, m$; and x_i, $i = 1, \ldots, n$.
An optimal solution is then defined by

$$\text{Max } f = f(g_1(\underline{x}), \ldots, g_m(\underline{x})), \text{ s.t.}$$

(6.3)

$$\underline{x} \in R$$

To simplify our exposition, we assume further

(6.4) $\qquad \frac{\partial f}{\partial g_i} > 0$ for $i = 1, \ldots, m$;

so that we presuppose a higher value of each of the goal variables is preferred to a lower value of (the same) goal variable.[1]

Step 1 - Successively maximize each of the m goal variables $g_i(\underline{x})$ separately and denote the maxima by g_i^* and the m corresponding combinations of the instrumental variables by $\underline{x}^{i*}$, $i = 1, \ldots, m$. It is usually not necessary to accept a value of $g_i(\underline{x})$ which is lower than g_i^{min}, defined as

(6.5) $\qquad g_i^{min} = \underset{j=1,\ldots,m}{Min} \{g_i(\underline{x}^{j*})\}$,

the lowest value of $g_i(\underline{x})$ resulting from the successive maximizations of the goal variables.[2] Then, the final solution $\underline{S}^*$ must be found between the 'ideal' (but usually infeasible) solution $\underline{I}$, and the 'pessimistic' solution $\underline{Q}$, which are defined respectively as

(6.6)
$$\underline{I} = [g_1^*, g_2^*, \ldots, g_m^*] \text{ and}$$
$$\underline{Q} = [g_1^{min}, g_2^{min}, \ldots, g_m^{min}]$$

1) Note, that this assumption is only made to simplify the exposition. All preference relations satisfying the conditions discussed in Section 6.1, can be included without any difficulties.

2) An obvious case, for which (6.5) is a valid limit on the choice of $\underline{S}^*$, is for m = 2, i.e. bicriterion optimization. Other cases are discussed in Appendix 6.a. If (6.5) is not applicable, the g_i^{min} might be assessed directly by the decision maker.

To facilitate the notation, we include the ideal solu-
tion $\underline{I}$ and the pessimistic solution $\underline{Q}$ in the (2xm)
'potency matrix' P.

Step 2 - For each goal variable $g_i(\underline{x})$, the decision maker may have
defined aspiration levels $g_{ij}(j=2,\ldots,k_i-1)$ with the
following property

(6.7) $g_i^{\min} < g_{i2} < g_{i3} < \ldots < g_{ik_i-1} < g_i^*$

Furthermore we define

$$g_{i1} = g_i^{\min} \quad \text{and}$$
(6.8)
$$g_{ik_i} = g_i^*$$

In the following steps these goal values are used in
constructing trial solutions $\hat{S}_i$ which have to be evaluated
by the decision maker. Because proposed goal levels are
sometimes regarded as too high, we need the auxiliary
vector δ with elements δ_j $(j=1,\ldots,m)$ corresponding to
the m goal variables. We define δ_j as the difference of
the lowest level of $g_j(\underline{x})$ being rejected by the decision
maker and the highest level of $g_j(\underline{x})$ being accepted thus
far. At the first stage of the procedure, no proposals
have been made and consequently, no goal level has been
rejected. Therefore we put $\delta_j = 0$ for $j = 1, \ldots, m$ during
the first step. However, if for a certain goal variable
j' no aspiration level has been specified, we define
$\delta_{j'} = g_{j'}^* - g_{j'}^{\min}$ for reasons which will become clear in
step 6.

Step 3 - Define the initial solution as

$$(6.9) \qquad \underline{S}_1 = [g_{11}, g_{21}, \ldots, g_{m1}],$$

which is thus equal to the pessimistic solution defined in
(6.6). Present this solution, together with the potency
matrix P_1, to the decision maker.

Step 4 - If the proposed solution is satisfactory for the decision
maker, he may accept it; if not, continue with step 5.
Define R_i as the subset of R defined by the goal levels
in $\underline{S}_i$.

Step 5 - The decision maker then has to answer the following question:
'Given the provisional solution $\underline{S}_i$, which goal variable
should be improved first'?[1]

Step 6 - Let us assume that the decision maker wants to augment the
j-th goal variable. Then construct a trial pessimistic so-
lution $\hat{\underline{S}}_{i+1}$, which differs with respect to $\underline{S}_i$ only as far
as the value of the j-th goal variable is concerned (deno-
ted by $g_j(\underline{x})_{\hat{\underline{S}}_{i+1}}$ and $g_j(\underline{x})_{\underline{S}_i}$ respectively).

If $\delta_j = 0$ no proposed value of $g_j(\underline{x})$ has been rejected thus
far, by which we can propose the next higher aspiration level
listed in step 2. If $\delta_j > 0$, a value of $g_j(\underline{x})$ which exceeds
the current solution by an amount δ_j has been rejected by
the decision maker. In this case, define[2]

$$(6.10) \qquad g_j(\underline{x})_{\hat{\underline{S}}_{i+1}} = g_j(\underline{x})_{\underline{S}_i} + \tfrac{1}{2} \cdot \delta_j$$

---

1) Later, we will discuss the case in which the decision maker
wants to raise more than one goal variable at one time.

2) Here, the decision maker may wish to define a new aspiration
level. In our opinion, it is wise to give him explicitly the
opportunity to do so.

When a provisional value for $g_j(\underline{x})$ has been calculated
in one of both above-mentioned ways, we introduce the
restriction:

(6.11) $$g_j(\underline{x}) \geq g_j(\underline{x})\,\hat{\underline{S}}_{i+1}$$

and proceed to step 7.

Step 7 - Combine the restriction formulated in step 6 or in step
9 with the set of restrictions describing the feasible
region R_i. Next calculate a new potency matrix, as in
step 2, but subject to the new set of restrictions. Label
this potency matrix $\hat{P}_{i+1}$.

Step 8 - Confront the decision maker with $\underline{S}_i$ and $\hat{\underline{S}}_{i+1}$ on the one
hand and with P_i and $\hat{P}_{i+1}$ on the other hand. The shifts
in the potency matrix can be viewed as a 'sacrifice' for
reaching the proposed solution. If (8b) the decision
maker considers this sacrifice to be justified, accept
the proposed solution by putting
$\underline{S}_{i+1} = \hat{\underline{S}}_{i+1}$ and $P_{i+1} = \hat{P}_{i+1}$. Furthermore, in the computer
algorithm (see Figure 6.3), put $\delta_j = \frac{1}{2}.\delta_j$ (which is only
relevant for $\delta_j > 0$) and return to step 4. If (8a) the
decision maker considers the sacrifice unjustified, the
proposed value of $g_j(\underline{x})$ is obviously too high. Therefore,
drop the constraint added in step 7 and proceed to step 9.

Step 9 - We now know that, in the decision maker's view $g_j(\underline{x})\,\underline{S}_i$
is too low and that $g_j(\underline{x})\,\hat{\underline{S}}_{i+1}$ is too high. By definition,
we thus may set δ_j equal to the difference between these
two values. A new proposal value $\underline{S}_{i+1}$ is then calculated
by defining

(6.12) $g_j(\underline{x})_{\hat{\underline{S}}_{i+1}} = g_j(\underline{x})_{\underline{S}_i} + \frac{1}{2}\cdot\delta_j$

As in step 6, we add the restriction that $g_j(\underline{x})$ must equal
or exceed the new proposal value and go to step 7 in order
to calculate a new potency matrix $\hat{P}_{i+1}$.

If the decision maker is unwilling to indicate a single goal variable which should be improved in value, one could present him the
option to define a set of goal variables which should be augmented
in value at the same time. Then, the procedure must be modified
slightly. These modifications have been included in Figure 6.3, and
are discussed below.

Changing more than one Goal Value Simultaneously.

Step 5*- Instead of one goal variable, more than one goal variable
to be augmented is chosen.

Step 6*- Find proposal values for all goal variables selected in 5*
in the way a new value was calculated for the single goal
variable in 6.

Step 7*- Before calculating the potency matrix $\hat{P}_{i+1}$ the set of
restrictions is extended with the restrictions formulated
in 6*.

Step 8*- If the decision maker considers the sacrifices too heavy
to approve the solution, he should indicate which of the
goal variables, having a higher value in $\hat{\underline{S}}_{i+1}$ than in $\underline{S}_i$,
should be reduced in 9*.

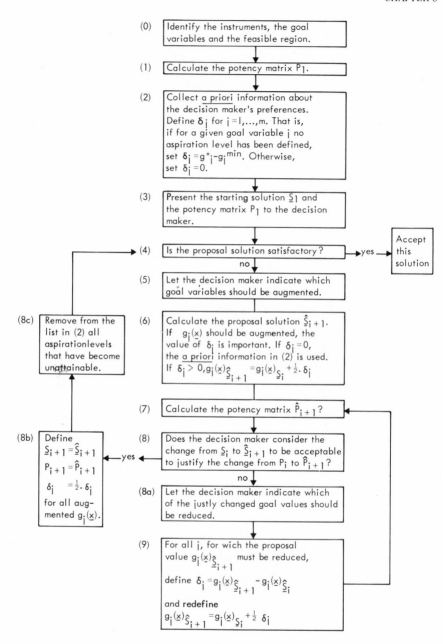

Figure 6.3. A flow chart of the extended interactive multiple goal programming procedure

Step 9*- Calculate a new proposal solution by reducing all goal variables indicated in 8* in the same way that the single goal variable was reduced in 9.

Other Options Available

In IMGP, there are more options available to the decision maker. One option considers the fact that, in general, interactive procedures induce learning effects (cf. Chapter 5). This implies that the decision maker may change his mind during the interactive process or may feel that he has made some errors. This is the main reason why the decision maker must have the opportunity to return to an earlier iteration or even to restart the whole process. As in most interactive procedures, these options can be given in IMGP without any difficulties.

An example of a learning effect occurs, for instance, when the decision maker recognizes that a proposed shift in a single goal variable is outweighted by a simultaneous shift in two or more other goal variables. He may then wish to return to the preceding solution to ask for such a simultaneous shift. He may also require additional information regarding the state of the problem. IMGP offers several possibilities. First, the total 'pay-off' matrix[1] underlying the potency matrix may be presented to the decision maker. Second, depending on the method used, the optimizations may produce a considerable amount of dual information on the state of the problem (cf. also Chapter 4). Third, to measure the above-mentioned simultaneous shifts of goal variables, one may introduce a proxy goal variable, such as, for instance, the sum of all other goal variables. Of course, many other devices to provide information regarding the state of the problem can be proposed.

1) The pay-off matrix is the matrix of goal values $g_i(x^{j*})$, with $i = 1, \ldots, m;$ and $j = 1, \ldots, m$.

6.3. IMGP in Linear Terms

Given the fairly modest requirements described in Section 6.1, many methods are available for use within the IMGP procedure[1]. For instance, many mathematical programming techniques may be useful. As an illustration, we describe IMGP in linear terms (with respect to the instruments $\underline{x}$), by which it becomes accessible for linear (goal) programming routines. The additional advantages of such a linear format of IMGP are discussed at the end of this section.

If the feasible region R can be described by means of linear restrictions, and the goal variables $g_i(\underline{x})$, $i = 1, \ldots, m$; are linear or piecewise linear and concave in the instruments $\underline{x}$, IMGP can use standard linear programming routines.

The calculatory steps in IMGP consist of the computation of the potency matrices. The first potency matrix, P_1, is calculated in step 1. Whenever the lower bounds on the values of one or more of the $g_i(\underline{x})$ are augmented (in step 6) or when some of these bounds are decreased (in step 9), the accompanying potency matrix is calculated in step 7. In all three cases the structure of the problem is identical. Each of the goal variables must successively be maximized (or minimized) within the feasible region R and conditioned by a set of lower bounds (or upper bounds) on the values of the goal variables. The problem can thus be written as

$$
\text{Max(c.q.Min)} \quad \{g_i(\underline{x})\}, \quad \text{s.t.}
$$

(6.13) $\underline{x} \in R$, and   for $i = 1, \ldots, m$;

$$
g_j(\underline{x}) \geq (\leq)\hat{g}_j \quad \text{for } j = 1, \ldots, m;
$$

[1] Even if all requirements are not fulfilled, IMGP can sometimes be used, although with a few modifications. For example, in Section 7.4, we demonstrate the use of IMGP in decision problems with a finite number of alternatives (a situation which is in conflict with the convexity condition on the feasible region).

where $\hat{g}_j$ denotes the proposed value of $g_j(\underline{x})$ for the problem at hand.

It is possible to formulate the set of problems in (6.13) in another, but also uniform way, i.e. as minimization problems differing only in the coefficients of the objective function. In this approach, which is closely related to the goal programming formulations in Chapter 4, we formulate for each of the goal variables two restrictions

(6.14)
$$g_j(\underline{x}) - \hat{y}_j^+ + \hat{y}_j^- = \hat{g}_j \qquad \text{for } j = 1, \ldots, m; \text{ and}$$

$$g_j(\underline{x}) - y_j^{*+} + y_j^{*-} = g_j^* \qquad \text{for } j = 1, \ldots, m;$$

where $\hat{g}_j$ denotes the proposed value of $g_j(\underline{x})$ in the problem at hand, and g_j^* its maximum value (or minimum value) in the first solution S_1 (thereby only constrained by $\underline{x} \in R$). The y^+ and y^- values measure the overattainment and underattainment with respect to the aspired levels $\hat{g}$ and g^*. The problem can then be formulated as a goal programming problem. Let us assume that $g_i(\underline{x})$ should be maximized, given a set of proposed values for the goal variables. This maximization problem can be translated as

(6.15)
$$\text{Min}\{M_1 \cdot \sum_{j=1}^{m} (\alpha_j^+ \cdot \hat{y}_j^+ + \alpha_j^- \cdot \hat{y}_j^-) + M_2 \cdot y_i^{*-}\} \text{ s.t.}$$

$\underline{x} \in R$ and s.t. (6.14)

$\alpha_j^+ = 1$ and $\alpha_j^- = 0$ if f is a decreasing function of $g_j(\underline{x})$

$\alpha_j^+ = 0$ and $\alpha_j^- = 1$ if f is an increasing function of $g_j(\underline{x})$

The non-Archimedean (cf. Charnes and Cooper [1977] and Chapter 4) weighing factors M_1 and M_2 have the property $M_1 >>> M_2$ by which pre-emptive priority is given to attain the proposal values $\hat{g}_j$, $j = 1, \ldots, m$, before $g_i(\underline{x})$ can be maximized by means of the minimization of y_j^{*-}. We assumed that the variables $g_j(\underline{x})$ could be formulated in such a way that f was monotone non-decreasing or monotone non-increasing in $g_j(\underline{x})$. In the first case, the proposal value $\hat{g}_j$ must be considered as a lower bound (which means $\hat{y}_j^-$ must be zero) and in the second case, $\hat{g}_j$ must be considered as an upper bound (by which $\hat{y}_j^+$ must be zero). In (6.15) we assumed $g_i(\underline{x})$ was to be maximized. Minimization of $g_i(\underline{x})$ can easily be achieved by replacing y_i^{*-} in (6.15) by y_i^{*+}.

Advantages Related to the Linear Format

As suggested in (6.14) and (6.15), IMGP can make straightforward use of goal programming routines. That is, for each proposal solution, a set of goal programs can be formulated. These differ mutually only with respect to one element in the objective function, being the y_i^{*-}, i = 1, ..., m to be minimized. By means of these goal programs, a potency matrix based on the proposal solution can be constructed. This has to be carried out for each new proposal solution. However, the goal programs belonging to different proposal solutions only differ with respect to some of the right-hand side constants, being the goal levels which have been changed. Clearly, this formulation gives access to specific goal programming routines as proposed for example by Lee [1972], (see also Chapter 4). However, standard linear programming packages can also be used. PL/I programs using IBM's MPSX - package are given by Ouwerkerk and Spronk [1978] and Hartog et al. [1979].

A main advantage of the linear format of the problem is that each solution of a goal program contains useful information about the effects of a shift of the right-hand side constants (see Chapter 4). In an extensive overview, Isermann [1977] argues that duality in multiple objective linear programming is even more relevant than in standard linear programming. Besides the economic implications of duality, he illustrates its decision-oriented relevance. He shows how information from the dual may be employed in the decision maker's search for a compromise solution. In the same sense Kornbluth [1978] proposes a method in which information from the (fuzzy) dual is systematically used in an interactive way.

Furthermore, the linear format of IMGP has all the advantages of goal programming, as discussed in Chapter 4. In its linear format, IMGP may also benefit from the widespread attention paid to linear programming, both in theory and practice. Special procedures developed for linear programming may also be useful in linear IMGP. As an example, procedures to identify redundant constraints in a linear programming problem may be used to identify 'redundant goal constraints' and redundant 'goal variables' (cf. Gal and Leberling [1977] and Spronk and Telgen [1979]).

6.4. Existence, Feasibility, Uniqueness and Convergency

A 'solution' is identified by a vector of minimum (or maximum) values imposed on the respective goal variables. It is easily seen, that given the ideal and the pessimistic solution, there is always at least one combination of the goal variables which is bounded by the ideal and the pessimistic solution, for which a feasible combination of the instrumental variables exists. For instance, consider the vector of goal values which is determined by $\underline{x}^{i*}$, the combination of instrumental variables which maximizes the i-th goal variable, $g_i(\underline{x})$. By definition, this vector is bounded both by the ideal and the pessimistic solution. By the convexity of R, also the convex combinations of the $\underline{x}_i^*$ are feasible.

During the successive iterations of IMGP, the goal values in the successive solutions are repeatedly shifted upwards by the decision maker, thus adding new constraints to the existing set of constraints. Because R is convex in $\underline{x}$ and because the newly added constraints are linear in $\underline{x}$, the part of the feasible region R which remains feasible after adding the constraints (denoted by R_i,

i=1,2,...;) remains convex in $\underline{x}$. This means that at each iteration
of IMGP there exists a vector of goal values, which is bounded by
the ideal and the pessimistic solution of the reduced feasible
region, for which a feasible combination of the instruments exists.

Given the assumptions underlying IMGP, a most preferred solution is not necessarily unique. Notably, the assumption that the
decision maker's preferences can be modelled by means of weakly
convex preference relations is not a sufficient condition to
guarantee a most preferred solution. For instance, even satisficing
behaviour can be represented by weakly convex preference relations.
However, if the preference relations have the *dominance* property[1],
it is easily seen that IMGP yields efficient solutions.

The next question is whether IMGP converges to a most preferred
solution (either unique or not). Of course, the convergency properties partly depend on the abilities of the decision maker. We therefore first assume that the decision maker is able to answer the
questions posed by IMGP, that his answers are consistent, correct
and finally that his preferences do not change during the interactive process of IMGP. Given these assumptions it can be shown that
IMGP terminates in a finite number of iterations within an ε-neigh-
bourhood of a most preferred solution.

First, starting from an accepted solution $\underline{S}_i$, the next solution will be accepted after a finite number of steps.
Let us define A_i as the subset of A (see Section 6.1) of which the
elements meet the minimally required goal levels defined by $\underline{S}_i$. We

---

1) A preference relation has the dominance property if for all
   pairs α,α' in A holds that α is preferred to α' if all goal
   values of α equal or exceed the corresponding values in α'.

know that $\underline{S}_i$ is preferred to all preceding solutions and that S_i can be improved. Thus the following condition must have been met.

(6.16) $\quad \exists \alpha' \in A_i [\alpha' \underset{\ominus}{\geq} \alpha, \quad \forall \alpha \in \{A - A_i\}]$

Let us next assume that the decision maker wants to improve $\underline{S}_i$ by raising the value of $g_k(\underline{x})$ thus obtaining a new solution $\underline{S}_{i+1}$. If the preferences of the decision maker can be modelled by means of a lexicographic ordering (see Section 6.1), the elements of A_{i+1} (the subset of A defined by $\underline{S}_{i+1}$) will satisfy condition

(6.17) $\quad \forall \alpha' \in A_{i+1} [\alpha' \underset{\ominus}{\geq} \alpha, \forall \alpha \in \{A_i - A_{i+1}\}]$

If the preferences of the decision maker can be modelled by means of a weakly convex ordering as defined in Section 6.1, the elements of A_{i+1} will satisfy

(6.18) $\quad \forall \alpha \in \{A_i - A_{i+1}\} [\exists \alpha' \in A_{i+1} [\alpha' \underset{\ominus}{\geq} \alpha]]$

Let us assume, that given $\underline{\delta}_i$ and given either (6.17) or (6.18), $g_k(\underline{x})$ can be increased by an amount of $\lambda > 0$. As described in Section 6.2, a first proposal solution $\hat{\underline{S}}_{i+1}$ is generated by augmenting the value of $g_k(\underline{x})$ in $\underline{S}_i$ by a given amount, which will be called d here. If $d \leq \lambda$, the proposal solution will be accepted; otherwise, the proposal will not be accepted[1]. Then a new proposal solution is calculated by halving the value of d. If $(d/2) \leq \lambda$ the proposal solution is accepted. If not, the value of d is divided by 2^2 and so forth. Clearly, the proposal solution is accepted as soon as $(d/2^n) < \lambda$ which for $\lambda > 0$ occurs at a finite value n. Thus we

---

1) Whether d exceeds λ has to be judged by the decision maker. For this evaluation, he uses, among other things, the information presented in the potency matrices.

have shown that each new solution $\underline{S}_{i+1}$ is reached in a finite number of steps.

Next, we show that only a finite number of solutions has to be calculated before a final solution is obtained, in which the values of the respective goal variables differ less than some predetermined $\varepsilon > 0$ from the respective goal values in a most preferred solution. At each iteration of IMGP at least the value of one goal variable is raised. Because there is a finite number (m) of goal variables, it is sufficient to show that an arbitrary goal variable $g_k(\underline{x})$ reaches a most preferred value g_k^O (ignoring a small distance of at most ε_k) within a finite number of iterations. Assuming, that the decision maker has not defined any aspiration level for $g_k(\underline{x})$, we only know that $g_k^{min} < g_k^O < g_k^*$, where g_k^* again is the maximum value of $g_k(\underline{x})$ for $\underline{x} \in R$. As described in Section 6.2, a proposal solution is calculated as $\hat{g}_k = (g_k^*-g_k^{min})/2$. From the (correct) answer of the decision maker we can deduce whether $g_k^O < \hat{g}_k$ or $g_k^O > \hat{g}_k$. We then know that either $g_k^{min} < g_k^O < \hat{g}_k$ or $\hat{g}_k < g_k^O < g_k^*$. At the next iteration in which g_k is chosen to be raised, a new proposal solution is chosen exactly in the middle of the chosen region. Thus, the range in which g_k^O must be found is exactly halved each time the decision maker is consulted. This means that the ε-neighbourhood of g_k^O is reached when

(6.19)
$$\frac{(g_k^*-g_k^{min})}{2^n} < \varepsilon_k,$$

where n is the number of times the decision maker gives his opinion on $\hat{g}_k$. In general, this ε_k-neighbourhood will be attained in less steps. This is because the aspiration levels which have been defined *a priori* may be of great help during the search procedure. Furthermore g_k^* is influenced by the values required for the other goal variables.

6.5. Concluding Remarks

In Chapters 3 and 5 we proposed several characteristics for describing interactive procedures, relating, among other things, to the class of problems which can be handled, the nature of the communication process between decision maker and decision model, and the technical properties.

First, we outline the type of problems which can be handled by interactive multiple goal programming. The convex set of feasible actions (R) is given and fixed over time. However, if this set changes over time, the interactive procedure should not be started all over again. This is because the solution obtained for the unchanged (old) problem can be used to make an advanced start. The set R needs to be convex. However, with the loss of some attractive properties of IMGP, mutually exclusive actions can also be handled (see Section 7.4). In IMGP, the goal variables are assumed to be measurable and known functions of the instrumental variables. The examples in Section 7.4 show how to include a goal variable which has to be measured on an ordinal scale. IMGP can be used (depending on the desires of the decision maker), to generate a unique final solution (within ε), an efficient solution or a satisficing solution. The method is not suitable for generating the complete set of efficient solutions. Instead, it aims at finding the efficient solution, which is considered (by the decision maker) to be the 'best' element within the set of all efficient solutions.

In IMGP, the communication process between decision maker and decision model has been structured in such a way that it has some attractive properties. The decision maker has only to provide a limited amount of information, although he has the option to give more information (and thus to command the interactive process) whenever he wishes to do so. Notably, if the decision maker has defined aspiration levels and pre-emptive priorities, these can be incorporated in the interactive process quite easily. Moreover, IMGP gives the decision maker the opportunity to reconsider this information during the interactive process. At each iteration, the method pro-

vides a large amount of information concerning the state of the problem. Depending on the decision maker at hand, this information may
be translated in various ways. An important advantage of IMGP (and
most other interactive procedures) is that the decision maker can
give his preferences on the basis of well-specified solutions and
is not obliged to answer any hypothetical question (cf. Chapter 5).

We can be very short about the technical properties of IMGP.
In the computational phases of IMGP any solution procedure which
meets the fairly modest requirements mentioned in sections 6.1 and
6.2 can be employed. As already mentioned in Section 6.4, IMGP converges within a finite number of iterations to a final solution
which is known to exist and to be feasible. The computer time per
iteration and the number of iterations needed to reach a final solution depends, among other things, on the problem to be solved and
the solution procedure chosen.

Appendix 6.a. <u>Suitable Starting Solutions</u>

The minimal goal levels g_{j1}, $j = 1, \ldots, m$; included in the
starting solution $\underline{S}_1$ (see (6.9)) determine the subset R_1 of the
feasible region R in which the final solution $\underline{S}^*$ is to be found.
Clearly, the size of R_1 co-determines the difficulty of the decision
problem. Therefore the time spent on finding values for g_{j1}, that
make R_1 as small as possible, may be worth-while. Of course the g_{j1}
must be chosen so as not to exclude any of the most preferred solutions. Given R and given some elementary knowledge of the decision
maker's preferences (see below), suitable values for g_{j1} can often
be derived in a straightforward manner. These mathematically derived
values for g_{j1} (which will be discussed in more detail below) may
offer valuable insight into the decision problem. For instance by
showing that certain solutions (those excluded by the g_{j1}) need
not be evaluated because they are dominated by solutions included
in R_1. On the other hand, the mathematically derived values for g_{j1}
have often no meaning at all for the decision maker, because he may
have defined higher values for the goal variable, which he considers
as 'necessary conditions' to be met by the final solution(s).

In this appendix we consider the case in which the decision
maker's preference ordering has the dominance property described in
Section 6.1. This means that we have to find maximal values for the
minimal goal levels g_{j1} in such a way as not to exclude any efficient
solution. In other words we have to find for each goal variable g_j,
$j = 1, \ldots, m$; its minimal value within the efficient set. The minimal value of a goal variable within the efficient set is sometimes
but not always, equal to its minimal value at the points for which
the other goal variables reach their maximum, as defined in (6.5).
Dessouki et al. [1979] show that the minimal value within the
efficient set can be found in the closed interval defined by the
minimal value within the feasible region R and the minimal value
defined by (6.5). The same authors propose a simple procedure to

find the minimal goal values within the efficient set:

(i)   Select an arbitrary vector of instruments $\underline{x}^1$ which yields an efficient solution and calculate the value of the goal variable concerned (say g_k).

(ii)   Select $\varepsilon^1 > 0$ and try to find a vector $\underline{x}^2$ for which

$$g_k(\underline{x}^2) \leq g_k(\underline{x}^1) - \varepsilon^1 \text{ and } \underline{g}(\underline{x}^2) \text{ is efficient.}$$

(iii) If a vector $\underline{x}^2$ exists, which yields an efficient solution, select $\varepsilon^2 > \varepsilon^1$.

       If no such $\underline{x}^2$ exists, select $\varepsilon^2 > \varepsilon^1$.

       In both cases, repeat step (ii).

The minimal goal values defined by (6.5) as well as the associated instrument vectors are obtained in the first step of IMGP. Clearly, these vectors of instruments can be used to define $\underline{x}^1$ in the above procedure. Dessouki et al. (Ibid) implement the second step of their procedure by solving a quadratic programming problem. The same task can be performed by maximizing $g_k(\underline{x})$ subject to

$$g_k(\underline{x}) \leq g_k(\underline{x}^1) - \varepsilon^1, \text{ and}$$

(6a.1)

$$\underline{x} \in R$$

and checking whether the resulting optimal solution $\underline{x}^2$ is efficient. Tests to check whether a given vector of instruments is efficient, are provided among others by Zionts and Wallenius [1980] and Wendell and Lee [1977].

References

Charnes, A.and W.W. Cooper (1977), Goal Programming and Multiple
  Objective Optimizations, Part I, European Journal of Operational
  Research.

Debreu, G. (1959), Theory of Value,Cowles Foundation Monograph, No.17,
  Wiley, New York.

Dessouki, M.I., M. Ghiassi and W.J. Davis (1979), Determining the
  Worst Value of an Objective Function within the Nondominated
  Solutions in Multiple Objective Linear Programming, Working Paper,
  University of Illinois at Urbana - Champaign, Urbana, IL 61801.

Gal, T. and H. Leberling (1977), Redundant Objective Functions in
  Linear Vector Maximum Problems and their Determination, European
  Journal of Operational Research, Vol.1, no.3, pp. 176-184.

Hartog, J.A., P. Nijkamp and J. Spronk (1979), Operational Multiple
  Goal Models for Large Economic Environmental Systems, Report
  7917/A, Centre for Research in Business Economics, Erasmus Univ.
  Rotterdam, Rotterdam.

Isermann, H. (1977), The Relevance of Duality in Multiple Objective
  Linear Programming, in Starr and Zeleny [1977], pp. 241-262.

Kornbluth, J.S.H. (1978), The Fuzzy Dual: Information for the Multiple
  Objective Decision Maker, Comput. Ops. Res., Vol.4, pp. 65-72.

Kuhn, H.W. and A.W. Tucker (1951), Nonlinear Programming, in Proceedings of the Second Berkeley Symposium on Mathematical Statistics
  and Probability, Jerzy Neyman (ed), University of California Press.

Lee, S.M. (1972), Goal Programming for Decision Analysis, Auerbach.

Nijkamp, P. and J. Spronk (1978), Interactive Multiple Goal Programming, Report 7803/A, Centre for Research in Business Economics,
  Erasmus University Rotterdam, Rotterdam.

Ouwerkerk, C. and J. Spronk (1978), A PL/I Computer Program for IMGP
  Using the MPSX Package, Centre for Research in Business Economics,
  Report 7823/A, Erasmus University Rotterdam, Rotterdam.

Rietveld, P. (1980), Multiple Objective Decision Methods and Regional Planning, North-Holland, Amsterdam.

Spronk, J. and J. Telgen (1979), A Note on Multiple Objective Programming and Redundancy, Report 7906/A, Centre for Research in Business Economics, Erasmus University Rotterdam, Rotterdam.

Starr, M.K. and M. Zeleny (1977), Multiple Criteria Decision Making, TIMS Studies in Management Sciences, Vol.6, North-Holland.

Takayama, A. (1974), Mathematical Economics, Dryden Press, Hinsdale.

Wendell, R.E. and D.N. Lee (1977), Efficiency in Multiple Objective Optimization Problems, Mathematical Programming, Vol.12, pp. 406-414.

Zionts, S and J. Wallenius (1980), Identifying Efficient Vectors: Some Theory and Computational Results, Operations Research, Vol. 28/3-II, pp. 785-793.

7. IMGP IN PRACTICE: EXAMPLES AND EXPERIENCES

In this chapter we present some examples of (potential)
applications of IMGP. These examples have been chosen deliberately
from fields other than capital budgeting and financial planning
(which are dealt with in more detail in Chapters 8, 9 and 10), in
order to demonstrate that the application potential of IMGP is not
limited to capital budgeting and financial planning. In fact, it
can be used in any decision situation which meets the fairly
unrestrictive requirements described in Chapter 6.

In Section 7.1 we demonstrate the use of IMGP by means of two
simple illustrations. In order to simulate the use of IMGP in
practice, we introduce in Section 7.2 an imaginary decision maker,
facing a portfolio selection problem. Section 7.3 describes some
of our experiences with the implementation of IMGP in combination
with large scale linear programming models. Section 7.4 gives two
examples of the use of IMGP in decision problems with discrete
choice alternatives. IMGP can be used fruitfully in this case,
though with some minor modifications. Our conclusions are given in
Section 7.5.

7.1. Two Simple Examples

In this section we demonstrate the use of IMGP by means of
two very simple examples. The first example concerns the choice
of an 'optimal' production combination of two product varieties
from an infinite number of alternatives. The second example deals
with a professor who has to decide how to allocate his time budget.

Example 1: A Production Planning Problem

A brick factory can produce two brick varieties, but due to
the limited capacity of machines, kiln and drying-room and to the
limited availability of skilled personnel, these products cannot
be produced in any desired combination. We show the area of
feasible production combinations in Figure 7.1, where x_1 and x_2
represent the quantity produced of variety one and two, respectively
(both in millions). For the planning period concerned management
is not able to define a profit function in terms of x_1 and x_2, due
to very uncertain conditions of the market and due to problems in
the factory, where a recently installed machine causes many
difficulties. Therefore management wants to consider both x_1 and
x_2 as goal variables. We thus have

$$(7.1) \qquad g_1(x_1,x_2) = x_1 \text{ and } g_2(x_1,x_2) = x_2$$

Although the maximum production of variety one is equal to
18,000,000 it is the 'problem machine' that causes difficulties
when the production of x_1 is raised over 14,000,000 units. In fact
this machine runs best when approximately 12,000,000 units are
produced with it. On the other hand, the factory has contracts to
deliver 8,000,000 units of variety one. Although this variety has
been estimated as less profitable than variety two, management wants
to meet the contractual obligations because the customers concerned
also buy a lot of variety two and offer a promising buying potential
in the near future. Thus the preferences for $g_1(\underline{x})$ seem to be
monotone non-decreasing for $g_1(\underline{x}) = x_1 \leq 12,000,000$ and monotone
non-increasing for $g_1(\underline{x}) = x_1 \geq 12,000,000$. Therefore it is reasonable to consider both $g_1^* = 12,000,000$ and $g_1 = 8,000,000$ as the
relevant aspiration levels for $g_1(\underline{x})$. There are no problems
whatsoever in the production of the fairly profitable second
variety. Management wants to produce as much as possible of this
second variety, thus to maximize $g_2(x_1,x_2)$.

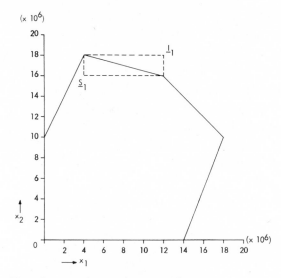

Figure 7.1. A production planning problem

When $g_2(\underline{x})$ is maximized, we have $g_2^* = 18$ and $g_1(\underline{x}) = 4$. Because this is a case of two goal variables (cf. Chapter 6), it is not necessary to accept a value of $g_1(x)$ lower than $g_1^{min} = 4$. No matter what minimal value for $g_2(\underline{x})$ is required by the decision maker (provided $\underline{x} \in R$), there is always a solution for which at the same time $g_1(\underline{x}) \geq 4$. By setting $g_1(\underline{x})$ equal to the most desired production volume $g_1(\underline{x}) = g_1^* = 12$, the value of $g_2(\underline{x})$ becomes $g_2(\underline{x}) = 16$, which is at the same time (by similar reasoning) the value of g_2^{min}. Therefore, we must find a final solution in which $4 \leq g_1(\underline{x}) \leq 12$ and $16 \leq g_2(\underline{x}) \leq 18$. Together with the information provided by the management we can list (step 2) the following aspiration levels. For $g_1(\underline{x})$ the values 4, 8 and 12; for $g_2(\underline{x})$ the values 16 and 18. The first potency matrix can be written as

$$(7.2) \qquad P_1 = \begin{bmatrix} 12 & 18 \\ 4 & 16 \end{bmatrix}$$

In the third step the first solution $\underline{S}_1$ is set equal to the pessimistic solution $\underline{Q}$ and presented to the decision maker, together with the potency matrix P_1. The pessimistic starting solution $\underline{S}_1$ and the ideal solution $\underline{I}_1$ are indicated in Figure 7.1. This solution has to be evaluated by the decision maker and subsequently integrated in the model. The successive steps towards the final solution are shown in Table 7.1. and illustrated in Figure 7.2.

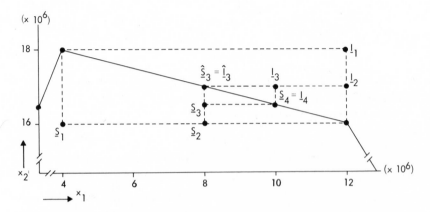

Figure 7.2. All solutions from the starting solution up to and including the final solution

In this relatively simple example we have omitted the definition and redefinition of the δ_j. To be complete we will now show how the δ_j's should have been defined during the successive iterations. At the beginning, in step 2, we have $\delta_1 = \delta_2 = 0$. The proposal solution (8,16) is accepted without modifying the proposed goal levels. Consequently, δ_1 and δ_2 remain unchanged. The proposal solution (8,17) is judged to have a too strong influence on the first goal variable. Thus δ_2 is set equal to 1. The new proposal solution (8,16.5) is subsequently accepted and δ_2 is halved to 0.5. Finally, the proposal solution (10, 16.5) is accepted without any problem, by which δ_1 remains zero. When this last proposal solution would not have been accepted directly, δ_1 would have also become positive.

Table 7.1. Successive (proposal) solutions together with the opinion of the decision maker

(proposal) solution to be evaluated	(proposal) potency matrix	steps	evaluation
$S_1 = [4,16]$	$P_1 = \begin{bmatrix} 12 & 18 \\ 4 & 16 \end{bmatrix}$	2,3,4,5	$\underline{S}_1$ not satisfactory, raise value $g_1(\underline{x})$
$\hat{S}_2 = [8,16]$	$\hat{P}_2 = \begin{bmatrix} 12 & 17 \\ 8 & 16 \end{bmatrix}$	6,7,8	shifts in P justified, set $\underline{S}_2 = \hat{S}_2$ and $P_2 = \hat{P}_2$
$S_2 = [8,16]$	$P_2 = \begin{bmatrix} 12 & 17 \\ 8 & 16 \end{bmatrix}$	4,5	$\underline{S}_2$ not satisfactory, raise value $g_2(\underline{x})$
$\hat{S}_3 = [8,17]$	$\hat{P}_3 = \begin{bmatrix} 8 & 17 \\ 8 & 17 \end{bmatrix}$	6,7,8	shifts in P not justified, lower value $g_2(\underline{x})$
$\hat{S}_3 = [8,16.5]$	$\hat{P}_3 = \begin{bmatrix} 10 & 17 \\ 8 & 16.5 \end{bmatrix}$	9,7,8	shifts in P justified, set $\underline{S}_3 = \hat{S}_3$ and $P_3 = \hat{P}_3$
$S_3 = [8,16.5]$	$P_3 = \begin{bmatrix} 10 & 17 \\ 8 & 16.5 \end{bmatrix}$	4,5	$\underline{S}_3$ not satisfactory, raise value of $g_1(\underline{x})$
$\hat{S}_4 = [10,16.5]$	$\hat{P}_4 = \begin{bmatrix} 10 & 16.5 \\ 10 & 16.5 \end{bmatrix}$	6,7,8	shifts in P justified, set $\underline{S}_4 = \hat{S}_4$ and $P_4 = \hat{P}_4$
$S_4 = [10,16.5]$	$P_4 = \begin{bmatrix} 10 & 16.5 \\ 10 & 16.5 \end{bmatrix}$	4	end of procedure

Example 2: Allocation of a Time Budget

A professor has to decide how many days a week on the average he will spend on research and on teaching and related activities (meetings, preparations, exams, etc.), respectively. We assume the number of courses and the number of students to be given and fixed. Therefore time spent on teaching influences only the quality of teaching and not the formal quantity. Let us denote the decision variables by x (days of teaching) and by y (days of research). Because a week has 7 days, we have

(7.3) $x + y \leq 7$

If he does not want to be dismissed in the long run, he has to spend at least one day a week on teaching activities. So we have

(7.4) $x \geq 1$

In his opinion, three days a week spent on teaching is optimal. He does not mind spending more time on this activity, but he feels that this additional effort will not contribute significantly to the quality of his teaching. Because he wants to maximize the quality of this teaching (by simultaneously minimizing the risk of being dismissed), one of his goals is:

(7.5) $\text{Min}\{g_1 = z_1^-\}$

$$\text{s.t. } x - z_1^+ + z_1^- = 3$$

Another desire is to minimize working during the weekends, although he does not mind working during the week. He does not have any problem in taking free days during the week.
These desires can be translated into

(7.6)   Min $\{g_2 = z_2^+\}$

$$\text{s.t. } x + y - z_2^+ + z_2^- = 5$$

A third goal variable is his current wealth, which he wants to be as high as possible. Let us assume that each additional day spent on research contributes 6 ducats to his wealth, where a day spent on teaching contributes 2 ducats. He therefore wishes to maximize

(7.7)   Max $g_3 = 2.x + 6.y$

A graphical representation of this problem is given in Figure 7.3. The elaboration by means of IMGP is shown in Figure 7.4.

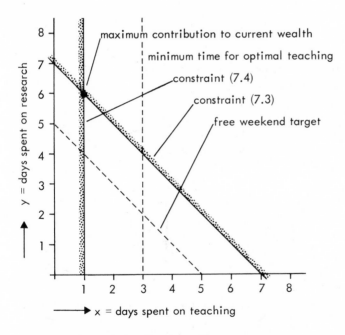

Figure 7.3. The time budget allocation problem

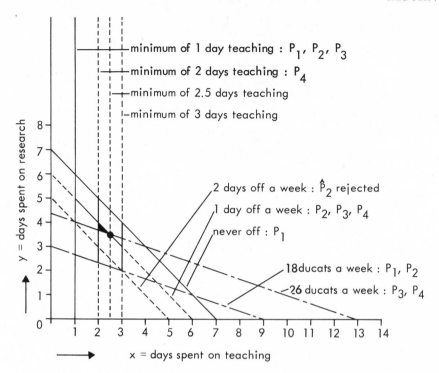

Figure 7.4. Successive IMGP steps for the time budget allocation problem

In order to discover whether (and if so, to what extent) these goal variables are conflicting, we construct (step 1) the following potency matrix P_1.

$$(7.8) \qquad P_1 = \begin{bmatrix} g_1^* & g_2^* & g_3^* \\ g_1^{min} & g_2^{min} & g_3^{min} \end{bmatrix} = \begin{bmatrix} 0 & 0 & 38 \\ 2 & 2 & 18 \end{bmatrix}$$

During the construction of this matrix, we deviated slightly from the procedure described in Chapter 6 (step 1) in order to take account of non-unique optimum solutions [1].

Let us assume that the professor (in step 2) has defined one aspiration level for each of the goal variables, which are respectively equal to 1 for g_1, 0 for g_2 and 26 for g_3, the latter value representing his estimation of the minimum welfare needed to survive.

In the third step, the most pessimistic solution, $\underline{S}_1 = (2,2,18)$, is presented to the decision maker, together with the potency matrix P_1. We assume that he is not satisfied with $\underline{S}_1$ (step 4) and that first (step 5) he wants to have a free weekend which is as long as possible (step 6). Thus we can construct the proposal solution $\hat{\underline{S}}_2 = (2,0,18)$. In step 7 we calculate the corresponding potency matrix $\hat{P}_2$ as

(7.9)
$$\hat{P}_2 = \begin{bmatrix} 0 & 0 & 26 \\ \\ 2 & 0 & 18 \end{bmatrix}$$

Comparing (in step 8) this matrix with P_1, the decision maker judges that his possibilities of increasing his wealth have critically deteriorated. We thus have to set (in step 9) a new, but less ambitious value for the second goal variable. By choosing this new value exactly between the corresponding value in $\underline{S}_1$ and the corresponding value in the rejected proposal solution, we get the new proposal solution $\hat{\underline{S}}_2 = (2,1,18)$ with the potency matrix

1) Note for instance that the minimization of $g_1 = z_1^-$ yields the complete area between points $(3,0)$, $(7,0)$ and $(3,4)$. We solved this problem by calculating a new pay-off matrix for the goal variables g_2 and g_3, given the optimum value for g_1. From this, the worst values of g_2 and g_3 were taken as corresponding to the optimum for g_1.

$$(7.10) \qquad \hat{P}_2 = \begin{bmatrix} 0 & 0 & 32 \\ & & \\ 2 & 1 & 18 \end{bmatrix}$$

Assuming that these shifts in the potency matrix are considered justified, we can define $\underline{S}_2 = \hat{\underline{S}}_2$ and $P_2 = \hat{P}_2$, leaving the decision maker with at least one free day a week.

Returning to step 4 and 5, the professor argues that if he cannot have a two-day weekend free he certainly has to increase his wealth by more than the current 18 ducats a week. Given this information and the list of aspiration levels, we propose $\hat{\underline{S}}_3 = (2,1,26)$ and calculate the corresponding potency matrix $\hat{P}_3$ (step 6 and 7), which is given by

$$(7.11) \qquad \hat{P}_3 = \begin{bmatrix} 0.5 & 0 & 32 \\ & & \\ 2 & 1 & 26 \end{bmatrix}$$

The professor judges these shifts in the potency matrix to be acceptable. Thus we define $\underline{S}_3 = \hat{\underline{S}}_3$ and $P_3 = \hat{P}_3$. Next, in this decision maker's opinion, the quality of his teaching should be ensured. Therefore, we propose $\hat{\underline{S}}_4 = (1,1,26)$ and calculate the potency matrix

$$(7.12) \qquad \hat{P}_4 = \begin{bmatrix} 0.5 & 2/3 & 28 \\ & & \\ 1 & 1 & 26 \end{bmatrix}$$

Because he judges 2 days a week on teaching (i.e. $z_1^- = 1$) a minimum to guarantee good (although not optimal) teaching, he accepts the shifts in the potency matrix implied by this requirement. Thus we have $\underline{S}_4 = \hat{\underline{S}}_4$ and $P_4 = \hat{P}_4$. Summarizing the current state of affairs, the professor has to work a maximum of six days a week, of which two days at least are spent on teaching. His increase in wealth will be at least 26 ducats a week. Given this

situation, he may continue to add requirements. For instance, he
may want to maximize time spent on teaching, which becomes 2.5
days of a six-day working-week, yielding 26 ducats. Similarly,
maximizing the increase in wealth yields 28 ducats a week, earned
with two days spent on teaching and four days on research. Minimizing
the length of the working-week implies two days of teaching and
$3\frac{2}{3}$ days of research with an increase in wealth of 26 ducats a week.

However, in our opinion it is unlikely that the decision maker
will choose such a razor-edge solution. It is more natural that he
accepts S_4 and P_4 as they are and decides, for instance, to work
$5\frac{2}{3}$ – 6 days a week, of which no more than 2 days spent on teaching,
earning 26 – 28 ducats a week.

7.2. Experiments with an Imaginary Decision Maker

In order to demonstrate some of the convergence properties of
IMGP, we introduce in this section the concept of an imaginary
decision maker, who makes the necessary managerial choices. We
assume that his preference structure can be described adequately
by a concave preference function exactly known to us. We assume
the decision maker to be able to give his judgements concerning
a solution proposed to him by the IMGP procedure, and moreover
to do so in a manner which is in complete accordance with the
preference function specified.

Given the *a priori* knowledge of the decision maker's preference
function, we can calculate an optimal solution of the problem at
hand. At the same time, we can execute the IMGP procedure by
'interacting' with the imaginary decision maker. Then, the solution
obtained from the *a priori* specified preference function can be
compared with the solution resulting from the interactive procedure.

In doing so we make three simplifying assumptions, each of which
can be relaxed quite easily. For the moment, we assume that the

decision maker does not specify any *a priori* information. Furthermore, we assume him to give consistent answers without any errors.
Finally, within the IMGP procedure, the decision maker has to
indicate, given an accepted solution, which goal value should be
raised. In the present case, we introduce the assumption that the
decision maker first tries to drive the first goal variable to its
optimal value, next the second, third and following goal variables
respectively. This procedure of changing the value of a given goal
variable is concluded as soon as it reaches a value which is
sufficiently close to the optimal value.

The computer program for the described experiment has been
run on an IBM 370/158 computer at the Technical University in Delft,
The Netherlands. In the program, which has been written in PL/1,
the MPSX package has been used to solve the linear programming
problems (see also Appendix 7.a).

Below, we give an example of an imaginary decision maker using
IMGP in order to find a solution for his portfolio selection problem.

Example 3: Selection of an Investment Portfolio

Several authors have formulated the problem of portfolio
construction as a multiple goal program. Baum and Carlson [1974]
showed how efficient solutions can be found. However, they did
not indicate how a final solution from the set of efficient
solutions should be chosen. Lee [1972], Lee and Lerro [1973],
Kumar, Philippatos and Ezzell [1978] and Bronsema and van de Kieft
[1978] formulated the problem as a standard multiple goal problem,
requiring complete *a priori* information on the decision maker's
preferences.

Lee [1972] formulated a model for selecting efficient mutual
funds portfolios. Given a budget constraint, a set of legal
constraints and a set of restrictions representing the maximum

allowable concentration in any industry, two goals must be strived
for. The first goal is to maximize the expected return of the
portfolio, E_p. The second goal is to minimize the risk of the
portfolio, as measured by its market volatility. The market volatility of a portfolio consisting of n securities is represented by

$$(7.13) \qquad B_p = \sum_{i=1}^{n} x_i \cdot B_i,$$

where x_i is the fraction of the budget invested in security i, B_i is
the market volatility of security i and B_p the market volatility
of the portfolio. The market volatility of a security or a portfolio measures its relationship with some stock market index common
to all securities. The market volatility (or beta) of a security
is often called the systematic risk of a security. Besides this
risk each security has its own unsystematic risk component, viewed
as a random variable with zero mean and standard deviation s_i. All
pairs of random variables representing the unsystematic risk are
assumed to have zero covariance and to be uncorrelated with the
market index. Lee wanted to account for the unsystematic risk of
the portfolio explicitly. Therefore, he introduced 'current dividend
yield' as an additional goal variable 'to help us compensate for
having the income fund suffer some unaccounted for risk' (Ibid.
pp. 227-228).

Given this framework, Lee formulated both a goal program for
a growth portfolio and a goal program for an income portfolio,
mutually only different with respect to their objective functions.
The first objective function was formulated to maximize expected
growth, to minimize market volatility and to maximize current
dividend yield in this order which was moreover pre-emptive. The
second objective function was also ordered by pre-emptive priority
factors, but in the reverse direction.

In the IMGP approach we replaced these two objective functions
by three separate objective functions, one to maximize

expected growth, one to minimize market volatility, and one to
maximize current dividend. The imaginary decision maker's preference
function was specified as

(7.14) $f(E_p, B_p, D_p) = 0.4E_p + 0.2B_p + 0.4D_p$,

where E_p, B_p and D_p are the portfolio's expected growth, market
volatility and current dividend yield respectively. For further
details on this experiment, we refer to Nijkamp and Spronk [1978].
All results are presented in Table 7.2, where the solution for the
a priori specified preference function (7.14), the solutions given
by Lee, and the unconditional optimal solutions for each of the
objective functions separately are also shown.

Besides the initial pessimistic solution, only nine proposal
solutions had to be evaluated by the imaginary decision maker.

Given the first proposed constraint for E_p, a pessimistic
solution follows in which the lower bound of D_p has also been
increased. Because the optimal solution (a) is not excluded by this
proposal solution, the latter has been accepted by the decision
maker. The second solution has been obtained by raising E_p. This
solution is unacceptable because it excludes a B_p value smaller
than 0.608 and a D_p value over 0.025. The next solution is obtained
by lowering the E_p value, which has been accepted. Then, the E_p
value is raised again, each time with a rise of half its previous
size (S_1), until the required accuracy for E_p is reached in
iteration 6. In step 7 the value of B_p is lowered with $\delta_2 = 0.68$.
In step 8 the value of B_p is lowered with a value which is not
equal to the δ_2 in step 7 divided by 2. This is because such a
value would have caused a B_p value outside the 'potency region' of
B_p specified in iteration 7. In this case δ_2 has been divided by
two until a feasible B_p value could be proposed in iteration 8.
The same happens in iteration 9. The solution proposed in iteration
9 is the final solution, because the required accuracy for B_p has
been attained and because the D_p value has been driven close enough

Table 7.2.　IMPG applied to Lee's model

description of the objective function	expected growth *	**	market volatility *	**	current dividend *	**	comment
(a) solution for (7.14)	0.4975		0.5844		0.00285		
(b) growth portfolio (Lee)	0.677		1.361		0.009		
(c) income portfolio (Lee)	0.105		0.922		0.033		
(d) max. expected growth	0.677		1.361		0.009		
(e) min. market volatility	0.0		0.0		0.0		
(f) max. current dividend	0.107		0.887		0.033		
(0) initial pessimistic sol.	0.0		1.361		0.0		
(1) proposed constraints	0.338		1.361		0.0		δ_1=0.338
pessimist. solutions		0.338		1.361		0.0027	
potential solutions		0.677		0.346		0.029	accepted
(2) proposed constraints	0.507		1.361		0.0027		δ_1=0.169
pessimist. solutions		0.507		1.361		0.0029	
potential solutions		0.677		0.608		0.025	rejected
(3) proposed constraints	0.423		1.361		0.0027		δ_1=0.085
pessimist. solutions		0.507		1.361		0.0023	
potential solutions		0.677		0.462		0.028	accepted
(4) proposed constraints	0.465		1.361		0.0023		δ_1=0.043
pessimist. solutions		0.465		1.361		0.0026	
potential solutions		0.677		0.471		0.026	accepted
(5) proposed constraints	0.486		1.361		0.0026		δ_1=0.021
pessimist. solutions		0.486		1.361		0.0028	
potential solutions		0.677		0.565		0.0268	accepted
(6) proposed constraints	0.497		1.361		0.0028		δ_1=0.011
pessimist. solutions		0.497		1.361		0.0028	
potential solutions		0.677		0.584		0.025	accepted
(7) proposed constraints	0.497		0.681		0.0028		δ_2=0.681
pessimist. solutions		0.497		0.681		0.0028	
potential solutions		0.534		0.584		0.013	accepted
(8) proposed constraints	0.497		0.596		0.0028		δ_2=0.085
pessimist. solutions		0.497		0.596		0.0028	
potential solutions		0.502		0.584		0.0048	accepted
(9) proposed constraints	0.497		0.585		0.0028		δ_2=0.011
pessimist. solutions		0.497		0.585		0.0028	
potential solutions (final solution)		0.498		0.584		0.0030	accepted
(a) solution for (7.14)	0.4975		0.5844		0.00285		

* goal values belonging to optimal solutions and proposed goal constraints.

** pessimistic and potential goal values.

to its optimal value.

The relatively favourable results with the above and other
examples (cf. also Nijkamp and Spronk [1978a]) cannot be generalized
without some reserves. Clearly, the number of iterations needed
depends on the number of goal variables, the exact shape of the
preference function and the required accuracy. Furthermore, we
assumed that the decision maker did not specify any *a priori*
information. If this is the case, the effect on the method's
convergence speed cannot be determined beforehand, because such
information may either accelerate or decelerate the process. Finally,
in this example we introduced an *ad hoc* hierarchical ranking of the
goal variables to be changed. First, the expected growth was driven
to its optimal value, then the market volatility and finally the
current dividend. It may be that another order of changing the goal
values may accelerate or decelerate the process.

7.3. Some Empirical Results

Just before the publication of this study, a project was started
in which IMGP was used to help investigating the conflicts between
a number of goal variables with respect to a large scale input-output
model describing the economic-environmental system of Western Europe.
First, a pilot study was carried out with a simplified version of
this input-output model (cf. Hartog, Nijkamp, and Spronk [1980]).
Because not all results of the main study were available at the
time of publication of the present study, we confine ourselves here
to a summary of the results of the pilot study. The simplified
version of the input-output model consists of 160 relations in 130
structural variables describing three conventional sectors and one
sector for the abatement of pollution (see for further details
van Driel et al [1980]). To start with, the following goal variables
have been defined by the analysts.

(1) wages

(2) consumption

(3) minimum growth of consumption

(4) maximum growth of capacity

(5) nuisance (defined as the amount of unabated pollution)

(6) production of the pollution abatement sector.

With this set of goal variables, a number of experiments have been carried out with decision makers (in this pilot study these were interested scientists being familiar with this kind of problems, both in theory and practice) trying to achieve a satisfactory solution for the problem at hand. The results of these experiments are rather encouraging. Each iteration costs some 30 seconds of CPU time (see Appendix 7.6 for details),needed to recalculate the potency matrix by means of solving 6 fairly similar linear goal programs [1]. Although it is not strictly necessary for interactive procedures to have such a low 'return time', it can be seen as an important advantage. This is because the decision maker, at the terminal display, can easily experiment with different combinations of the goal variables, without high costs and within a relatively short period. In Table 7.3, we give a condensed description of the third session at the terminal desk of a decision maker (see Hartog et al [1980] for a more detailed description).

It is not necessary for a decision maker to continue the interactive procedure to the extent that the present decision maker did, i.e. to proceed until a unique (or nearly unique) final solution occurs. One might as well stop at an earlier iteration, being left with a number of 'scenarios' all satisfying the minimum conditions specified by the decision maker. The choice out of these scenarios

---

1) This fairly good performance can be ascribed to the relative simplicity of IMGP, combined with some attractive properties of the MPSX-package. Note for instance, that from iteration to iteration the goal programs change only with respect to some right-hand side values, so that each optimization can greatly benefit from earlier optimal solutions.

Table 7.3. A session with a decision maker investigating the goal conflicts within an economic-environmental system

			iteration number					
	1	2	3	4	5	6	....	14
(1) pess. value	793*	1500	1500	1500	1500	1696		1600
ideal value	3292	3292	3091	2024	1993	1991		1600
(2) pess. value	1000	1000	1000	1000	1225*	2000		1890
ideal value	2810	2810	2643	2274	2241	2241		1890
(3) pess. value	0	0	0	0*	5	5		10
ideal value	20	20	19	19	19	16		10
(4) pess. value	2751	2751*	500	500	500	500		252
ideal value	79	79	79	79	80	87		251
(5) pess. value	290	290	255*	30	30	30*		15
ideal value	0	12	12	12	12	18		15
(6) pess. value	0	0	9704	9704	9704	11316		13545
ideal value	28189	28189	28189	19977	19042	18094		13556

* Goal value chosen to be improved

174

can be made by a committee or otherwise.

An examination of the detailed results associated with the final result attained by this decision maker showed that nearly all instrumental variables within the model behaved according to smooth growth paths. However, because no goal variable had been included to take care of a balanced distribution of activity over the industrial sectors, some undesired effects occurred in this respect. In fact, this was one of the learning effects mentioned in Chapters 5 and 6, which resulted in discussions and proposals for new goal variables. Other learning effects have led among others to the proposal to delete the sixth goal variable as being an improper one because its value can be raised by switching to heavily polluting sectors. Furthermore, the nuisance goal variable was proposed to be defined differently.

On the basis of the results of this pilot study, it has been decided to continue the experiments, using the full version of the abovementioned input-output model, a slightly revised set of goal variables, and with the aid of decision makers who are responsible for the kind of decisions simulated by the model (see Hartog and Spronk [1980]).

7.4. IMGP Applied to Discrete Decision Problems

With some minor modifications, IMGP can also be applied to discrete decision problems with explicitly given alternatives. In this section we give two illustrative examples. The first example concerns the selection of a single alternative from a set of mutually exclusive investment projects, each of which is described by its performance with respect to four criteria. The second example concerns an enterprise which is planning to build a new factory. There are 20 candidate locations, all of which are described in terms of seven criteria, some of which are measured on an ordinal scale.

Example 4: Selecting a Capital Investment Project

This example [1] of a multiple criteria decision problem with
only a limited number of alternatives involves a laundry which is
opening a new laundrette, to be equipped with 20 washing machines.
For the latter, a number of alternative types is available. The
decision maker believes four goal variables to be relevant in the
choice from the set of alternatives, i.e. purchase price, electricity
consumption, water consumption, and washing time. Each of these goal
variables is to be minimized. There are 33 different types of washing
machines, which are described in Table 7.4.

Although Interactive Multiple Goal Programming loses one of its
attractive properties in this case (i.e. by the simple calculation
of the respective optima of the goal variables no reduction of the
set of alternatives can be obtained here), it can still be used as
a systematic procedure to reduce the set of feasible actions by
adding and tightening constraints on the values of the goal variables
and showing the consequences. An 'ideal solution' is defined as before.
A 'pessimistic solution' now lists, for each of the goal variables,
the worst (in the present case, the highest) value amongst <u>all</u>
available alternatives. The solutions are represented by row vectors
with their elements representing the price of a washing-machine,

---

1) The case on which this example is based has been designed by
   Professor A. Törn. A more detailed description of this case,
   together with its solution by means of various procedures
   other than IMGP, can be found in Carlsson et al.[1980].

Table 7.4. Alternative types of washing machines

alternative number	unit price in dollars	total washing time* in minutes	electricity consumption* in kwh	water consumption* in litres	(proposal) solutions by which alternative is rejected
1	509	74	1.4	114	S_2, S_2
2	425	80	1.4	110	S_3, S_3
3	446	72	1.5	135	S_3, S_3
4	564	65	1.5	118	S_2, S_2
5	547	53	1.7	140	S_2, S_2
6	450	68	1.5	135	S_3, S_5, S_5
7	473	65	1.5	130	S_3, final solution
8	484	56	1.6	115	S_4, S_4
9	456	68	1.5	130	S_3, S_6, S_6
10	488	72	1.5	114	S_3, S_3
11	530	55	1.6	135	S_2, S_2
12	477	76	1.4	110	S_3, S_3
13	589	53	1.5	130	S_2, S_2
14	534	61	1.3	122	S_2, S_2
15	536	57	1.6	110	S_2, S_2
16	494	72	1.4	135	S_3, S_3
17	425	65	1.7	120	S_3, S_4, S_4
18	555	53	1.6	125	S_2, S_2
19	543	57	1.5	120	S_2, S_2
20	515	68	1.4	130	S_2, S_2
21	452	76	1.4	112	S_3, S_3
22	547	68	1.4	120	S_2, S_2
23	421	76	1.3	130	S_3, S_3
24	498	68	1.5	120	S_2, S_2
25	467	65	1.6	130	S_3, S_4, S_4
26	595	50	1.7	135	S_2, S_2
27	414	68	1.6	125	S_3, S_4, S_4
28	431	66	1.6	110	S_3, S_4, S_4
29	452	72	1.4	115	S_3, S_3
30	408	77	1.5	119	S_3, S_3
31	478	59	1.7	110	S_4, S_4
32	395	76	1.4	120	S_3, S_3
33	543	57	1.4	135	S_2, S_2

* For the most used program

its total washing time, its electricity consumption and water
consumption, respectively. The first potency matrix is given by

$$
(7.15) \qquad P_1 = \begin{vmatrix} 395 & 50 & 1.3 & 110 \\ 595 & 80 & 1.7 & 140 \end{vmatrix}
$$

Given the pessimistic solution, i.e. the lower row of P_1 the decision
maker has to indicate which goal value should be decreased in value.
Let us assume that he wants the price to be lower than $ 595 per
machine but that he does not specify how much lower. We then set a
proposal price of ($ 595 + $ 395) / 2 = $ 495 (all other (pessimis-
tic) goal values remaining equal) and calculate the potency matrix
associated with this proposal solution as

$$
(7.16) \qquad \hat{P}_2 = \begin{vmatrix} 395 & 56 & 1.3 & 110 \\ 494 & 80 & 1.7 & 135 \end{vmatrix}
$$

Thus by taking $ 495 as an upper bound for the price the decision
maker is willing to pay for one machine, one has to drop the alternatives with a lower washing time than 56 minutes (i.e. alternatives
5, 11, 13, 18 and 26). On the other hand, by accepting this bound
on the price level, alternatives with a higher water consumption
than 135 litres (alternative 5) can also be left out of consideration.
Of course, it is up to the decision maker to accept this restriction
on the price level and its consequences. If he does not accept this
restriction we calculate a new proposal price limit exactly between
$ 595 (which was too high) and $ 495 (which appeared to be too low).
However, let us assume that the decision maker accepts this solution.
Besides the already mentioned alternatives, we can also drop the
numbers 1, 4, 14, 15, 19, 20, 22, 24 and 33. Thus, in total, the
number of alternatives is reduced from 33 to 19 (cf. Table 7.4).

Given the lastly accepted pessimistic solution, the decision
maker again has to indicate which goal value should be reduced in

value. Let us assume that he wants to reduce the total washing time
for the mostly used program and that, during this run, he is able
to specify the desired reduction. Let the upper bound on washing time
be 60 minutes, which gives

$$
(7.17) \qquad \hat{P}_3 = \begin{bmatrix} 478 & 56 & 1.6 & 110 \\ 484 & 59 & 1.7 & 115 \end{bmatrix}
$$

Confronted with this proposal solution, the decision maker argues
that the minimal electricity consumption (1.6 kwh for the most used
program) is too high. This means that the imposed maximum value on
washing time (60 minutes) was chosen too low. (We already know that
the maximum value on washing time in the preceding accepted solution
(80 minutes) was considered to be too high). Therefore, given the
lastly accepted solution (i.e. the lower row of (7.16)), we propose
a new solution by limiting washing time to an upper limit of 70
minutes. The implied potency matrix is given by

$$
(7.18) \qquad \hat{P}_3 = \begin{bmatrix} 414 & 56 & 1.5 & 110 \\ 484 & 68 & 1.7 & 135 \end{bmatrix}
$$

Assuming that the decision maker accepts this proposal and its
consequences (if he does not, the upper bound on washing time is
further reduced to $(70+80)/2 = 75$ minutes), the number of alternatives remaining to be analyzed becomes 9 (10 alternatives are
to be dropped: 2, 3, 10, 12, 16, 21, 23, 29, 30 and 32).

Let us next assume that the decision maker, given the accepted
solution in (7.18), wants to limit electricity consumption to 1.5
kwh at most for the most intensive washing program.
This implies

$$
(7.19) \qquad \hat{P}_4 = \begin{bmatrix} 450 & 65 & 1.5 & 130 \\ 473 & 68 & 1.5 & 135 \end{bmatrix}
$$

The decision maker accepts this proposal (so that only alternatives 6, 7 and 9 remain) and wants to reduce water consumption to at most 130 litres per washing program. We then get

$$(7.20) \qquad \hat{P}_5 = \begin{vmatrix} 456 & 65 & 1.5 & 130 \\ 473 & 68 & 1.5 & 130 \end{vmatrix}$$

This proposal is also accepted. Only two alternatives, 7 and 9 are retained. The decision maker decides to choose the alternatives with the lowest electricity consumption, given by

$$(7.21) \qquad S_6 = [473 \quad 65 \quad 1.5 \quad 130]$$

This is also the final solution.

Example 5: Locating a Factory

An enterprise is planning to build a new factory for the production of storage batteries. There are twenty possibilities for the location of this new factory. Each alternative has been described in terms of its contributions to the goal variables which management considers to be relevant in this situation. These goal variables are

g_1 = capacity of the factory, expressed as the annual number of units produced (in millions). Between certain limits, management wants the capacity to be as large as possible.

g_2 = costs of establishing the new factory (purchase of land and cost of construction). Of course management wants a value of this variable which is as low as possible.

g_3 = score for the quality of the facilities provided by the local government (subsidies, advice, licences). These scores are presented on an ordinal scale of increasing priority: --, -, 0, +, ++. The element -- represents a strongly negative outcome

for the local facilities concerned, whereas the element ++
represents a strongly positive outcome.

g_4 = score for the possibilities to attract skilled labour (again
represented on an ordinal scale with --, -, 0, +, ++).

g_5 = score for the quality of the transportation network to be used
by the factory (again represented on an ordinal scale with
--, -, 0, +, ++).

g_6 = estimated size of the total local market (measured in millions
of units sold per year). Of course, management prefers a more
voluminous market to a smaller one.

g_7 = score for the possibilities to enter the local market (again
represented on an ordinal scale with --, -, 0, +, ++).

The 'industrial profiles' (see Paelinck and Nijkamp [1976]) of the
20 possible locations are given in Table 7.5. None of the alternatives
is *a priori* dominated by another. The first potency matrix can be
written as

$$(7.22) \qquad P_1 = \begin{bmatrix} 30 & 20 & ++ & ++ & ++ & 55 & ++ \\ 11 & 50 & -- & -- & -- & 10 & -- \end{bmatrix}$$

and the first solution as

$$(7.23) \qquad \underline{S}_1 = [11,50,--,--,--,10,--]$$

Assume management's first wishes are that the quality of the local
governmental facilities should not be too low ($g_3 \geq -$) and that there
are not too many difficulties in attracting labour ($g_4 \geq -$). We then
have

$$(7.24) \qquad \hat{\underline{S}}_2 = [11,50,-,-,--,10,--]$$

As can be seen in Table 7.5, the profile numbers 2, 8, 10 and 18

Table 7.5. Profiles of the location alternatives

profile number	(scoring) values of the goal variables							(proposal) solutions by which profile is rejected
	g_1	g_2	g_3	g_4	g_5	g_6	g_7	
1	30	48	0	–	+	40	–	$\hat{\underline{S}}_3$, $\hat{\underline{S}}_4$, $\underline{S}_4$
2	29	50	–	– –	++	25	++	$\hat{\underline{S}}_2$, $\underline{S}_2$
3	28	44	0	+	+	45	– –	$\hat{\underline{S}}_3$, $\hat{\underline{S}}_4$, $\underline{S}_4$
4	27	40	++	++	– –	·20	–	$\hat{\underline{S}}_3$(two times), $\underline{S}_3$
5	26	41	–	0	+	55	+	$\hat{\underline{S}}_3$, final solution
6	25	46	0	0	++	10	++	$\hat{\underline{S}}_5$, $\underline{S}_5$
7	24	40	+	++	0	10	++	$\hat{\underline{S}}_3$, $\hat{\underline{S}}_4$, $\underline{S}_4$
8	23	43	– –	+	++	10	0	$\hat{\underline{S}}_2$, $\underline{S}_2$
9	22	38	–	+	+	10	– –	$\hat{\underline{S}}_3$
10	21	37	–	– –	–	15	+	$\hat{\underline{S}}_2$, $\underline{S}_2$
11	20	35	0	+	0	50	++	$\hat{\underline{S}}_3$, $\underline{S}_3$
12	19	41	+	+	++	20	+	$\hat{\underline{S}}_3$, $\underline{S}_3$
13	18	36	–	+	+	25	0	$\hat{\underline{S}}_3$, $\underline{S}_3$
14	17	32	0	0	– –	35	++	$\hat{\underline{S}}_3$, $\underline{S}_3$
15	16	28	0	0	+	45	+	$\hat{\underline{S}}_3$, $\underline{S}_3$
16	15	25	0	0	0	30	0	$\hat{\underline{S}}_3$, $\underline{S}_3$
17	14	26	0	++	++	15	+	$\hat{\underline{S}}_3$, $\underline{S}_3$
18	13	24	– –	–	–	30	–	$\hat{\underline{S}}_2$, $\underline{S}_2$
19	12	23	+	++	+	10	+	$\hat{\underline{S}}_3$, $\underline{S}_3$
20	11	20	0	+	0	15	–	$\hat{\underline{S}}_3$, $\underline{S}_3$

do not meet these requirements. The accompanying potency matrix is

$$(7.25) \qquad \hat{\underline{P}}_2 = \begin{bmatrix} 30 & 20 & ++ & ++ & ++ & 55 & ++ \\ 11 & 48 & - & - & -- & 10 & -- \end{bmatrix}$$

As can be read from $\hat{P}_2$ and Table 7.5 we have, by rejecting profile number 2, rejected the factory with the highest construction costs. Therefore we define

$$(7.26) \qquad \underline{S}_2 = [11,48,-,-,--,10,--], \text{ and } P_2 = \hat{P}_2$$

Management next wants a capacity of at least 20 million units per year to meet the export orders $(g_1 \geq 20)$. For the same reason, it would like to have the best possible transportation facilities $(g_5 \geq ++)$. We thus get

$$(7.27) \qquad \hat{\underline{S}}_3 = [20,48,-,-,++,10,--]$$

As can be seen in Table 7.5, there is only one profile (number 6) left in this solution, by which the potency matrix reduces to

$$(7.28) \qquad \hat{\underline{P}}_3 = \begin{bmatrix} 25 & 46 & - & - & ++ & 10 & -- \\ 25 & 46 & - & - & ++ & 10 & -- \end{bmatrix}$$

Management judges this loss in potency too heavy and is interested in the results of a less perfect transportation system. The model then proposes the solution

$$(7.29) \qquad \hat{\underline{S}}_3 = [20,48,-,-,0,10,--]$$

There are more profiles left in this solution, viz. the numbers 1, 3, 5, 6 and 7. The potency matrix can be written as

$$(7.30) \quad \hat{\underline{P}}_3 = \begin{bmatrix} 30 & 40 & + & ++ & ++ & 55 & ++ \\ 24 & 48 & - & - & 0 & 10 & -- \end{bmatrix}$$

Management considers the proposal good enough to justify the shifts in the potency matrix, by which we can formulate

$$(7.31) \quad \underline{S}_3 = [24,48,-,-,0,10,--] \text{ and } P_3 = \hat{\underline{P}}_3$$

In the following step, transportation is required to be slightly better and the possibility to enter the local market must be 'not too bad' ($g_7 \geq 0$). This solution is judged to 'outweigh' the shifts in the potency matrix. Then the fourth solution is determined as

$$(7.32) \quad \underline{S}_4 = [25,46,-,0,+,10,+],$$

for which the fifth and sixth profiles are still feasible. Finally management wants to face a local market which exceeds the 10 million units sales in $\underline{S}_4$. Consequently, the final solution becomes

$$(7.33) \quad \underline{S}_5 = [26,41,-,0,+,55,+],$$

which is the fifth profile.

7.5. Conclusions

To illustrate the (potential) use of IMGP, we have presented some examples. Many more examples could have been given, as IMGP can be used for any linear programming problem with two or more goal variables or with one goal variable and some 'soft' constraints, and also for any other problem which meets the fairly unrestrictive requirements described in Chapter 6. In addition, IMGP can be used for some problems which do not meet these requirements (such as discrete evaluation problems), though with a minor modification.

Nevertheless, these and other examples are not well suited to draw a balanced conclusion on the merits and demerits of IMGP in practice. As is the case with most other interactive procedures, the number of experiences with IMGP in practice is still very limited. Although many practitioners appear to be very interested in interactive procedures, it will take some time before the performance of these procedures can be evaluated in practice. In the meantime, the evaluation of IMGP and other interactive procedures might be based on a theoretical framework, e.g. as provided in Section 5.1.

We are convinced that this type of interactive procedures can be used fruitfully in practice, provided the organizational setting of the decision problem and the wishes of the decision makers are taken into consideration. IMGP has a number of properties which, from a practical point of view, seem to be attractive. A detailed evaluation of IMGP based on both practical and theoretical considerations is given in Section 10.1.

At this point, it is important to note that a fully operational set of computer programs has become available for the implementation of IMGP in linear goal programs. These computer programs have been developed for a specific problem (see Section 7.3), but may be used for any other linear goal problem. The set of computer programs has been designed such that the decision maker can use a computer terminal display and thus be in conversational contact with the computer system. In this way the decision maker can evaluate the outcomes implied by his earlier choices, and can accordingly express the desired changes in the linear programs, which are then solved by the computer. A description of this set of interrelated computer programs is given in Appendix 7.b.

Appendix 7.a. <u>Computer Program Used for the Experiments with an</u>
<u>Imaginary Decision Maker</u>

In this appendix, we describe [1] the structure of the computer program used for the experiments involving an imaginary decision maker using IMGP. As mentioned in Section 7.2, we assume here that the imaginary decision maker's preference function is linear in the goal variables. The program consists of three subprograms, written in PL/I and using the MPSX-package. The first subprogram reads the data and generates the input for the MPSX-package. MPSX expects input in a certain format and in a certain order. To fulfil these requirements, we use the input generator ETMIC (cf. Lebret [1977]). The second subprogram calculates an optimal solution for the imaginary decision maker's preference function and saves the basis of their simplex solution for subsequent problems. These first two subprograms can also be used for standard linear and multiple goal programming. The third subprogram simulates the decisions made by an imaginary decision maker using IMGP.

In each of the three subprograms, the following 'standard' terms are used.

NP   = number of problems, i.e. number of goal variables
DD   = data set name
PP   = problem name: there are always NP+1 problem names. Problem names PP||1 up to and including PP||NP correspond with the NP goal variables. Problem name PP||NP+1 corresponds with the imaginary decision maker's preference function.
TT   = name of the right-hand side column
BB   = name of the 'bounds' which can be used within MPSX

1) A full description of this computer program can be found in Ouwerkerk and Spronk [1978].

AAGOAL = common name of the first NP+1 rows of the input tableau,
          describing the NP goal variables (AAGOAL||1 up to and
          including AAGOAL||NP) and describing the imaginary decision
          maker's preference function (AAGOAL||NP+1).

AAGOAP = common name of row(NP+1) up to and including row(2xNP)+1
          of the input tableau, describing the upper limits for the
          NP respective goal variables to be minimized.

In broad lines, the chart in Figure 7a.1 shows the structure of the
total program. Next, in Figure 7a.2, we present a flow chart of the
subprogram for an imaginary decision maker using IMGP. Below, we
explain in order of occurrance, the most important names used within
this subprogram.

SOLOPT = vector of goal values for the optimal solution of the
          imaginary decision maker's preference function

SOLACC = vector of pessimistic goal values

POTACC = vector of ideal goal values

DELTA   = vector of step sizes for the shifts in SOLACC

ACCUR   = vector of accuracies

VAL   = vector of changed right-hand side values for the AAGOAP
          restrictions

HMAT   = matrix of goal values obtained during the respective
          minimizations of the NP goal variable

SOLPROP = vector of pessimistic goal values after the proposed
          shift in one of the AAGOAP restrictions

POTPROP = vector of ideal goal values corresponding with SOLPROP

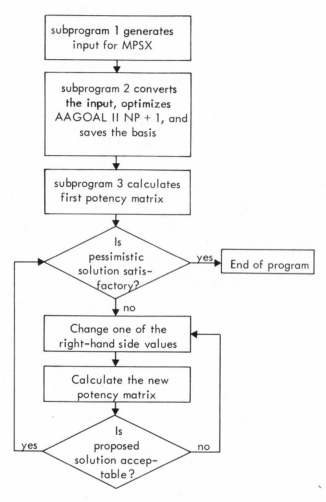

Figure 7a.1. Structure of the computer program

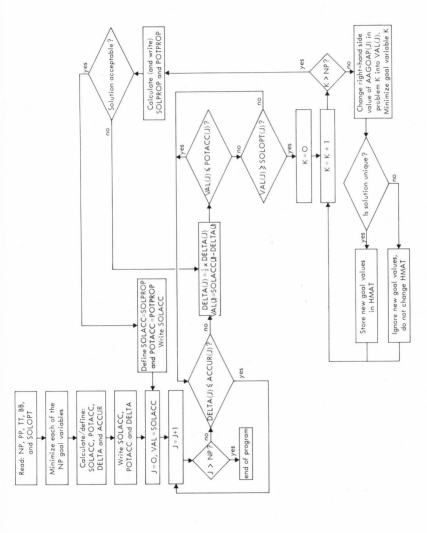

Figure 7a.2. Flow chart of the subprogram used for the experiments with an imaginary decision maker

189

Appendix 7.b. An Operational Computer Program for IMGP

In this appendix we give a brief description of the computer programs (and their interrelationships) which can be used for the implementation of IMGP. The design of this interrelated set of programs is such that the decision maker, using a computer terminal, is in conversational contact with the computer system (in the case of our experiments the IBM 370/158 at the University of Technology in Delft, The Netherlands). Structured programming has been used, having the advantage that parts of the program can be tested (and changed) independently of other parts. The linear programs are solved by means of calls to the IBM's MPSX/370-package [1977], embedded in PL/I computer programs. These modules are coordinated by means of command procedures.

In Figure 7b.1 we give a sketch of the system of programs. Given a new multiple criteria decision problem, the following programs have to be carried out once. The data have to be transformed into the required MPSX input format by means of a matrix generator. Then a PL/I computer program using MPSX, calculates the first potency matrices. The outcomes of the linear programs, which have to be solved in order to calculate this potency matrix, are stored in the dataset PROBFILE A. The potency matrix itself is stored in a dataset which can be displayed to the decision maker.

After these initial operations, the decision maker can choose between two command procedures, 'START' and 'RESUME', which are essentially the same, except for one point, START copies the data of the linear programs underlying the first potency matrix (stored in PROBFILE A) to the dataset PROBFILE B and displays the first potency matrix to the decision maker. RESUME does not include such a copy command, thus leaving the dataset PROBFILE B as it was after the last iteration of the preceding session. Accordingly, it displays the accompanying potency matrix to the decision maker. Clearly, START is used when a new decision maker starts tackling the problem, or when a decision maker wishes to recommence the entire interactive

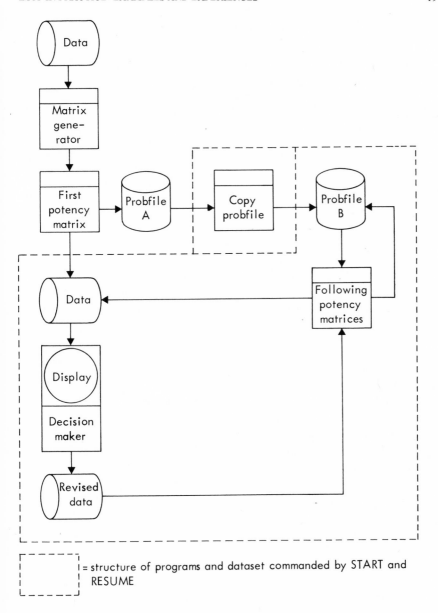

Figure 7b.1. The system of computer programs used for the implementation of IMGP

procedure. RESUME is used when a decision maker wants to continue
the session after a break.

Thus both START and RESUME display a potency matrix, together
with a sequence of questions which have to be answered by the
decision maker. The first question is whether the presented solution
is satisfactory or not. If the decision maker states it is
satisfactory, he can subsequently ask for a detailed (hardcopy)
description of the results. If not, he has to indicate which goal
variable should be changed in value and to what amount. These data
and the data of PROBFILE B are then used in a PL/I program (again
calling the MPSX-package) which calculates the new potency matrix.
The dataset PROBFILE B is changed. It now contains the data of the
linear program underlying the last calculated potency matrix. The
potency matrix itself is stored in a dataset, which again is
displayed to the decision maker. The procedure terminates when the
decision maker states that the presented solution is satisfactory.

References

Baum, S. and R.C. Carlson (1974), Multi-goal Optimization in Management Science, Omega, pp. 607-623.

Bronsema, H.J.J. and B.V.H. van de Kieft (1978), Enkele Risico-maatstaven en Beslissingscriteria voor het Beleggingsprobleem onder Risico: een doelprogrammeringsformulering, in Jonkhart et al. [1978].

Carlsson, C., M. Zeleny and A. Törn (1980), Three Cases in Multiple Criteria Decision Making, (forthcoming).

Despontin, M. and J. Spronk (1979), Comparison and Evaluation of Multiple Criteria Decision Models - first Results of an International Investigation, Report 7923/A, Centre for Research in Business Economics, Erasmus University Rotterdam, Rotterdam.

Driel, G.J. van, J.A. Hartog and C. van Ravenzwaaij. (1980), Limits to the Welfare State, Martinus Nijhoff, Boston.

Fandel, G and T. Gal (eds) (1980), Multiple Criteria Decision Making, Theory and Application, Springer, Berlin.

Hartog, J.A. and J. Spronk (1980), Een Modelstudie naar de Relatie Milieu-Economie, WRR, Serie "Voorstudies en Achtergronden", Staatsuitgeverij, Den Haag.

Hartog, J.A., P. Nijkamp and J. Spronk (1980), Operational Multiple Goal Models for Large Economic Environmental Models, in K. Iracki, K. Malanowski, S. Walukiewicz (eds), Optimization Techniques, Part 2, Berlin, Springer, pp.502-512.

IBM (1977), Mathematical Programming System Extended/370 (MPSX/370) Program Reference Manual (3rd edition).

Jonkhart, M.J.L., J.W.R. Schuit and J. Spronk (eds)(1978), Financiering en Belegging, Stand van Zaken anno 1978, Stenfert Kroese, Leiden.

Khairullah, Z. and S. Zionts (1980), An Experiment with Some Approaches for Solving Problems with Multiple Criteria, in Fandel, G. and T. Gal [1980].

Kumar, P.C., G.C. Philippatos and J.R. Ezzell (1978), Goal
Programming and the Selection of Portfolios by Dual-Purpose
Funds, Journal of Finance, March 1978.

Lebret, M.D. (1977), EIMIC-Equation to MPS - Input Conversion,
Rekencentrum T.H.- Delft, User's Guide RC-TWA-77004, Delft,
April 1977.

Lee, S.M. (1972), Goal Programming for Decision Analysis, Auerbach.

Lee, S.M. and A.J. Lerro (1973), Optimizing the Portfolio Selection
for Mutual Funds, Journal of Finance, pp. 1087-1101.

Nijkamp, P. and J. Spronk (1978), Interactive Multiple Goal Pro-
gramming; Method and Application, Report 7812/F, Centre for
Research in Business Economics, Erasmus University Rotterdam,
Rotterdam.

Nijkamp, P. and J. Spronk (1980), Three Cases in Multiple Criteria
Decision-Making: An Interactive Multiple Goal Programming
Approach, in Carlsson et al. [1980].

Ouwerkerk, C. and J. Spronk (1978), A PL/I Computer Program for IMGP,
Using the MPSX-Package, Centre for Research in Business Economics,
Report 7823/A, Erasmus University Rotterdam, Rotterdam.

Paelinck, J.H. and P. Nijkamp (1976), Operational Theory and Method
in Regional Economics, Saxon House, Farnborough (jointly with
D.C. Heath, Lexington).

8. CAPITAL BUDGETING AND FINANCIAL PLANNING
WITH MULTIPLE GOALS

In this chapter we first review some applications of multiple
criteria decision methods in capital budgeting and financial planning, as reported in the literature. We list a number of general
problems occurring in these applications. In Sections 8.2 - 8.4
these problems are discussed in more detail. It is especially shown
how IMGP might help to solve these problems. Our conclusions are
given in Section 8.5.

8.1. A Brief Survey of the Literature

In this section we present some examples of capital budgeting
and financial planning models which explicitly incorporate multiple
goals. These models have been chosen from the literature, so that
we will be able to demonstrate a series of technical problems often
occurring in this field of applications.

Non-interactive Models

One of the easiest ways to deal with multiple goals is to
single out one of them which then has to be maximized, while requiring minimum values for the other goal variables. Such an approach
was followed e.g. by Robichek et al. [1969], who extended the capital
budgeting problem by imposing constraints on each period's level of
earnings induced by the accepted projects. The objections to such
a procedure are clear. It assumes that all goals formulated as
constraints are *ex ante* equally important, and moreover, that they
have absolute priority over the goal variable which is being maximized.

During the very early stages of the development of goal programming it was frequently suggested that this technique could be an important means in dealing with capital budgeting and financial planning involving multiple objectives. For instance, Ijiri et al.[1963] argue that their linear programming model for budgeting and financial planning could be combined with goal programming approaches to break-even budgeting. Indeed, a considerable number of authors have employed goal programming in financial planning and capital budgeting models (an extensive list of references can be found in Nijkamp and Spronk [1979]). There are some practical reasons to use goal programming in these fields. In this respect, Ashton and Atkins [1977] state that 'it is natural in financial planning to speak in terms of targets and goals; many of the indicators of company performance such as dividend cover, liquidity, or return on capital employed have target ratios adopted by customs and practice'. Nevertheless, the employment of goal programming is not without difficulties. Notably, its need of a considerable amount of *a priori* information to be given by the decision maker should be mentioned. This shortcoming of goal programming clearly paved the way for other procedures.

It has also been proposed that the concept of efficient solutions (see Chapter 3) be used in financial planning problems incorporating multiple goals. Sealey [1978] describes a bank financial planning model which has been formulated as a vector maximum problem. The relevant goal variables are assumed to be 'profit' and 'solvency', where the latter is defined by two distinct (although related) goal variables: (1) the capital adequacy ratio (defined as the ratio of required to actual bank capital) and (2) the risk asset to capital ratio. The instruments are the amounts to be invested in each of the six available types of assets. Furthermore, the model is subject to a number of constraints, relating to capital adequacy, diversification, required reserves, and to the balance sheet. For this example, Sealey has found a set of 17 efficient solutions, from which the decision maker has to choose a final solution.

This approach seems attractive. Nevertheless, a few important

disadvantages should be mentioned. For instance, one may wonder
whether for a given goal variable, more is always preferred to less
(or *vice versa*). In many financial planning problems goal variables
such as 'growth size', 'level of liquidity', 'amount of leverage' and
several (other) ratios are considered important. For none of these
goal variables is it obvious whether they should be maximized or
minimized. Of course, one may maximize (or minimize) these kinds
of goal variables subject to additional constraints on their range
of values. As will be shown in Section 8.3, there are more flexible
solutions to this problem. A more serious problem is the fact that,
in general, the number of efficient solutions is very large. The
identification thus requires a considerable (and sometimes even
prohibitive) amount of computer storage and time. Furthermore, the
number of efficient solutions easily exceeds the information processing capacity of the decision maker. This problem may be solved
by means of interactive procedures.

Interactive Models

Candler and Boehlje [1971] describe a two-period capital
budgeting model in which the alternative activities consist of (a)
two investment projects, to be undertaken either in period 1 or in
period 2, (b) the 'opportunity to put cash in the bank', (c) net
tax-free cash at the end of the planning horizon, (d) the value
of the assets at the end of the planning horizon, (e) dividends paid
to shareholders and (f) pollution. At the same time, the latter four
acitivities have been defined as goal variables, each of which has
to be maximized or minimized. Furthermore, the dividends have been
restricted to increase at a given (linear) rate. The outcomes of
existing operations have been assumed to be given and fixed and
consequently, independent of the investment projects. This problem
has been formulated as a deterministic vector maximum problem. The

feasible region of the acitivity vectors $\underline{x}$ is described by linear
(in-) equalities in $\underline{x}$. Some of the elements of $\underline{x}$ are integer. Because
the goal variables $g_j(\underline{x})$, $j = 1, \ldots, 4$; are at the same time activity
variables, they can only be expressed on a linear scale. Candler and
Boehlje aim at efficient (Pareto-optimal) solutions. The ultimate
solution is to be found by an (unstructured) iterative and interactive
approach.

Chateau [1975] gives a numerical example of a capital budgeting
problem with multiple goals. The problem is to choose from a set of
investment projects, some of which are indivisible. Internal capital
rationing is assumed to have the highest priority. Furthermore, three
other goals are assumed (an acceptable level of cash, a desired level
of dividend disbursement, and a minimum target asset value).

This problem has been formulated as a deterministic, mixed-
integer, goal programming model, employing pre-emptive priority
factors. Chateau shows the results for a variety of objective functions, including the one originally used by Weingartner. Although
Chateau finds merit in the goal programming model's flexibility, he
also mentions a number of its disadvantages. In his opinion, 'the
ordering and weightings on *a priori* ground and in absolute or relative terms may constitute a rigidity factor of the goal programming
approach'.[1] Not surprisingly, he proposes an interactive procedure.
However, for this he has chosen an approach which also requires very
detailed information from the decision maker, i.e. marginal rates of
substitution for multiple criteria.

With regard to multiple objective decision models, many interactive procedures have shown to be very powerful tools in the process
of searching for a final (compromise) solution. However, as mentioned
above, financial planners are accustomed to expressing their

1) Furthermore, Chateau seems to suggest that goal variables should
   be expressible in monetary terms. In our opinion, this is not always true for the goal programming formulation.

preferences in terms of goals and targets. Therefore it seems useful to search for interactive procedures which correspond to this use. An attempt in this direction was made by Ashton and Atkins [1977]. They describe an interactive procedure based on goal programming, in which both weights and targets are changed parametrically. Two important technical problems they have encountered are the choice of the distance metric in the goal program and the considerable number of goals which are being used in their financial planning model. They developed a three-stage methodology which could deal with these problems in an *ad hoc* way. In their opinion (with which we wholeheartedly agree) a specific methodology is necessary for financial planning problems involving multiple objectives. Moreover, in view of the possible applications in this field, the efforts to find such a methodology seem to be justified.

Ashton and Atkins describe an eight-period financial planning model incorporating a set of investment opportunities and financing alternatives available to the firm. Furthermore, this model includes a number of accounting variables which correspond with the U.K. tax law and accounting standards. For each of the planning periods, eight goal variables are defined (six of which are ratios). Thus the problem contains a total of 64 goal variables. Such a large number of goal variables constitutes a source of difficulties in using multiple objective programming methods.

In the above and in other financial planning and capital budgeting models, several technical problems may occur. In Section 8.2 we will pay attention to the problem of large numbers of goal variables. Section 8.3 is devoted to goal variables requiring special treatment. Notably, this is the case for goal variables defined as ratios or as chance constraints, and also for goal variables which are neither to be maximized nor minimized. In Section 8.4 we discuss the problems caused by the occurrence of $(0,1)$ variables, which are used to represent indivisible capital investment projects.

8.2. Large Numbers of Goal Variables

In capital budgeting and financial planning, the number of
goal variables can easily become unmanageable. Even if the firm
considers a small number of goal variables to be important (say two
or three), these goal variables may need to be formulated for each
of the time periods within the planning horizon. It may also be
necessary to define the same kind of goal variables separately for
different divisions of the firm. It is clear that in this way, the
number of goal variables becomes considerably greater than 'the
magical number seven plus or minus two', which is often mentioned
in the literature on multiple criteria decision making, to be the
maximum number of goal variables which can be handled by the decision
maker (see Miller [1956] and Tell [1978]).

As far as we can see, there are three main ways to tackle this
problem:

(a) reduction of the number of goal variables, by replacing each
    set of analogous goal variables by some kind of aggregate.
(b) reduction of the number of goal variables by removing
    'insignificant' goal variables.
(c) division of the total set of goal variables in subsets, which are
    considered sequentially.

We will next discuss each of these approaches in greater detail.

Replacing Sets of Goal Variables by Aggregates

A straightforward procedure to reduce the number of goal variables is to replace each set of analogous goal variables by some kind
of aggregate. Most aggregation procedures have no firm theoretical
basis. Nevertheless, some aggregators may be useful in practice. To
mention just a few, one could use the goal variables' average, or
only the goal variable defined for the end of the planning horizon,

or the maximum growth rate of the goal variable, or the minimum, and so on. Of course it is necessary that the chosen aggregate has some practical meaning to the decision maker. If such an aggregate cannot be found for all sets of analogous goal variables, one has to accept the presence of non-aggregated goal variables beside goal variables which are aggregates of other goal variables.

An important objection to most aggregates is that the mutual differences between the values of the goal variables concerned are neglected. For instance, maximizing the average per period number of employees over a given planning period may result in a very erratic time-pattern of the employment. We will demonstrate an aggregate which partly meets this objection. This alternative aggregate, which is generally to be minimized, is defined as the maximum deviation from target (growth) values defined for the set of analogue goal variables concerned. As an example, let us assume a firm planning its capital investment expenditures for the periods t, t = 1, ..., T. Assume that the firm wants a growth rate of its cash flows C_t, t = 1, ..., T; of at least 10 per cent a period. The cash flow in the period before the first planning period is denoted by C_0. One way to formulate the firm's growth target is represented by

$$(8.1) \qquad C_t - y_t^+ + y_t^- = (1.1)^t \cdot C_0 \qquad \text{for } t = 1, \ldots, T.$$

The aggregate mentioned above is, in this case, defined by

$$(8.2) \qquad d = \operatorname*{Max}_{t=1}^{T} \{y_t^-\},$$

which can be calculated for any sequence of cash flows C_0, C_1, ..., C_T. In normal planning models, several sequences of cash flows are available, in which case the aggregate d might be minimized over the set of alternatives. As pointed out in Chapter 4, this in fact minimaxing procedure can also be adopted within a

programming framework. In the present case, this can be achieved
by adding the constraints (8.1) and furthermore

$$(8.3) \qquad\qquad d \geq y_t^- \qquad\qquad \text{for } t = 1, \ldots, T;$$

after which d can be treated as a normal goal variable.

Although this formulation is rather straightforward, some slight
but significant modifications can be made. To start with, the constraints (8.1) are often replaced by the constraints

$$(8.4) \qquad C_t - y_t^+ + y_t^- = 1.1 \, C_{t-1} \quad \text{for } t = 1, \ldots, T.$$

In (8.1), the growth targets are completely determined *a priori*,
whereas in (8.4) the targets depend on the preceding cash flow.

In connection with either (8.1) or (8.4), one might consider
to 'scale' the deviational variables y_t^+ and y_t^-. For instance, in
the case of (8.1), this could be achieved by multiplying all variables y_t^+ and y_t^- in (8.1) with a factor $(1.1)^t$. The effect is that
the deviations from the targets are measured in proportion to the
target values, whereas the deviations in the unadapted form of
(8.1) are measured in a unit which is not.

Finally it should be stressed that, in our example, only the
negative deviations from the aspired growth levels were judged to
be undesirable. Of course, other possibilities do exist. Instead
of negative deviations, either positive deviations alone or both
the negative and the positive deviations[1] might be used.

---

1) In a slightly different way, Theil [1968, pp.265-271] shows how
   to reduce the possibility of undesirably large fluctuations of
   variables over time. The procedure he proposes is to add to
   the objective function (to be minimized) the sum of the squares
   of the successive period-to-period differences of the variables.

Alternatively, the decision maker may wish to formulate two target
growth levels, i.e. a minimally and a maximally desired level.

Removing insignificant goal variables

Generally speaking, goal variables specified in a decision
problem are not of equal importance. On the contrary, some goal
variables may be so important that they completely determine the
solution of the decision problem, dominating the other goal variables.
It would be of great help if these less important goal variables
could be detected before solving the decision problem.

Another situation arises if all feasible solutions of a
decision problem score almost equally well with respect to a given
goal variable. Also in this case, it might help to eliminate this
goal variable before solving the decision problem for its optimum.

These and other examples suggest that decision problems exist,
in which the use of a subset of the complete set of goal variables
leads to the same (or approximately the same) solution as would
have been found by using the complete set of goal variables.

One approach to detect goal variables which might be omitted
has been proposed by Gal and Leberling [1977] for the linear vector
maximum problem. They give a procedure to identify redundant goal
variables, defined as goal variables which can be omitted without
changing the set of efficient solutions. The identification of
redundant goal variables in linear vector maximum problems turns
out to be equivalent to the identification of redundant constraints
in linear systems (see Spronk and Telgen [1979]). These authors also
discuss some other relationships between multiple objective programming and redundancy.[1)]

---

1) For an in depth treatment of redundancy and linear programs,
   see Telgen [1979].

For instance they show that goal constraints, either formulated
a priori or during an interactive process, may be technically redundant. The advantage of identifying redundant goals and goal
variables is that the decision maker has to provide less information
about his preferences. However, it may be that the decision maker
does not want to remove this 'technical' redundancy, because he may
be accustomed to expressing part of his preferences in terms of these
redundant entities, or even that he cannot be convinced of their
redundancy.

     As shown by Tell [1978], factor analysis constitutes another
method for reducing the number of goal variables in a multiple
criteria decision problem. In this approach all original goal variables are transformed into a smaller set of factors, which are
subsequently treated as goal variables. This reduction of the number
of goal variables results in a loss of information. Because the
procedure provides insight into the amount of information lost
(see Tell [1978]),this loss can be traded off against the reduction
in the number of goal variables. However, in our opinion the amount
of information lost cannot be a reliable indicator of the importance
of the information which is lost.

Subdividing the set of goal variables in subsets

     Another possibility for dealing with a large number of goal
variables is to divide the set of goal variables in a number of
subsets, each containing goal variables of approximately the same
importance. Several approaches to the thus defined problem have been
proposed.

     Analogous to the hierarchical optimization methods (see Section
5.4), one might - as in goal programming (see Chapter 4) - try to
obtain a lexicographic ordering over the subsets of goal variables.
For example, it could be argued that the goal variables relating

to the first planning period have pre-emptive priority over those relating to the second planning period, and so forth. If such an ordering has been obtained, the set of decision alternatives can be reduced sequentially by evaluating this set first in terms of the subset of the most important goal variables, then in terms of the second most important goal variables, and so on.

The generalized interactive procedure proposed by Spronk and Zionts [1980] offers another possibility to deal with the above-mentioned subsets of goal variables. In this procedure, minimally desired values for the goal variables in one subset are determined, subject to constraints on the values of the goal variables in the other subsets, by means of one of the usual interactive procedures. The outcomes for one subset of goal variables are defined as constraints, subject to which the desired goal values in the other subsets must be found. If no satisfactory solution can be found for one subset of goal variables, the constraints posed by one or more of the other subsets must be relaxed, and each of the subsets concerned must be reconsidered.[1]

8.3. Goal Variables Requiring Special Treatment

In this section we deal with three types of goal variables which require special treatment. Goal variables defined as ratios of two linear functions of the instrumental variables become non-linear in the instruments, but can be handled by IMGP. Similarly, chance constraints can be treated as goal constraints being modified in an interactive manner. Finally, goal variables that are neither to be maximized nor minimized can also be handled by IMGP.

---

1) Although no such application has been made yet, it seems that this generalized interactive procedure is useful in solving decentralization problems.

Ratio Forms

In financial planning it is not unusual to use goal variables that are defined as ratios (see Ashton and Atkins [1977]). Well-known examples are 'return on investment','price-earnings ratio', 'quick ratio', 'debt to equity ratio', 'times interest earned' and 'inventory turnover ratio'. Ratios, being non-linear functions of the instrumental variables, can generally not be treated by means of linear multiple objective programming methods. Linear goal programming (and consequently IMGP) are exceptions, as they can deal with ratios of linear functions of the instrumental variables, be it in a less straightforward way than is often assumed. Consider for example the goal variable

$$(8.5) \qquad\qquad g(x) = \frac{3x+2}{2x+4} \ ,$$

and assume that a target value of $g(x) = 1$ has been defined. This might be translated by the non-linear goal restriction

$$(8.6) \qquad\qquad \frac{3x+2}{2x+4} - y^+ + y^- = 1$$

An incorrect, but often proposed formulation of the some problem would yield

$$(8.7) \qquad\qquad (3x+2) - u^+ + u^- = (2x+4),$$

which can be written as

$$(8.8) \qquad\qquad x - u^+ + u^- = 2$$

As shown for example by Awerbuch et al. [1976], substituting the linear formulation (8.8) for the non-linear formulation (8.6) is not, in general, correct. In our example, multiplication of both

sides of (8.6) by the factor (2x+4) shows that (8.6) and (8.8) are
equivalent only if $u^+ = (2x+4).y^+$ and $u^- = (2x+4).y^-$, in which case
(8.8) again becomes non-linear in the instrumental variable x.

If aspired goal levels are defined as 'hard' constraints, little
problems arise with the non-linearity of ratios.[1] For instance, considering the target in the above example as a hard constraint would
yield

(8.9) $3x+2 \geq 2x+4$, or $x \geq 2$

Problems arise only if the deviations from the target ratio are
either to be maximized or minimized. In that case, the deviational
variables become relevant, and the fractional form of the ratios
and the deviational variables should be taken into account.

Fortunately, several procedures for dealing with fractional
forms are available. Because IMGP uses a separate programming model
for each goal variable, any procedure intended for the maximization
of only one fractional goal variable might be considered. For
instance, Charnes and Cooper [1962] transform the fractional problem
into a straight linear programming problem, Joksch [1964] proposes
parametric methods to solve the fractional problem, and Bitran and
Novaes [1973] solve the problem by solving a series of linear
programs differing with respect to the objective function only.

If there is more than one fractional goal variable to be
optimized within the same program, the problem becomes more complicated. In fact, most multiple objective programming methods cannot
really cope with it. Kornbluth [1973] provides a survey of the pro-

1) Provided that the denominator of the ratio assumes either positive
   values only or negative values only. Probably all ratios used in
   capital budgeting and financial planning have denominators assuming positive values only. Cases in which the denominator can become both positive and negative may give rise to disjunctive constraints.

blems and suggests some solution procedures. Kornbluth and Steuer
[1980] discuss the nature of the efficient set if several, fractional
goal variables are involved. They also provide an algorithm to find
all weakly efficient[1] solutions if several fractional goal variables are involved.

As mentioned above, IMGP circumvents the problem of several
fractional goal variables by defining a separate goal program for
each goal variable, which is to be optimized subject to hard constraints on the values of the other goal variables. Nevertheless,
situations may arise in which the number of fractional goal variables becomes too large to handle. As shown by Ashton and Atkins
[1980] and Charnes and Cooper [1977], the minimax metric can be used
to solve this simultaneous occurrence of the ratio problem and the
problem of large numbers of goal variables. This will be illustrated
in Chapter 9 by means of a financial planning model.

Uncertainty and Chance Constraints

As is the case with many other planning and decision problems,
financial planning is beset with uncertainty. Besides the uncertainty
with respect to the technical coefficients and the availability of
resources, the specification of the goal variables and the specification of the targets may also be of an uncertain nature.

A straightforward way to deal with uncertainty is to use the
expected values ('best estimates') of the uncertain parameters to
calculate a solution which would be 'optimal' for a risk-neutral
decision maker, and to carry out a postoptimality analysis to give

---

1) Defined as solutions for which no other solutions can be found
   that are strictly better with respect to all goal variables. For
   instance, two solutions with goal value vectors (7,3,2) and
   (7,4,2) are both weakly efficient. However, only the first
   solution is efficient in the sense defined in Chapter 3.

the presumably risk-averse decision maker an idea of the risks he
is running. Deshpande and Zionts [1980] and Gal [1980] among others,
have paid special attention to the postoptimality analysis of the
goal variable specification.

From a theoretical point of view a more elegant approach would
be to treat all uncertain parameters as random variables, for which
a well-defined probability distribution function can be specified.
Given such information, stochastic programming methods might be used.
Several research efforts have been directed towards the translation
of random goal variables into stochastic goal programming models
(see e.g. Charnes and Cooper [1963], Contini [1968], Lane [1970],
and Leclercq [1979]). A well-known example is the use of *chance
constraints*. Assume that the target value b of the goal variable
$\tilde{g}(\underline{x})$ has to be reached with a probability of at least $1-\varepsilon$. We thus
have

(8.10) $P(\tilde{g}(\underline{x}) \geq b) \geq 1-\varepsilon$

Assuming that $\tilde{g}(\underline{x})$ is normally distributed, or employing a non-
parametric relationship such as Tchebysheff's inequality, this desire
can be translated by means of the deterministic equivalent

(8.11) $E(\tilde{g}(\underline{x})) + k_{\varepsilon}.\sigma(\tilde{g}(\underline{x})) \geq b$

It is easily seen that such a formulation can be adopted within a
goal programming framework, and can thus be handled by means of
IMGP. Minimization of ε, i.e. minimizing the probability of not
achieving the target value b, can be accomplished by repeatedly
solving

(8.12) $\text{Min}\{y^-\}$, s.t.

                 $E(\tilde{g}(\underline{x})) + k_{\varepsilon}.\sigma(\tilde{g}(\underline{x})).+y^- \geq b,$

while systematically changing k_ε. Obviously, if $\bar{y} > 0$ the k_ε value should be lowered. If $\bar{y} = 0$, k_ε might be raised.

Many other stochastic problems can, and have been formulated in goal programming. For an overview we refer to the authors mentioned above. Notwithstanding the existence of these stochastic goal programming models, very few applications have been reported in the literature thusfar. This may be explained by the fact that stochastic programming methods are relatively complicated. Furthermore, the input data required by these methods are generally hard to obtain. Notably, the decision maker has to specify a probability distribution function (or, in some cases, two or three parameter values of this function) for any uncertain entry in the goal programming model, and has to specify the interdependencies between these uncertain entries. Furthermore, he should specify his risk attitude. Therefore, despite their theoretical attractiveness, these stochastic goal programming models easily become unmanageable in practice.

Nevertheless, uncertainty should not be neglected. Depending upon organizational setting of the planning problem (time available, budget, information processing capacity of decision maker etc.), any possibility to deal with uncertainty should be considered. In some situations, the assessment of probability distribution functions may be feasible. In other cases, postoptimality analysis may be carried out fruitfully. However, it should be stressed that, in a given planning problem, the decision maker himself may have developed his 'own' measures and procedures for coping with uncertainty. A clear example in financial planning is the widespread use of several ratios as representatives of the flexibility, profitability and endurance of the financial structure. Instead of trying to convince the decision maker not to use his (perhaps) crude measures, one might as well try to translate these measures so as to incorporate them within the planning model. What is the correct procedure to follow depends largely upon the planning situation at hand, the evaluation of which will be one of the analyst's most difficult and hazardous tasks. In any case, if the 'practical' solution is chosen,

one might consider adopting the decision maker's measures of risk
as additional goal variables in the programming model.

More not always preferred to less and Vice Versa

Several goal variables may occur in financial planning problems,
which are neither to be maximized nor minimized. Goal variables as
the 'growth of accounting earnings over time', 'the amount of cash
held', as well as several goal variables defined as ratios will
generally not have to be maximized or minimized. Instead, the values
of these goal variables will have to meet certain upper and lower
limits defined by the decision maker or, alternatively will have
to be as close as possible to a given target value. It may even be
that the decision maker cannot define such lower limits, upper
limits and target values *a priori*. A clear example of the latter
type is formed by capital rationing constraints. The exact positioning
of the latter constraints depends upon the evaluation and preferences
of the decision maker, and thus should be considered as an output
rather than an input of the decision proces.

Most interactive procedures can only deal with these situations
in a fairly crude way, i.e. by maximizing a goal variable, subject
to a rigid *a priori* defined constraint on the goal variable's value,
or by minimizing the distance to such a constraint. Since it is based
on goal programming. IMGP offers a much more flexible approach. An
overview of possible objective functions in goal programming has been
given in Section 4.2. In Chapter 9 we will illustrate how IMGP can
handle goal variables which are neither to be maximized nor minimized.

8.4. Indivisibility of Projects

Financial planning models very often include discrete (0,1)
variables to represent the yes-no options inherent in the selection
of capital investment projects. As is well-known, the inclusion of

these types of variables calls for the use of special solution procedures other than the simple rounding of continuous solutions obtained after neglecting the discrete nature of the (0,1) variables. Obviously, this does not only hold for single objective programming models, but for multiple objective programming methods as well. For example, consider the case with goal variables

$g_1(\underline{x}) = x_1 + 1\frac{1}{2}.x_2 + 3x_3$, and $g_2(\underline{x}) = x_1 - x_3$. Assume that the following integer solutions are feasible:

$$\underline{x}_A = (0,0,0)$$
$$\underline{x}_B = (1,0,0)$$
$$\underline{x}_C = (0,1,0)$$
$$\underline{x}_D = (0,0,1)$$

The representation of these solutions in goal value space is given in Figure 8.1. It is obvious, that solutions B', C', and D' are

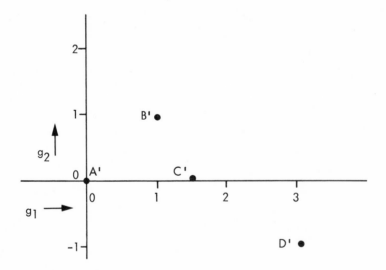

Figure 8.1. The set of feasible (0,1) solutions represented in goal value space

non-dominated. The example also shows that the set of efficient solutions cannot be obtained in the same way as in the corresponding continuous problem, i.e. by means of a parametric analysis of the weights in a linear combination of the goal variables. Such an analysis would yield the solutions B' and D', but would neglect solution C'. Procedures to generate all efficient solutions in integer multiple objective programming methods have been proposed by Bowman [1976], and by Bitran [1978] for the (0,1) integer problem. The computational experiences reported thus far are not very promising. Furthermore, the set of all efficient solutions may again be too extensive to be of much value to the decision maker (see Chapter 3).

Very few interactive multiple objective programming methods have been adapted for the integer case. For instance, Zionts [1977] has proposed an extension of the Zionts-Wallenius algorithm (see Chapter 5), in order to include integer variables. The extension consists mainly of a branch and bound procedure connected with the interactive procedure. These ideas have been developed further by Villarreal et al. [1980]. A difficulty to bear in mind in these branch and bound procedures is the implicit nature of the decision maker's preference function. However, Villarreal et al. (Ibid) suggest that after exploring a certain number of nodes, the decision maker's preference function may have been approximated precisely enough to consider the problem comparable with single objective problems.

Lee [1978] and Lee and Morris [1977] studied the integer version of goal programming including pre-emptive priorities. They presented integer goal programming methods based on the cutting plane, branch and bound, and implicit enumeration approaches. The performance of these methods in a series of test problems was measured by means of two indicators :the number of iterations and the computation time (on an IBM 370-158) required for solving a problem. On the basis of their experiments, Lee and Morris (Ibid) conclude that the branch and bound algorithm of goal programming is far more efficient than the cutting plane method, especially for the mixed integer case.

Furthermore, 'in the implicit enumeration method, the time required
for solution increases dramatically as the number of variable increases'.For example, a problem with 25 constraints, 19 (0,1)-varia-
bles, and 10 pre-emptive priority factors was only solved after 919
seconds of CPU-time and 19855 iterations. For problems having more
than twenty variables, Lee and Morris found it difficult ' to obtain
the optimal solution within a reasonable time limit'.

Although these results are discouraging, especially for
applications in large-scale financial planning and capital budgeting
models, some hope does exist. That is because many variants of the
above-mentioned integer programming methods do exist, which have not
yet been studied for their capability to tackle goal programming
with pre-emptive priorities .

After the above exposition, it will be clear that one cannot
expect IMGP handling integer variables without any problems. Nevertheless, we believe that IMGP is relatively promising for the solution
of integer multiple objective programming problems. Since the computational steps of IMGP consist of the solution of a series of single
objective optimization problems, any normal integer programming
method can be employed.[1] Within these integer programming methods,
the constraints on the values of the goal variables formulated during
the interactive process can often be used fruitfully to facilitate
the search for an optimal solution. In this respect, the results of

---

1) The same holds for other interactive goal programming methods
   of type c (cf. Section 5.4), as for instance the hierarchical
   procedure proposed by van Delft and Nijkamp [1976].

our experiments with a financial planning model including 21 (0,1)-variables and 163 constraints are rather encouraging (see Section 9.4). Nevertheless, more experiments are necessary in order to be able to draw more definite conclusions about the computational performance of IMGP in integer multiple objective programming problems.

As has already been indicated, the presence of integer variables also causes some difficulties in IMGP. A first problem is how to find a suitable solution to start the interactive process. As shown in Appendix 6.a, the minimal (maximal) values of the goal variables reached within the efficient set constitute a good starting point. Because the calculation of the efficient set for integer programming problems in general, and for the (0,1) programming problem in particular, is not yet technically feasible for problems of a more than very moderate format, this method of finding a starting solution should be disregarded. Instead, one might proceed by asking the decision maker to define 'least attractive' values for the goal variables. If an integer solution can be found which satisfies these very modest conditions, the vector of 'least attractive' values can be nominated as the starting solution. Alternatively, the starting solution can be defined as the minimal (maximal) values of the goal variables within the feasible region.

As argued above, the calculation of the potency matrix consisting of a series of individually optimal goal values obtained, subject to a set of minimally desired goal values, is no more difficult than the solution of the corresponding single objective integer programming problem. However, compared with the continuous case, it is often more difficult to interpret the meaning of the potency matrices, and of shifts in these matrices after a change in a minimally desired goal value. To illustrate this point, let us return to the example in Figure 8.1. Assume that the first potency matrix is given by

$$(8.13) \qquad P_1 = \begin{bmatrix} 3 & 1 \\ 1 & -1 \end{bmatrix}$$

If the decision maker wants a value for g_1 of at least 2, the
potency matrix

$$(8.14) \qquad P_2 = \begin{bmatrix} 3 & -1 \\ 3 & -1 \end{bmatrix}$$

will result. Assume next, that alternative C' in Figure 8.1 does
not exist, that the same potency matrix as in (8.13) is used, and
furthermore, that the decision maker again desires a value for g_1
of at least 2. In this case the same potency matrix as in (8.14)
occurs! Thus from the shifts in the potency matrix it cannot be
concluded that the tightening of the goal value excludes possibly
valuable alternatives. This can only be verified by recalculating
the potency matrix P_2 for a series of values for g_1 (e.g. using
the δ procedure described in Chapter 6, yielding the g_1 values
1.5, 1.25, 1.125, etc.).

The above shows that the implementation of IMGP in integer
problems appears to be technically quite simple, but is certainly
not without some pitfalls. In our opinion, the integer case
constitutes a fruitful area for further research.

8.5. Conclusion

In this chapter, a number of capital budgeting and financial
planning models explicitly dealing with a multiplicity of goals
were discussed. It appeared that a series of technical problems
frequently occur in this field of application. These problems relate
to the number of the goal variables, the nature of the goal variables, and to the existence of indivisible projects. It was suggested

that IMGP can fruitfully be used to tackle a number of these problems. This ability will be illustrated in the following chapter.

References

Ashton, D.J. and D.R. Atkins (1977), Multicriteria Programming for
Financial Planning, Paper presented at the XXIII International
Meeting of TIMS, Athens.

Ashton, D.J. and D.R. Atkins (1980), Multicriteria Programming for
Financial Planning: Some Second Thoughts, in Nijkamp, P. and
J. Spronk (eds) [1980].

Awerbuch, S., J.G. Ecker and W.A. Wallace (1976), A note: Hidden
Nonlinearities in the Application of Goal Programming, Management
Science, Vol. 22/8, pp. 918-920.

Bitran, G.R. (1978), Theory and Algorithms for Linear Multiple
Objective Programs with Zero-One Variables, Report 150, Operations
Research Center, Massachusetts Institute of Technology, May 1978.

Bitran, G.R. and A.G. Novaes (1973), Linear Programming with a
Fractional Objective Function, Operations Research, Vol. 21/1,
pp. 22-29.

Bowman, V.J. (1976), On the Relationship of the Tchebycheff's Norm
and the Efficient Frontier of Multiple-Criteria Objectives, in
Thiriez, H. and S. Zionts (eds)[1976].

Charnes, A. and W.W. Cooper (1962), Programming with Linear Fractional
Functionals, Naval Res. Log.Quart., Vol. 9, pp. 181-186.

Charnes, A. and W.W. Cooper (1963), Deterministic Equivalents for
Optimizing and Satisficing under Chance Constraints, Operations
Research, Vol. 11/1.

Charnes, A. and W.W. Cooper (1977), Goal Programming and Multiple
Objective Optimizations, Eur. Jnl. of Op. Res., Vol.1, pp. 39-54.

Chateau, J.P.D. (1975), The Capital Budgeting Problem under Conflicting Financial Policies, Journal of Business Finance and Accounting, Vol. 2/1, Spring 1975, pp. 83-103.

Contini, B. (1968), A Stochastic Approach to Goal Programming, Operations Research, Vol. 16/3.

Delft, A. van and P. Nijkamp (1976), Multicriteria Analysis and Regional Decision-Making, Martinus Nijhoff, Boston.

Deshpande, D.V. and S. Zionts (1980), Sensitivity Analysis in Multiple Objective Linear Programming: Changes in the Objective Function Matrix, in Fandel, G. and T. Gal (eds) [1980, pp.26-39].

Fandel, G. and T. Gal (1980), Multiple Criteria Decision Making-Theory and Application, Springer, Berlin,

Gal, T. (1980), Postefficiency Analysis in Linear Vectormaximum Problems in Nijkamp, P. and J. Spronk (eds) [1980].

Gal, T. and H. Leberling (1973), Redundant Objective Functions in Linear Vector Maximum Problems and their Determination, European Journal of Operational Research, Vol. 1/3, pp. 176-184.

Ijiri, Y., F.K. Levy and R.C. Lyon (1963), A Linear Programming Model for Budgeting and Financial Planning, Journal of Accounting Research, pp. 198-212.

Joksch, H.C. (1964), Programming with Fractional Linear Objective Functions, Nav. Res. Log.Quart., Vol. 11, pp. 197-204.

Kornbluth, J.S.H. (1973), A Survey of Goal Programming, Omega, Vol. 1/2, pp. 193-205.

Kornbluth, J.S.H. and R.E. Steuer (1980), On Computing the Set of All Weakly Efficient Vertices in Multiple Objective Linear Fractional Programming, in Fandel and Gal [1980].

Lane, N. (1970), Goal Programming and Satisficing Models in Economic Analysis, Xerox University, Microfilms, Ann Arbor, Michigan.

Leclerq, J.P. (1979), Résolution de Programmes Lineaires Stochastiques par des Techniques Multicritères, Doctoral Dissertation, Facultés Universitaires N.D. de La Paix.

Lee, S.M. (1978), Interactive Integer Goal Programming: Methods and Applications, in Zionts, S. [1978, pp. 362-383].

Lee, S.M. and R.L. Morris (1977), Integer Goal Programming Methods, in Starr, M.K. and M. Zeleny [1977, pp. 273-289].

Miller, G.A. (1956), The Magical Number Seven, Plus or Minus Two:
    Some Limits on Our Capacity for Processing Information,
    Psychological Review, Vol. 63/2, pp. 81-97.
Nijkamp, P. and J. Spronk (1979), Goal Programming for Decision
    Making, Ricerca Operativa, Vol. 12,pp. 3-49.
Nijkamp, P. and J. Spronk (eds)(1980), Multicriteria Analysis:
    Practical Methods, Gower Press Inc., London.
Robichek, A., D. Ogilvie and J. Roach (1969), Capital Budgeting: A
    Pragmatic Approach, Financial Executive, pp. 26-38.
Sealey, C.W. (1978), Financial Planning with Multiple Objectives,
    Financial Management, Winter 1978, pp. 17-23.
Spronk, J. and J. Telgen (1979), A Note on Multiple Objective
    Programming and Redundancy, Report 7906/A, Centre for Research
    in Business Economics, Erasmus University Rotterdam, Rotterdam.
Spronk, J. and S. Zionts (1980), Multiple Criteria Problem Solving
    with Substantially more than 'seven plus or minus two' Objectives,
    Working Paper in Preparation.
Starr, M.K. and M. Zeleny (eds)(1977), Multiple Criteria Decision
    Making, North-Holland (TIMS Studies in the Management Sciences,
    Vol. 6), Amsterdam.
Telgen, J. (1979), Redundancy and Linear Programs, Mathematical
    Centre, Amsterdam.
Tell, B. (1978), Factor Analysis - A Method for Reducing the Number
    of Criteria in a Multiple Criteria Model, Research Paper 6146,
    Ekonomiska Forskningsinstitutet vid Handelshögskolan, Stockholm.
Theil, H. (1968), Optimal Decision Rules for Government and Industry,
    North-Holland, Amsterdam.
Thiriez, H. and S. Zionts (eds)(1976), Multiple Criteria Decision
    Making, Springer, Berlin.
Villarreal, B., M.H. Karwan and S. Zionts (1980), An Interactive
    Branch and Bound Procedure for Multicriterion Integer Linear
    Programming, in Fandel, G. and T. Gal (eds) [1980, pp. 448-467].
Zionts, S. (1977), Integer Linear Programming with Multiple Objectives,
    Annals of Discrete Mathematics, Vol. 1, pp. 551-562.

Zionts, S. (ed.) (1978), <u>Multiple Criteria Problem Solving</u>, Springer, Berlin.

9. USING IMGP FOR A FINANCIAL PLANNING MODEL: AN ILLUSTRATION

In this chapter we present a financial planning model including multiple goals, and we show how a financial plan might be selected by using IMGP. The financial planning model has been constructed so as to demonstrate the potential of IMGP with respect to the technical problems discussed in Chapter 8. At the same time, we have tried to include some features of financial planning, which are in practice rather usual. Nevertheless, the resulting model - as is probably the case for all financial planning models described in the literature - can be no more than an example, and certainly does not claim to be applicable to all financial planning problems. Every financial planning problem in reality has its own peculiarities. The purpose of this chapter is to show how IMGP might help to cope with some of those peculiarities occurring frequently.

In Section 9.1 we describe the assumptions underlying the present financial planning model. A detailed description of the model is given in Section 9.2. In Section 9.3 we demonstrate a session with a decision maker, using IMGP to find a solution for the above financial planning model. In this section we ignore the go/no-go nature of capital investment projects. In Section 9.4 we therefore describe how the results change when this factor is taken into account. Our conclusions are given in Section 9.5.

9.1. Introductory Remarks

In the model, management has to evaluate a set of capital investment projects, simultaneously considering a series of financing decisions. For the sake of simplicity we have assumed no equity issues and no dividend payments during the planning period. Thus the only financing decisions concern a series of debt issues. Next to these investment and financing decisions, management has to decide upon the amount of cash to be held in each period.

One of the most important goal variables in this case is assumed
to be the firm's total market value. Following Myers and Pogue [1974,
p.580], we adopt two propositions of modern capital market theory:
  (a) The possible effect on the firm's market value, induced by
      the stochastic dependencies between a capital investment
      project and other projects (including the firm's existing
      assets), can be ignored by the firm.
  (b) The total market value of the firm equals its unlevered value
      plus the market value of tax savings implied by debt finan-
      cing.
By means of these two assumptions, the market value of the firm's
portfolio of capital investment projects can be defined as the sum
of the *unlevered present values* of the projects included plus the
market value of the tax savings implied by debt financing (see
Myers and Pogue [1974]). The unlevered present value of a project
(assumed to be estimated directly by the management independently
of the model) is defined as the market value of the project, if
it were financed exclusively with equity (see also Myers [1974]).
The firm's total market value is now defined as the market value of
the firm's portfolio of investments plus correction terms for its
cash holdings and lendings (see Section 9.2). In the absence of
equity issues, the firm's total market value does not have to
include a term for the costs of such issues. Similarly, the costs
of possible bankruptcy have been ignored.

The financial planning model of this chapter is semi-
deterministic. This means that the uncertainly which is inherent in
financial planning is to be accounted for exogeneously. For instance,
the unlevered present values of the projects already include the
value of the risks associated with the projects. As will be shown
below, other risks will be accounted for by managerial decisions
with respect to the values of goal variables relating to the amount
of debt issued, and relating to the liquidity position of the firm.

The choice of a deterministic financial planning model is not an
essential one, but is mainly inspired by the desire to not complicate
the example too much, and to limit computer time. As shown in Chapter
8, goal programming - and consequently IMGP - can handle uncertainty
by means of, among other things, chance constraints.

As argued in Chapter 2, the neglicence of certain goal variables
can affect the firm's total market value adversely. Instead of
accounting for the goal variables either by translating them into
'cost factors' in the total market value definition, or by means
of constraints on their respective values, we prefer to deal with
these goal variables explicitly and separately. As such we have
chosen the stability of the accounting earnings over time, the
amount of debt outstanding (limited through the 'times interest
earned' ratio), the minimum cash level over time and the maximum
cash level.

Another goal variable adopted in this model relates to the
firm's employment level. Of course, this goal variable may be
selected so as to avoid possible negative effects on the firm's total market value. However, it can be equally seen as a goal variable in its own right along with the above goal variables.

In the following section we will describe how the above data
can be translated into a goal program, which can be handled by IMGP.

9.2. Description of the Model

In this section we give a formal description of the financial
planning model which is based on the considerations of the preceding
section. First we specify some of the general features of the model.
Then we succesively present the instrumental variables, the definitional equations and the goal variables.

General

As shown in Chapter 8, IMGP can handle a number of those problems often occurring in financial planning models. Because inclusion of all potential problems would make our example rather complicated (and consequently less illustrative), we illustrate the capacity of IMGP with respect to only some of the problems.

The present financial planning model covers ten periods. All data are assumed to be given and fixed. Consequently, a deterministic model can be developed. The instruments are a number of capital investment projects, the amount of debt issued in each period, the amount of cash hold in each period and the amount lent out in each period. There are no dividends and no equity issues, although each of these options can be included quite easily. The goal variables regarded as relevant in this example relate to the firm's market value, the stability of the accounting earnings over time, the amount of debt issued, the liquidity position and the employment offered by the firm.

The tax rate is assumed to be 40 percent. The interest rate assumed to be relevant for the type of debt this firm issues, is 10 percent. Moreover, this rate is assumed to be fixed over time and to be independent of the amount of debt issued.

Instruments

In this example, the firm can choose from a set of twenty capital investment projects. The relevant project effects, consisting of the present values, the per period after tax cash flows, the contribution to the per period earnings before interest and taxes, and the contribution to the firm's total employment level are given in Tables 9.1, 9.2, and 9.3. These tables also show the

corresponding figures for the existing firm, if no projects were
to be adopted.

In the programming model, the possibility of adopting a project
is translated by means of the $(0,1)$ variables x^n, $n = 0, \ldots, 20$;
where $x^0 (x^0=1)$ represents the existing firm. [1] All projects are
assumed to be economically independent, both mutually and from the
existing operations.

Another instrumental variable is the amount of debt issued in
each period. For the sake of simplicity, only one kind of debt is
assumed for which the borrowing rate is independent of the amount of
debt issued and constant overtime. In consequence, the market value
of debt equals its book value. Furthermore, all debt issues can be
seen as one period loans D_t, representing the principal borrowed
at the beginning of period t, and repaid at the end of the same
period. Denoting the interest rate by r, and the tax rate by T, the
market value of the tax savings due to a shift from all-equity
financing to (partial) debt financing, is given by

$$(9.1) \qquad \sum_{t=0}^{10} r.T.D_t/(1+r)^t,$$

where $r.T.D_0$ represents the tax savings caused by the debt issued
in the period before the first planning period, $D_0 = 400$. In the
model, debt to be issued in the first period after the planning
horizon is limited to 1.5 times D_{10}.

Besides the option to borrow, we also assume that the firm
can lend out an amount Z_t at the beginning of each period. Essentially, these lendings are assumed to be the exact counterparts
of the loans D_t. Thus the market value of the lendings is equal to
minus the value in (9.1), replacing D_t by Z_t. Z_0 is assumed to be
zero, whereas Z_{11} is limited to 1.5 times Z_{10}.

---

1) In general, superscripts relate to the projects. Subscripts
relate to time periods.

Table 9.1. Unlevered present values and net cash flows of the projects

no. n	PV A^n	c_0^n	c_1^n	c_2^n	c_3^n	c_4^n	c_5^n	c_6^n	c_7^n	c_8^n	c_9^n	c_{10}^n
0	1000	130	130	130	120	120	120	120	110	110	110	110
1	10	−10	2	2	2	2	2	2	2	2	2	2
2	9		−10	2	2	2	2	2	2	2	2	2
3	8			−10	2	2	2	2	2	2	2	2
4	7				−10	2	2	2	2	2	2	2
5	6					−10	2	2	2	2	2	2
6	60	−50	10	10	10	10	10	10	10	10	10	10
7	−40	−200	18	18	18	18	18	18	18	18	18	18
8	40		−300	100	100	100	100	100				
9	10		−100	40	40	40	−60	40	40	40	40	−60
10	20			−100	50	40	30	20	10	10	10	10
11	10				−100	50	40	30	20	20	10	0
12	20	−100	50	50	50							
13	10				−100	50	50	50				
14	5							−100	50	50	50	
15	0										−100	50
16	15			−100	40	40	40	40	40	40	40	40
17	−10					−20	8	6	4	2		
18	−15						−20	8	6	4	2	
19	−20							−20	8	6	4	2
20	30		−50	10	11	12	13	14	15	15	15	15

* All cash flows are assumed to occur at the end of the period. The cash flows c_0^n are assumed to occur at the beginning of period 1.

Table 9.2. Earnings contributed by the projects

no.	contribution to earnings before interest and taxes of projects n in periods t = 1, ..., 10.*										
n	E_0^n	E_1^n	E_2^n	E_3^n	E_4^n	E_5^n	E_6^n	E_7^n	E_8^n	E_9^n	E_{10}^n
0	100	103	105	112	108	110	115	120	125	130	135
1		1.5	1.5	1.5	1.5	1.5	1.5	1.5	1.5	1.5	1.5
2			1.5	1.5	1.5	1.5	1.5	1.5	1.5	1.5	1.5
3				1.5	1.5	1.5	1.5	1.5	1.5	1.5	1.5
4					1.5	1.5	1.5	1.5	1.5	1.5	1.5
5						1.5	1.5	1.5	1.5	1.5	1.5
6		7	7	7	7	7	7	7	7	7	7
7		-2	-2	-2	-2	-2	-2	-2	-2	-2	-2
8			-50	70	80	90	100				
9			20	20	20	20	20	20	20	20	20
10				20	20	20	20	20	20	20	20
11				20	20	20	20	20			
12		10	15	25							
13					10	15	25				
14								10	15	25	
15											10
16				-10	0	0	10	20	30	30	20
17					0	0	0	0	0		
18						0	0	0	0	0	
19							0	0	0	0	0
20		0	2	4	6	8	10	12	14	15	15

* All earnings are assumed to occur at the end of the period. The earnings E_0^n are assumed to occur at the beginning of period 1.

Table 9.3. Project effects on the firm's total employment

no. n	W_1^n	W_2^n	W_3^n	W_4^n	W_5^n	W_6^n	W_7^n	W_8^n	W_9^n	W_{10}^n
0	100	100	100	100	100	100	100	100	100	100
1		-1	-1	-1	-1	-1	-1	-1	-1	-1
2			-1	-1	-1	-1	-1	-1	-1	-1
3				-1	-1	-1	-1	-1	-1	-1
4					-1	-1	-1	-1	-1	-1
5						-1	-1	-1	-1	-1
6		-5	-5	-5	-5	-5	-5	-5	-5	-5
7	20	20	20	20	20	20	20	20	20	20
8		-10	-10	-10	-10	-10	-10	-10	-10	-10
9		-3	-3	-3	-3	-3	-3	-3	-3	-3
10			0	0	0	0	0	0	0	0
11				0	0	0	0	0	0	0
12	5	5	5							
13				5	5	5				
14							5	5	5	
15										5
16			0	0	0	0	0	0	0	0
17				3	3	3	3	3		
18					3	3	3	3	3	
19						3	3	3	3	3
20	5	4	2	0	-2	-2	-2	-2	-2	-2

* Measured as the average number of man-years per period.

** The total employment in period t, defined as W_t, can be found by adding the W_t^n values of all accepted projects ($W_0 = 100$).

Finally, the set of instrumental variables includes liquid assets, assumed to consist exclusively of the amounts of cash hold in each period. L_0 represents the amount of cash at the beginning of period 1, L_1 is the amount hold during period one, L_2 is the amount hold during period 2, and so forth. As an investment, the holding of cash is not very lucrative. Consider a dollar, put in cash at the beginning of period t, and withdrawn at the end of the same period. The current market value of this operation is

$$(9.2) \qquad -1/(1+r)^{t-1} + 1/(1+r)^{t} = -r/(1+r)^{t},$$

where we choose r as discount rate, because the cash could have been used to repay debt. The current market value of holding the planned cash balances L_t, $t = 0,1, \ldots, 10$; is defined by

$$(9.3) \qquad L_0 - \sum_{t=1}^{10} r.L_t/(1+r)^{t}.$$

Obviously, the book value of L_0 - the beginning cash - equals its market value. In this case, $L_0 = 15$. In the model, cash to be held in the first period after the planning horizon is limited to $1.5L_{10}$.

Definitional equations

The definitional equations in this model are almost self-explanatory. E_t, the firm's total accounting earnings before interest and taxes in period t, $t = 1, \ldots, 10$; are given by

$$(9.4) \qquad E_t = \sum_{n=0}^{20} E_t^n . x^n \qquad \text{for } t = 1, \ldots, 10;$$

where E_t^n is the part of the period t earnings, contributed by project n. Likewise, the total after tax cash flows are defined as

$$(9.5) \qquad C_t = \sum_{n=0}^{20} c_t^n . x^n \qquad \text{for } t = 0, \ldots, 10;$$

where C_0 is the total cash flow at the beginning of the first planning period. The average number of employees in period t is defined as

$$(9.6) \qquad W_t = \sum_{n=0}^{20} W_t^n . x^n \qquad \text{for } t = 1, \ldots, 10.$$

The sources and uses of funds constraints are given by

$$(9.7) \quad C_t + D_{t+1} + [r.T-(1+r)].D_t + L_t - L_{t+1} + [(1+r)-r.T].$$

$$Z_t - Z_{t+1} = 0. \qquad \text{for } t = 0, \ldots, 10.$$

Goal Variables

1. Current Market Value

In this example, the firm's current market value is assumed to be one of its most important goal variables. Obviously, this goal variable is to be maximized. Because no bankruptcy costs and no equity issues and thus no issue costs are assumed, the current market value can be defined as [1]

$$(9.8) \quad V = \sum_{n=0}^{20} A^n . x^n + \sum_{t=0}^{10} r.T.D_t / (1+r)^t - D_0 - \sum_{t=1}^{10} r.L_t / (1+r)^t + L_0,$$

where A^n is the base case present value of project n, T is the

1) See the preceding section

tax rate, and r is the interest rate assumed to be relevant in this case. Note that $A^{\circ} . x^{\circ}$, $r.D_{o}$ and L_{o} are constants, which can be disregarded in the programming model. Furthermore, all effects of borrowing, lending and holding cash after the planning horizon are ignored.

2. Stability of the Earnings Overtime

Although efficient capital markets should be insensible to erratic time patterns of the firm's accounting earnings, we assume here that the firm wants to smoothen the time path of their total accounting earnings before interests and taxes per period, E_{t}, $t = 0,1, \ldots, 10$. Let us assume that the firm has defined the following target growth path:

$$(9.9) \qquad E_{t}^{*} = E_{o} . (1+g_{E})^{t} \qquad \text{for } t = 1, \ldots, 10;$$

where E_{t}^{*} is the target for earnings in period t, and g_{E} is the target growth rate defined by the management ($g_{E} = 0.05$). In order to allow for possible deviations from this target growth path, the goal con-straints

$$(9.10) \qquad E_{t} - e_{t}^{+} + e_{t}^{-} = E_{t}^{*} \qquad \text{for } t = 1, \ldots, 10;$$

are defined. In our example, the firm only concerns itself with negative deviations from the growth targets. Therefore, the firm has expressed the desire to minimize the maximum deviation from the growth targets. This desire can be translated by introducing the minimax constraints.

$$(9.11) \qquad e_{max}^{-} \geq e_{t}^{-} / (1+g_{E})^{t} \qquad \text{for } t = 0,1, \ldots, 10;$$

and defining e_{max}^{-} as a goal variable to be minimized. In (9.11), the deviations e_{t}^{-} have been divided by the factors $(1+g_{E})^{t}$ because pro-portional rather than absolute deviations were thought to be relevant.

3. Debt Outstanding

If the firm's only goal would be its current market value, then
ignoring bankruptcy costs, the firm should finance its operations
completely with debt (see Jonkhart [1980]). However, firms in reality
do not finance completely with debt, because bankruptcy costs cannot
be ignored or for other reasons (see Chapter 2). Myers and Pogue
[1974] formulate debt constraints such that 'the probability that
the firm will get into trouble reaches an unacceptable level'. As
shown in Chapter 8, IMGP can handle these kinds of chance constraints,
giving the decision maker the option to define - interactively - what
is an unacceptable probability of trouble. In our example we have
chosen an approach, which is more familiar in practice; that is, to
limit the risk of being unable to pay interests on debt out of
current earnings, the *interest cover* (or *times interest earned*),
defined as the ratio of earnings before interest and taxes to the
interest charges, should be maximized. Thus we have

$$(9.12) \qquad \text{Max}\{E_t/r.D_t\} \qquad\qquad \text{for } t = 1, \ldots, 10.$$

Within IMGP, these 10 goal variables might be maximized separately
(see Chapter 8). However, to avoid a too large number of goal
variables, we have chosen to adopt an approach suggested by Charnes
and Cooper [1977]:

$$
\begin{aligned}
&\text{Max } \lambda, \text{ s.t.} \\
(9.13) \qquad & \qquad\qquad\qquad\qquad \text{for } t = 1, \ldots, 10. \\
&\lambda \leq E_t/(r.D_t)
\end{aligned}
$$

Assuming $r.D_t > 0$ for $t = 1, \ldots, 10$; the following heuristic method
to maximize λ can be used. First, fix $\lambda = \bar{\lambda}$. Then solve

$$
\begin{aligned}
&\text{Max } v, \text{ s.t.} \\
(9.14) \qquad & v \leq E_t - \bar{\lambda}.r.D_t \qquad \text{for } t = 1, \ldots, 10. \\
&v \text{ unrestricted in sign.}
\end{aligned}
$$

If the maximum v^* is negative, $\bar{\lambda}$ is infeasible. A lower value for $\bar{\lambda}$ should be chosen and a new v^* should be calculated. If v^* is positive, $\bar{\lambda}$ is feasible and can be raised. A zero value for v^* corresponds with the optimal value for λ. A set of pessimistic values for the ratios $E_t/r.D_t$ is defined at the beginning as

(9.15) $E_t/r.D_t \geq 1.0$ for $t = 1, \ldots, 10$.

Of course, these pessimistic values can be raised during the interactive process.

4. Minimum Cash Level

We assume that a minimum cash level of 5 per cent of the per period cash flow plus 5 per cent of the per period interest charges is desirable. Similar to the preceding goal variable, this can be formalized as

(9.16)
$$\text{Min } \lambda, \text{ s.t.}$$
$$L_t/(C_t+r.D_t) + \lambda \geq 0.05 \qquad \text{for } t = 1, \ldots, 10.$$

Assuming that $(C_t+r.D_t) > 0$ for $t = 1, \ldots, 10$, the same heuristic method as used for the third goal variable, can again be used. Thus, fixing $\lambda = \bar{\lambda}$, and solving

(9.17)
$$\text{Min } \xi, \text{ s.t.}$$
$$L_t + (\bar{\lambda}-0.05).(C_t+r.D_t) + \xi \geq 0 \qquad \text{for } t = 1, \ldots, 10;$$

gives either a positive or a zero value for ξ. If $\xi > 0$, the specified 'tolerance' $\bar{\lambda}$ in meeting the target ratio value 0.05 is too tight and should consequently be relaxed. On the other hand if $\xi = 0$, the tolerance measure $\bar{\lambda}$ can be tightened. Note that the best value of $\bar{\lambda}$ which can be conceived is $\bar{\lambda} = 0$, corresponding with the case that L_t equals or exceeds $0.05.(C_t+r.D_t)$ for all t. Together with this goal variable, we propose the following set of pessimistic values:

(9.18) $L_t > \lambda^{min} \cdot (C_t + r \cdot D_t)$ for $t = 1, \ldots, 10$.

At the start of the interactive process we set $\lambda^{min} = 0$.

5. Maximum Cash Level

We assume that the amount of cash in each period must be less than or equal to 15 per cent of the cash flow plus interest charges. Furthermore, we assume that management wants the amount of cash to be as low as possible. These desires can be translated as

(9.19)
$$\text{Max} \sum_{t=1}^{10} \eta_t$$

$$L_t - 0.15(C_t + r \cdot D_t) + \eta_t = 0 \qquad \text{for } t = 1, \ldots, 10.$$

6. Employment

As an example of an organizational factor which may influence the firm's investment decisions, we have chosen the number of employees in this firm. Both to promote the conditions of employment and to avoid work disputes, management wants to minimize the maximum number of dismissals per period. This can be translated by introducing the goal constraints.

(9.20) $W_t - w_t^+ + w_t^- = W_{t-1}$ for $t = 1, \ldots, 10$;

and in addition by introducing the 'minimax' constraints

(9.21) $w_{max}^- \geq w_t^-$ for $t = 1, \ldots, 10$;

and defining w_{max}^- as a goal variable to be minimized. Note that in this case, the targets are defined implicitly. Furthermore, the

deviations are measured in absolute rather than proportional terms.
Note also that the firm in this case pays more attention to the
avoidence of work disputes than to the firm's total employment level.
The latter can benefit more than in the current formulation, by
minimizing $\sum\limits_{t=1}^{10} \bar{w}_t$ or alternatively, by maximizing $\sum\limits_{t=1}^{10} W_t$.

9.3. Selection of a Financial Plan (Continuous Case)

In this and in the following section we show how a financial
plan might be selected by using IMGP. In this section we assume the
variables x^n, $n = 0, 1, \ldots, 20$; to be continuous. Section 9.4 will
deal with the discrete case. In both cases, the decisions necessary
in order to reach a final solution were - in this fictitious
example - made by ourselves.

The most important results of the first iteration are presented
in Tables 9.4 and 9.5. We trust that these results are self-
explanatory, and therefore confine ourselves to a few remarks. First,
it should be noted that the solutions which are optimal in the first
iterations are mutually significantly different. Each project occurs
in at least one of these solutions. Only one project (number 3)
occurs in all solutions. In none of the solutions is debt issued
after the fifth period. This is caused by the fact that the cash
outflows exceed the cash inflows (one might say that there is a lack
of new projects) and by the absence of dividend payments. In the
model, the surplus of funds is lent out. The plan which gives a
maximal market value might be rejected because (a) the earnings
goal is not attained, (b) the interest cover is in some periods too
low, (c) no cash is held, and (d) the maximal number of dismissals
is too high.

Table 9.6 shows how the final solution is reached. First, minimal
values for the cash hold, the interest cover and the market value
are ensured, respectively. Then, it is decided to formulate the
earnings goal as a restriction (iteration 5), after which the maximal
number of dismissals is limited and the restriction on the interest

Table 9.4. Investment projects chosen when different goal variables are optimized, first iteration

project	goal variable optimized					
n	market value	underatt. min. earnings	interest cover	underatt. min. cash level	cash below upper limit	max. number discharges
0	1.0	1.0	1.0	1.0	1.0	1.0
1	1.0	1.0			1.0	
2	1.0	1.0			1.0	
3	1.0	1.0	1.0	1.0	1.0	1.0
4	1.0	1.0	1.0		1.0	
5	1.0		1.0		1.0	
6	1.0				1.0	
7	1.0			0.09	1.0	0.30
8	0.63		0.05		0.17	
9		1.0			1.0	
10	1.0	1.0		0.48	1.0	0.58
11	1.0		0.22	0.65	1.0	1.0
12	1.0	0.2			1.0	
13	1.0		1.0	1.0	1.0	0.51
14	1.0		1.0		1.0	0.51
15	1.0		1.0			0.51
16	1.0	0.72	0.11	0.47	1.0	
17				1.0	1.0	
18		1.0	0.17	1.0	1.0	
19			1.0		1.0	
20	1.0				1.0	

Table 9.5. Some outcomes when different goal variables are optimized, first iteration

goal variable	E_1	E_2	E_3	E_4	E_5	E_6	E_7	E_8	E_9	E_{10}	D_1	D_2	D_3	D_4	D_5	D_6–D_{10}
1	120	105	205	226	242	276	215	227	233	213	639	717	685	586	120	0
2	105	130	153	153	155	167	179	184	196	194	308	292	348	120		0
3	103	103	116	129	138	155	141	151	163	152	279	201	80	113		0
4	103	105	118	142	149	169	154	158	155	155	304	190	170	215		0
5	120	143	192	208	221	249	235	247	253	223	639	677	649	555	213	0
6	102	104	124	145	150	160	157	165	155	152	340	238	173	218		0

goal variable	w_1	w_2	w_3	w_4	w_5	w_6	w_7	w_8	w_9	w_{10}	λ_1	λ_2	λ_3	λ_4	λ_5	λ_6–λ_{10}
1	130	117	113	111	108	107	107	107	107	107	1.87	1.46	3.34	2.60	3.70	0.0
2	101	98	97	95	97	97	97	97	97	94	3.41	4.44	4.39	12.7		0.0
3	100	99	99	103	103	105	105	105	105	104	3.69	5.11	14.45	11.43		0.0
4	102	102	102	109	112	112	107	107	104	101	3.38	5.52	6.95	6.61		0.0
5	130	118	115	115	115	117	117	117	114	106	1.87	2.12	2.96	3.76	10.34	0.0
6	106	106	106	108	108	108	108	108	108	108	3.01	4.38	7.18	6.98		0.0

goal variable	L_1	L_2	L_3	L_4	L_5	L_6	L_7	L_8	L_9	L_{10}	$\bar{E}_{max}$	$\bar{W}_{max}$	V
1	0.0	0.0	0.0	0.0	0.0	0.0	0.0	0.0	0.0	0.0	4.83	13.33	849.1
2	9.1	4.4	43.0	37.0	15.7	33.4	30.1	29.8	30.0	9.9	0.0	3.0	588.1
3	0.0	20.0	1.2	29.3	28.6	11.0	2.1	27.2	11.6	25.2	6.93	0.51	610.1
4	8.1	6.8	2.6	36.8	33.1	35.3	8.0	23.4	12.8	17.8	4.70	5.0	601.8
5	0.0	0.0	0.0	0.0	0.0	0.0	0.0	0.0	0.0	0.0	0.0	11.67	797.9
6	0.0	13.8	2.6	37.1	31.4	21.5	0.0	25.2	16.1	22.2	14.87	0.0	626.1

Table 9.6. Potential goal values during the interactive process

goal variable	potential goal values		iteration number										
		1	2	3	4	5	6	7	8	9	10	11
current market value	pess.	588.108	588.108	588.108*	700.0*	700.0	700.0	700.0*	750.0*	775.0	762.5	762.5
	ideal	849.097	843.743	838.817	838.817	838.817	790.86	775.19	775.19	775.19	775.19	765.08
underattainment min. earnings	pess.	14.87	14.87	5.79	1.90*	0.0	0.0	0.0	0.0	0.0	0.0	0.0
	ideal	0.0	0.0	0.0	0.0	0.0	0.0	0.0	0.0	0.0	0.0	0.0
interest cover	pess.	1.0	1.0*	2.0	2.0	2.0	2.0*	3.0	3.0	3.0	3.0*	3.25
	ideal	3.69	3.68	3.68	3.68	3.58	3.58	3.58	3.48	3.03	3.32	3.32
underattainment min. cash level	pess.	0.5*	0.0	0.0	0.0	0.0	0.0	0.0	0.0	0.0	0.0	0.0
	ideal	0.0	0.0	0.0	0.0	0.0	0.0	0.0	0.0	0.0	0.0	0.0
amount of cash below upper limit	pess.	0.0	0.0	0.0	0.0	0.0	0.0	0.0	0.0	0.0	0.0	0.0
	ideal	647.15	431.43	323.32	323.32	323.32	306.44	257.93	257.93	204.13	253.74	224.4
max. number of discharges	pess.	13.33	13.0	12.15	12.15	12.15*	5.0	5.0	5.0	5.0	5.0	5.0
	ideal	0.0	0.0	0.0	0.48	0.48	0.48	0.81	2.88	4.98	3.87	4.76

* Goal value chosen to be improved.

cover is further tightened. In iterations 8 and 9, the minimally
desired market value is raised. However, given the solutions in
iteration 9, this minimally desired value is pushed back in step 10.
In the final iteration, the interest cover is raised further,
leaving us with six, in this case only slightly different solutions.

In Table 9.7 we show the solution which gives a maximum market
value, given the constraints formulated in the final iteration. Both
the earnings and the minimum cash goal are attained. The market
value and the interest cover appear to be quite satisfactory. The
maximum number of dismissals (five) occurs in one period only. This
number is not considered to be too serious, if management attracts
the additional labour required in period one on basis of a one-year
contract.

Table 9.7. Some outcomes when the market value is maximized, final iteration

n	x^n	n	x^n
0	1.0		
1		11	1.0
2	1.0	12	0.13
3	1.0	13	1.0
4	1.0	14	1.0
5	1.0	15	1.0
6	0.8	16	0.56
7		17	
8		18	
9		19	
10	1.0	20	1.0

time	D_t	Z_t	L_t	C_t	E_t	W_t	λ_t
0	400.0		15.0	76.67		100.0	
1	338.26		5.92	84.67	109.93	105.67	3.25
2	269.93		1.34	8.93	116.10	100.67	4.30
3	295.12		2.07	11.90	142.37	97.67	4.82
4	315.34		16.49	298.24	174.10	99.0	5.52
5	34.27		14.73	291.24	184.60	96.0	53.87
6		261.04	8.61	172.24	207.16	95.0	
7		445.39	12.16	243.24	204.72	95.0	
8		715.35	12.16	243.24	216.72	95.0	
9		1007.01	6.66	133.24	218.28	95.0	
10		1197.28	10.05	201.00	202.72	95.0	

$V = 765.08$

$\bar{e}_{max} = 0.0$

$E_t \geq 3.25 \ (r \cdot D_t)$

$L_t \geq 0.05 \ (C_t + r \cdot D_t)$

$\bar{w}_{max} = 5.0$

9.4. Selection of a Financial Plan (Discrete Case)

In this section we repeat the experiment of the preceding section, while taking account of the discrete nature of the project variables x^n, $n = 0,1, \ldots, 20$. In this discrete case the amount of cash below the upper limit was not maximized anymore because, after considering the results of the continuous case, this goal variable appeared to be less relevant to us.[1] The decision to drop this goal variable can be viewed as being based on the insights obtained by using the interactive procedure.

The first pessimistic solution is chosen to be equal to the pessimistic solution of the fifth iteration in the continuous case.[2] This implies that the underattainment of the earnings target and of the minimal cash level target are respectively restricted to zero, the market value is at least 700 and the interest charges are covered at least two times. Table 9.8 shows the potential goal values of the fifth iteration in the continuous case and of all iterations in the discrete case. In the second iteration, the maximal number of dismissals is restricted to 5, whereas the interest cover becomes at least 3 in the third iteration. Because the potential market value has been reduced too much during these two iterations, it is decided to revise the decision made in the second iteration. That is, the maximal number of dismissals is restricted to 7 in the fourth iteration. Next, the minimally desired market value is set at 750 (iteration 5). The interest cover becomes at least 3.25 in iteration 6. In the final iteration, the maximal number of dismissals is reduced to 6.

We have found four different solutions satisfying the minimally desired goal levels formulated in the final iteration. One solution

---

1) Because the maximum cash level is defined as a percentage of cash flows plus interest charges (see (9.19)), the underattainment of this maximum cash level can be enlarged by simply raising the debts D_t and the loans Z_t simultaneously by equal amounts.
2) This first integer solution was found by simply rounding the continuous solution. In other problems, the identification of an integer starting solution may be more difficult.

Table 9.8. Potential goal values during the interactive process, integer case

goal variable	potential goal values		iteration number						
		5(cont.)	1	2	3	4	5	6	7
current market value	pess.	700.0	700.0	700.0	700.0	700.0*	750.0	751.907	751.907
	ideal	838.817	824.452	759.799	724.498	771.827	771.827	760.897	760.897
underattainment min. earnings	pess.	0.0	0.0	0.0	0.0	0.0	0.0	0.0	0.0
	ideal	0.0	0.0	0.0	0.0	0.0	0.0	0.0	0.0
interest cover	pess.	2.0	2.74	2.87*	3.0	3.0	3.0*	3.25	3.25
	ideal	3.58	3.31	3.26	3.26	3.29	3.29	3.29	3.29
underattainment min. cash level	pess.	0.0	0.0	0.0	0.0	0.0	0.0	0.0	0.0
	ideal	0.0	0.0	0.0	0.0	0.0	0.0	0.0	0.0
max. number of discharges	pess.	12.15	10*	5	5*	7	7	7*	6
	ideal	0.48	1	1	5	5	6	6	6

* Goal value chosen to be changed.

which was found by maximizing the market value subject to the minimally desired goal levels, yields the ideal values for each of the
goal variables. This solution is described in Table 9.9. Of course,
it might be argued that this solution is better than the other
solutions since the latter are dominated. On the other hand, if it
is not certain that all goal variables important to the decision
maker have been included in the analysis, it is better to present
all four solutions to the decision maker.

We can be quite positive with regard to the computational aspects of
IMGP in this integer case. We used MIP, the standard package for mixed
integer programming offered by IBM, for solving each of the integer programs described in this section. The branch and bound procedure used
in MIP offers several options which appear to be quite useful in the
present case. For instance, if the value of the goal variable to be
optimized is known to be bounded, such a bound can be inserted -
generally simplifying the branching process. Because IMGP repeatedly
shifts the minimally desired goal levels, this option is very useful.
Another possibility to lighten the computational burden is to start
each iteration of IMGP with an integer solution which is known to be
feasible, subject to the newly added constraint. To this end, the
preceding optimal integer solution of the goal variable, of which
the minimum value is raised in the new iteration can be used. For
instance, assume an integer solution exists for which the market
value is 760. Clearly, this solution remains feasible if a constraint
requiring a market value of at least 750 is added.

Using an IBM 370/158 computer, the CPU-time necessary for each
iteration was on average less than one minute. In our opinion this
already satisfactory performance can be improved quite considerably,
because in our case we had to cope with an incidentally limited amount
of real storage. Furthermore, the similarity of the optimization
problems, both within and between each iteration, might offer
additional possibilities to simplify the computational process.

Table 9.9. Some outcomes when the market value is maximized, final iteration, integer case

projects				time	D_t	z_t	L_t	C_t	E_t	w_t	λ_t
n	x^n	n	x^n								
0	1			0	400.0		15.0	80	110.0	100	3.29
1	1	11	1	1	334.67		5.67	80	115.5	105	4.24
2	1	12	1	2	272.54		3.46	42	146.0	99	5.97
3	1	13	1	3	244.41		0.97	-5	174.0	96	6.25
4		14	1	4	278.29		15.19	276	184.5	98	106.46
5	1	15	1	5	17.33		13.54	269	201.5	96	
6	1	16		6		256.67	7.5	150	193.5	95	
7		17		7		418.52	11.05	221	205.5	95	
8		18		8		664.63	11.05	221	201.5	95	
9		19		9		931.0	5.55	111	191.5	95	
10	1	20	1	10		1093.36	10.05	201		95	

$V = 760.90$

$\bar{e}_{max} = 0.0$

$E_t \geq 3.29 \ (r.D_t)$

$L_t \geq 0.05 \ (C_t + r.D_t)$

$\bar{w}_{max} = 6$

9.5. Conclusion

The example described in this chapter suggests that IMGP can be
a valuable tool for financial planning with multiple goals. Some of
the technical peculiarities inherent in financial planning models can
be tackled in a straightforward manner. Neither the presence of several ratio forms in the goal variables, nor the presence of integer instrumental variables appears to deliver any serious problems.

Furthermore, IMGP offers all advantages of interactive procedures. As such, the method is conceptually rather simple and thus quite
comprehensible for both analyst and decision maker.

In the following chapter we will discuss some of the problems
that might accompany the implementation of IMGP.

References

Charnes, A and W.W. Cooper (1977), Goal Programming and Multiple Objective Optimizations - Part I, European Journal of Operational Research, Vol. 1/1, pp. 39-54.

Jonkhart, M.J.L. (1980), Optimal Capital Structure and Corporate Debt Capacity, dissertation, Erasmus University Rotterdam, Rotterdam.

Myers, S.C. (1974), Interactions of Corporate Financing and Investment Decisions - Implications for Capital Budgeting, Journal of Finance.

Myers, S.C. and G.A. Pogue (1974), A Programming Approach to Corporate Financial Management, Journal of Finance.

10. EVALUATION

10.1. Implementation of IMGP

When IMGP is implemented in practical capital budgeting and
financial planning problems, it should be made clear to all actors
that the method is not intended to provide an 'optimal' plan which
may be forced upon the organization. It should be stressed that the
method is primarily a tool to help one understand the decision problem. In addition, it can be used as a means of communication between
the actors. If the method is used to select one or more investment
plans, it can only be claimed that these plans are 'good', 'optimal',
or 'efficient' (depending on the decision maker's choices) given the
relations depicted in the model of the planning problem and given the
set of goal variables defined by the decision maker. Once again, this
stresses the fact that IMGP and similar methods are more a learning
tool than a tool for optimization. With the help of these methods, the
decision maker can gain more insight into the alternative plans
available in the goals he is striving for, and into the possible
effects of the modelled parameters.

In order to implement IMGP in practice, it is necessary to verify not only whether the characteristics of the problem at hand and
its organizational setting meet the technical requirements for the
procedure (cf. Chapter 6), but also whether its implementation is
really desired and at least not counteracted by the participants
involved in the decision problem. The importance of the latter can
hardly be overstressed, as is suggested by various reports on applications of normative decision methods. For instance, managers may
be quite reluctant to even mention their goals, let alone specify
them in such a way that they can be incorporated within a multiple
criteria decision model.

For a successful implementation it is necessary to overcome
this type of resistance. In our opinion, the only way to get a
method accepted is to inform all participants concerned about the
aim, the assumptions and the operation of the method. One should
try to avoid that either the decision maker or any of the other
participants feel they are being manipulated by the method.
For the same reason, the decision maker should be given every
opportunity to change and rechange his mind and as a possible
consequence, his earlier choice, during the interactive process.
This implies that the computer programs should be designed to be
as flexible as possible.

To stimulate the learning effects resulting from the use of
interactive methods, the computer programs should be provided with
options in order to get information on the values of instrumental
variables, on shadow-prices of restrictions, and so forth.
Furthermore, we would like to advocate short response times
between the choices of the decision maker on the one hand and the
display of the consequences of these choices on the other hand.
With short response times, it becomes feasible for the decision
maker to sit at the terminal desk and to experiment with several
combinations of the goal variables. It should be stressed, however,
that short response times are beneficial but not strictly necessary
for using these interactive procedures.

10.2. Main Advantages of IMGP

In this section we will summarize the main advantages of IMGP.
Its possible disadvantages are discussed in the following section,
together with some areas for further research. The present survey
will be brief, as most of the items have already been discussed in
detail in the preceding chapters.

As indicated by its name, IMGP is interactive. It thus has all
of the advantages of interactive methods discussed in Section 5.1.

The class of problems for which IMGP can be used is quite
large. In fact, IMGP can handle all those problems which can be
handled by goal programming. As shown in Chapters 8 and 9, some
technical problems that may occur in capital budgeting and financial planning with multiple goals can be tackled in a straightforward way. Because the assumptions about the decision maker's
preferences are quite weak, IMGP can be used (depending on the
needs of the decision maker), to generate a unique final solution,
a series of efficient solutions, or a set of satisficing solutions.

IMGP is a relatively simple method, easy to understand for
both decision maker and analyst. This is an important advantage in
itself. Furthermore, the simplicity of the method implies that it
can easily be computerized, and that the required computer is relatively short. This implies that it becomes feasible in terms of
both time and costs to carry out many iterations within a short
period. As explained in the preceding section, this feature of IMGP
ensures that the decision maker can extensively benefit from the
learning effects of using interactive methods.

The types of questions to be answered by the decision maker
appear to be rather simple: (1) is the given solution acceptable
or not? (2) which goal value needs to be improved? (3) how much at
the least should this goal value be improved? (Optional) (4) do you
accept the consequences of the proposed improvement of the value of
the indicated goal variable? If the decision maker wishes to answer
the third question, his answer need not be very precise, because
he only has to specify 'a' lower bound for the size of the goal
value improvement. In addition, the last question gives the opportunity to revise the answer on the third question. Finally, as
already mentioned above, it is feasible to repeat some or all iterations of the interactive process several times.

10.3. Some Disadvantages and Areas for Further Research

In this study we made the assumption that the model describing

the available alternatives, the set of goal variables and the
relationships between goal variables and instruments is given or
can be established without insurmountable difficulties. In many
decision situations this assumption is rather strong. Moreover,
because of the learning effects which result from the use of IMGP,
the model may have to be revised during the interactive process.
In its present form, IMGP can handle these revisions on an *ad hoc*
basis only.

It was also assumed that the decision maker's preferences can be
described, at least in principle, by means of the preference relations
discussed in Section 6.1. However, decision situations may exist in
which this assumption is not satisfied. This holds especially true
when the single decision maker assumed in this study is replaced
by a team of decision makers. In the latter case, it may be hard if
not impossible to find a preference ordering (for the team as a
whole) which has the properties of transitivity and completeness.

The fact that the decision maker may change his mind during
the interactive process is, as such, certainly not a disadvantage.
However, there is no formal guarantee that the decision maker will
stop changing his mind.

Many of the topics discussed in this study offer possibilities
for further research. With respect to IMGP, it might be interesting
to investigate whether solution procedures other than the simplex
method can be used within the IMGP framework. For instance, Spronk
and Telgen [1980] proposed the use of the ellipsoidal method of
linear programming. The use of non-linear programming methods constitutes another subject for further study. In addition, it would be
interesting to know whether these methods could be used if the
set of alternatives is non-convex. As suggested by the use of IMGP
for the mixed integer financial planning model described in Chapter
9, at least some methods can be used to solve non-convex problems.
However, to be more conclusive, much more study should be carried
out in this direction.

The non-empirical computational analysis of multiple criteria decision methods is still a generally neglected subject, and therefore deserves more attention.

On a more practical level, it might be useful to search for possibilities to easify the calculatory steps in IMGP. One such possibility is the removal of redundant (goal) constraints, both before and during the interactive process (see Spronk and Telgen [1979]). As already mentioned in Section 10.1, one should try to make the response times between the decision maker's choices and the presentation of the results as short as possible. In this respect, quite satisfactory results have already been obtained (see Appendix 7b). Nevertheless, further improvements are certainly possible. The same holds for the optional access to different kinds of information (for which multi-level computer programs might be designed), and for the presentation of the results (for which graphical display techniques might be considered).

As discussed in Chapter 8, some technical problems may arise in capital budgeting and financial planning with multiple goals. By means of IMGP, most of these problems can be tackled. However, we feel that some of them need further attention. For instance, studying the problem of the (0,1) instrumental variables and that of large numbers of goal variables might yield valuable results. Furthermore, it should be realized that most of the problems described in Chapter 8 may occur simultaneously. This phenomenon is another area for further research.

Besides the rather technical subjects mentioned in this section, much work needs to be done with respect to the organizational setting of capital budgeting and financial planning in relation to the role of the kind of normative decision methods discussed here. Can these methods be used if there are several decision makers, possibly on different hierarchical decision levels? How can these methods best be implemented? Are there any consequences for the administrative system?

Most of these questions are rather difficult to answer. Nevertheless, if the implementation of interactive methods in capital
budgeting and financial planning is to be successful, these questions should not be ignored.

10.4. Concluding Remarks

The title of this study might suggest that our only purpose is
to promote the use of IMGP in capital budgeting and financial planning. Although we feel that IMGP is relatively well-suited to handle
these kinds of problems, we expect and hope that in the near future,
new methods will be developed which are better suited to tackle
capital budgeting and financial planning problems with multiple
goals.

A more important purpose of this study is to stress the idea
of considering capital budgeting and financial planning as decision
problems involving multiple goals. Furthermore, we have tried to
show that the way of thinking inherent in multiple criteria decision
making offers new and promising tools to tackle these problems.
Finally, it was stressed that, in general, normative decision methods
cannot claim to offer 'the optimal solution for all your problems'.
Instead, these methods can help the decision maker to understand his
decision problem and, in some cases, help him to find a few solutions which might be considered relatively good. In our opinion,
normative decision methods can only be helpful if their underlying
assumptions do not deviate too much from the decision problem at
hand. This was one of the reasons for developing IMGP, in addition
to the already existing range of methods. We hope that our modest
attempt to tackle capital budgeting and financial planning by means
of multiple criteria decision methods will encourage others to
follow.

References

Spronk, J. and J. Telgen (1979), A Note on Multiple Objective
  Programming and Redundancy, Report 7906/A, Centre for Research
  in Business Economics, Erasmus University Rotterdam, Rotterdam.
Spronk, J. and J. Telgen (1980), An Ellipsoidal Interactive Multiple
  Goal Programming Method, Working Paper 97, College of Business
  Administration, University of Tennessee, Knoxville, TN 37916.

AUTHOR INDEX

SUBJECT INDEX